AF754043

Data Analytics using Machine Learning Techniques on Cloud Platforms

Data Analytics using Machine Learning Techniques on Cloud Platforms examines how machine learning (ML) and cloud computing combine to drive data-driven decision-making across industries. Covering ML techniques, loud-based analytics tools and security concerns, this book provides theoretical foundations and real-world applications in fields like healthcare, logistics and e-commerce. It also addresses security challenges, privacy concerns and compliance frameworks, ensuring a comprehensive understanding of cloud-based analytics.

This book:

- Covers supervised and unsupervised learning, including regression, clustering, classification and neural networks.
- Discusses Hadoop, Spark, Tableau, Power BI and Splunk for analytics and visualization.
- Examines how cloud computing enhances scalability, efficiency and automation in data analytics.
- Showcases ML-driven solutions in e-commerce, supply chain logistics, healthcare and education.

This book is an essential resource for students, researchers and professionals who seek to understand and apply ML-driven cloud analytics in real-world scenarios.

Data Analytics using Machine Learning Techniques on Cloud Platforms

Seema Rawat, Neelu Jyothi Ahuja, Avita Katal,
Praveen Kumar and Shabana Urooj

CRC Press
Taylor & Francis Group
Boca Raton London New York

CRC Press is an imprint of the
Taylor & Francis Group, an **informa** business

Designed cover image: Shutterstock

First edition published 2026
by CRC Press
2385 NW Executive Center Drive, Suite 320, Boca Raton FL 33431

and by CRC Press
4 Park Square, Milton Park, Abingdon, Oxon, OX14 4RN

CRC Press is an imprint of Taylor & Francis Group, LLC

© 2026 Seema Rawat, Neelu Jyothi Ahuja, Avita Katal, Praveen Kumar, Shabana Urooj

Reasonable efforts have been made to publish reliable data and information, but the author and publisher cannot assume responsibility for the validity of all materials or the consequences of their use. The authors and publishers have attempted to trace the copyright holders of all material reproduced in this publication and apologize to copyright holders if permission to publish in this form has not been obtained. If any copyright material has not been acknowledged please write and let us know so we may rectify in any future reprint.

Except as permitted under U.S. Copyright Law, no part of this book may be reprinted, reproduced, transmitted, or utilized in any form by any electronic, mechanical, or other means, now known or hereafter invented, including photocopying, microfilming and recording, or in any information storage or retrieval system, without written permission from the publishers.

For permission to photocopy or use material electronically from this work, access www.copyright.com or contact the Copyright Clearance Center, Inc. (CCC), 222 Rosewood Drive, Danvers, MA 01923, 978-750-8400. For works that are not available on CCC please contact mpkbookspermissions@tandf.co.uk

Trademark notice: Product or corporate names may be trademarks or registered trademarks and are used only for identification and explanation without intent to infringe.

ISBN: 978-1-032-49146-2 (hbk)
ISBN: 978-1-032-50067-6 (pbk)
ISBN: 978-1-003-39677-2 (ebk)

DOI: 10.1201/9781003396772

Typeset in Times
by Apex CoVantage, LLC

Contents

Preface

During this era of digital change, the possibilities that data analysis, ML and cloud computing present to industries are limitless. These technologies, when brought together, enable businesses to capture enormous amounts of data, gain insight into them and improve their business processes. This book is an attempt to address the issues surrounding all three areas, by providing a worthy source that integrates theory and practice.

The journey begins with insights into what data analytics are like, where it started, how it looks like in a big data era. The book then turns to relevant challenges that industries are currently facing in the data management sphere, analysing necessary tools and technologies such as Apache Hadoop, Tableau and Power BI, which are crucial for analytical processes. The emphasis on statistical methods and ML toolchains equips the audience with the necessary skill set to comprehend predictive analytics models and the deployment of such models.

The book discusses the potential of ML by introducing methods like neural networks, supervised and unsupervised learning, regression, clustering and others and demonstrating how they are used in many fields. Along with describing cloud computing's architecture, advantages and integration with analytics to promote scalability and agility, it also examines the revolutionary role of cloud computing. Examples from e-commerce, logistics, healthcare and education highlight the transformative potential of combining data analytics, ML and cloud computing, and driving innovation and efficiency across industries. These technologies empower businesses to make data-driven decisions, optimize operations and improve user experiences. The book also focuses on important aspects such as security and privacy concerns which are very important in the cloud age. Also, it provides a good exploration of new advancements that are expected to give a beacon of hope on the advancements of AI analytics in businesses and the society as a whole.

The unique highlights that distinguish this book and demonstrate its transformative potential in the intersection of data analytics, ML and cloud computing are as follows:

- It provides thorough insights into the potent fusion of cloud computing, ML and data analytics, fusing theoretical knowledge with real-world applications.
- It highlights the enormous potential of these technologies by discussing real-world use cases in a variety of industries, including e-commerce, healthcare, education and logistics.
- It provides a thorough examination of state-of-the-art ML tools and algorithms, highlighting how they may optimize data analytics for better decision-making.
- It discusses the most recent developments, difficulties and security issues in the rapidly changing field of data analytics using cloud computing and ML.
- It offers a forward-looking perspective by examining the revolutionary effects of AI, ML and big data technologies on several sectors, paying particular attention to new advancements.

This book is appropriate for students, researchers and professionals who would like to enhance their knowledge of these interrelated forms of technology. With its structured approach and practical insights, it serves as both a learning tool and a reference for navigating the complexities of the data-driven world. This book is aimed at encouraging readers to become actively involved in the development of data analytics, ML and cloud computing.

One of the most significant areas that now affect decision-making across a range of industries, including government, business, healthcare and education, is data analytics. It entails examining unprocessed datasets to identify novel approaches to decision-making that will assist the company in resolving intricate issues using the information gathered. Chapter 1, "Data Analytics: An Overview", explores the development of data analytics, from conventional methods to the fusion of data science and big data. It focuses on how ML and AI-driven techniques have replaced descriptive and predictive analytics. Furthermore, this chapter examines how big data analytics has transformed several sectors and looks at where it is going in the coming years because of developments in edge computing, IoT and AI.

Big data technologies have revolutionized analytics, visualization and data processing in a variety of sectors. Scalable distributed processing and storage are offered by Apache Hadoop, which includes HDFS, MapReduce and YARN. Hadoop 2 enhancements like YARN and HDFS federation provide more flexibility, scalability and performance. Real-time processing and sophisticated analytics are supported by Apache Storm and Spark, allowing for dynamic and quick data operations. Data representation is improved by visualization tools like Tableau and Lumify, with Tableau being particularly good at statistical analysis and predictive modelling and Lumify combining multimedia and geographic analytics for team insights. Splunk is unique in log management because it offers real-time analytics for compliance, security and IT operations. Chapter 2, "Data Analytics: Tools and Technologies", focuses and discusses in detail these technologies. When combined, these technologies enable sectors including government, healthcare and telecommunications to extract useful insights from complex and varied data, promoting creativity, operational effectiveness and well-informed decision-making.

Statistical approaches are crucial because prior to ML, they provided some frameworks for integrating data analysis, hypothesis testing and prediction techniques. Statistical approaches continue to play a significant role in data analytics today. These techniques are the foundation of modern ML and are still essential for identifying patterns, correlations and trends of interest in your data, despite being outdated by today's standards. Chapter 3, "Data Analytics: Statistical Approach", explores the statistical approach to data analytics, with a focus on the ML toolkit and some fundamental statistical analysis techniques. Additionally, this chapter provides instances of how statistical techniques might enhance ML processes.

Chapter 4, "Supervised and Unsupervised Methods of Machine Learning for Data Analytics", covers the different ML techniques for data analytics with suitable examples. The topics covered include regression, clustering, classification, neural networks and deep neural networks algorithms used for data analytics.

There is enormous promise for enhancing decision-making, automation and predictive skills across a range of sectors through the confluence of data analytics and

ML. The computing needs, data quality problems, interpretability of the model, ethical considerations and the difficulty of incorporating ML into current data analytics systems are some of the major obstacles that this integration brings. Organizations may gain a competitive edge and uncover new solutions by tackling these issues and utilizing ML.

Chapter 5, "Opportunities and Challenges for Data Analytics Integrated with Machine Learning", focuses on the many potentials and difficulties for data analytics combined with ML.

Cloud computing has completely changed the face of IT infrastructure, providing scalable, adaptable and affordable solutions for all the demands of enterprises worldwide. Chapter 6, "Cloud Computing: A Change in the IT Infrastructure Landscape", focuses on the development of cloud computing, its primary value proposition and the general ideas that distinguish it from conventional IT systems. The authors have examined cloud computing architecture, paying particular attention to the hardware and software components as well as important considerations while moving towards a cloud infrastructure. The chapter goes on to describe how cloud computing enables companies to be more flexible and develop more quickly. The chapter ends with the new developments including edge-to-cloud integration, hybrid clouds and serverless computing.

Rapid data development in the digital age has prompted new methods of data analytics, where cloud computing and ML are essential. Chapter 7, "Redefining Data Analytics with Machine Learning and Cloud", presents the revolutionary effects of these developments on data processing and analysis. To manage big and varied datasets, it starts by examining contemporary data architecture with an emphasis on scalable and adaptable solutions. The chapter then explores how ML is used in data analytics, emphasizing how it may extract valuable insights from complicated and unstructured data. The function of serverless data analytics pipelines is also covered, demonstrating how they simplify data workflow management.

The combination of cloud computing, ML and data analytics is revolutionizing company operations by fostering efficiency and creativity. Chapter 8, "Data Analytics and Cloud Together: A Powerful Combination for E-Commerce and Supply Chain Logistics", examines the combined effects of these technologies on supply chain logistics and e-commerce. These technologies provide real-time fraud detection, inventory optimization, consumer sentiment analysis and tailored customer experiences in e-commerce. It helps with demand forecasting, warehouse management, supply chain optimization and predictive maintenance in logistics. This chapter also includes case studies demonstrating the implementation of supply chains, e-commerce and their architecture backed by cloud platforms such as AWS.

The healthcare and education sectors now have more streamlined, individualized and easily available platforms because of the combination of data analytics, ML and cloud computing. Predictive analytics has several advantages for the health industry, such as improved patient outcomes, cost savings, personalized treatment approaches, preventative illness identification and increased operational performance. To further enhance student results, ML and data analytics also make it possible for individualized learning experiences, adaptive learning environments and data-driven decision-making in the classroom. Although cloud computing facilitates scalable infrastructure to manage large volumes of data and efficiently execute sophisticated algorithms, it ignores ethical concerns such as algorithmic bias and data privacy, necessitating alternatives like explainable AI and federated learning. Chapter 9, "Data Analytics, Machine Learning and Cloud Together: A Powerful Combination for Healthcare and Education", highlights current applications, case studies and emerging trends of these technologies' convergence into healthcare and education. It ends with a look to the future and how these innovations might create fair, intelligent systems that support efficiency, accessibility and a customized experience in both fields.

Although more and more businesses are using the cloud to manage their data, those responsible for guaranteeing data availability, confidentiality and integrity face a difficult challenge. Chapter 10, "Security and Privacy Issues for Data Analytics Using Machine Learning in Cloud Computing", covers the difficulties with privacy and security that come up while utilizing cloud-based data analytics pipelines. The shared responsibility model serves as the foundation for the chapter's introduction of the main security issues, outlining how security duties are divided between cloud service providers and users. It discusses infrastructure security, data security in transit and at rest, multi-tenant setups and challenges related to data origin, history and retention. The study of application security involves tackling the problems of protecting cloud-native apps, online apps and APIs in addition to operating system security. The scrutiny goes towards AWS security controls, security auditing and compliance management endures, as well as security of AI ML pipelines under safeguard of Google SAIF and Generative AI security controls. This chapter offers vital insights for protecting cloud-based data analytics pipelines using ML, with a focus on critical areas such as infrastructure, data, application security and privacy concerns.

Cloud computing and ML are transforming data analytics, which benefits organizations by enabling them to manage large datasets quickly, scalable and affordably. The convergence of these technologies enables increased anticipatory potential, stimulates innovation and supports operational excellence as enterprises address complex data challenges.

Chapter 11, "Future Trends for ML-Based Data Analytics in the Cloud", examines the origins of cloud-based ML and its revolutionary effects on a variety of sectors, including healthcare, retail and urban planning. The chapter discusses new developments that are anticipated to influence analytics in the future, including explainable AI, federated learning, edge AI and hyper automation. These advances are accompanied by discussions of the issues of environmental sustainability, skills shortages and data privacy, along with workable answers. The chapter concludes with a discussion of a more thorough use of ML in the cloud using blockchain and quantum computing, along with suggestions for businesses looking to fully leverage these technologies.

Author Biographies

Dr. Seema Rawat | Professor | AI & Data Science | Innovation & Entrepreneurship

Dr. Seema Rawat, Professor in the Department of Information Technology at Amity School of Engineering and Technology, Amity University Uttar Pradesh Noida, is a distinguished academician and researcher. She has specialization in Deep Learning, Artificial Intelligence, Data Science, Machine Learning, Cloud Computing.

Dr. Seema holds a PhD and M. Tech in Computer Science and Engineering and has 20 years of teaching experience in leading engineering institutes across India and abroad. Dr. Seema has an impressive research portfolio, with high-impact SCI-indexed journal papers and Scopus-indexed research papers/book chapters. She has published 70+ research papers, authored books with Elsevier and Springer, and holds more than 15 Indian patents. She serves as a reviewer for top-tier Scopus-indexed journals and editor of various books. She is supervising 5 PhD Scholar in India and 02 Foreign PhD research Scholars.

She is actively involved in professional organizations such as IEEE, ACM, and CSI. Beyond her academic and research accomplishments. Dr. Seema recognized with the Faculty Innovation Excellence Award 2019 by DST, Government of India, she actively contributes to AI research, innovation, and entrepreneurship. Dr. Seema dominates real-world impact as Vice President of UP's Entrepreneurship Council (WICCI). She is Senior Technical Advisor Technical Advisor to DeetyaSoft, Ennoble IP, and MyDigital360.

Dr. Neelu Jyothi Ahuja | Professor & Associate Dean (Academics), School of Computer Science, UPES, Dehradun, Uttarakhand, India

Dr. Neelu Jyothi Ahuja is a professor and associate dean (Academics) at the School of Computer Science, UPES, Dehradun. She earned her PhD in 2010, focusing on developing a rule-based expert system for seismic data interpretation. With 24+ years of experience in teaching, research and project development, she has led numerous AI and machine learning-driven projects addressing real-world challenges.

From 2010 to 2017, she headed the Computing Research Institute, fostering interdisciplinary research. She has successfully delivered R&D projects worth over ₹1.5 crores, funded by the Department of Science and Technology (DST), GOI. Her current research focuses on AI-based tutoring tools for learning disabilities and an AI-driven snake trapper. She has supervised 10 PhD scholars and is currently guiding five more.

Dr. Ahuja has received prestigious recognitions, including the Himayan Nari Sakhti Award (2020), IGEN Women Achievers Award (2021), Leading Women Researcher Award (2022) and a research felicitation by UCOST (2022). She has been an invited speaker at national and international forums and serves on key committees such as WHO's Promotion of Assistive Products and DST's Expert Committee for CORE projects. She has also chaired conference sessions and various academic panels.

Her research interests include machine learning, intelligent tutoring systems, AI, expert systems, ICT and object-oriented development. She is an active member of IEEE, ACM and ACM-Women. Passionate about innovative teaching and student engagement, she emphasizes holistic learning beyond classroom boundaries.

Dr. Avita Katal | Associate Professor and Program Leader, School of Computer Science, UPES, Dehradun, Uttarakhand, India

Dr. Avita Katal is a highly regarded academic and researcher in the fields of cloud computing, Internet of Things (IoT) and artificial intelligence. She holds a PhD in the domain of cloud computing, has completed her MTech and BE in computer science engineering. Dr. Avita Katal is currently Associate Professor in the School of Computer Science at the University of Petroleum and Energy Studies (UPES) in Dehradun, Uttarakhand, India. She serves as the program leader for the BTech program in Computer Science & Engineering with specialization in Cloud Computing and Virtualization Technologies. Dr. Avita Katal holds a Postgraduate Certificate in Academic Practice (PGCAP), enhancing her educational expertise. With over a decade of research experience, Dr. Katal has contributed significantly to the development of advanced algorithms and systems in cloud computing environments, with particular focus on optimization techniques, resource management and cloud security.

Dr. Katal has published extensively in reputed international journals and conferences, where her work has been recognized for its innovation and practical applications. She also serves as a reviewer for numerous prestigious journals and conferences in her field, demonstrating her leadership and expertise in cloud computing, IoT and AI. Her ongoing research aims to bridge the gap between theoretical advancements and their implementation in real-world cloud infrastructures, particularly in the context of scalability, reliability and efficiency.

Dr. Praveen Kumar | Director and Professor in Astana IT University, Astana, Kazakhstan

Dr. Praveen Kumar received his PhD and MTech in Computer Science and Engineering. Currently, he is working as a director and professor in Astana IT University, Astana, Kazakhstan. He has more than 18+ years of experience in teaching and research. He has been awarded the Best PhD thesis, Best Researcher award and

Fellow Member of the Indian Institute of Machine Learning for outstanding contribution in AI and ML, recognized by the Government of West Bengal, India. His areas of interest include big data analytics, data mining, ML. etc.

He has to his credit 10 Patents/Copyright and has published more than 140+ research papers in International Journals and Conferences (Scopus Indexed) with Scopus H-Index 16. He is supervising five PhD research scholars in AI, big data analytics and data mining. He has delivered invited talk and guest lecture in Jamia Millia Islamia University, Maharaja Agrasen College of Delhi University, Duy Tan University Vietnam, ECE Paris, France, etc. He has been associated with many conferences throughout the world as a TPC member and session chair, etc.

He has visited various countries like Uzbekistan; Tokyo, Japan; London, UK; Paris, France; Da Nang, Vietnam; Dubai; Russia and Kazakhstan. He is a senior member of IEEE, lifetime member of IETE, member of ACM and member of IET (UK) and other renowned technical societies. He is associated with Corporates, and he is a technical adviser of DeetyaSoft Pvt. Ltd. Noida, IVRguru, MyDigital360, etc.

Prof. (Dr.) Shabana Urooj | Professor, College of Engineering, Princess Nourah Bint Abdulrahman University

Prof. (Dr.) Shabana Urooj (Senior Member, IEEE) presently working as a full professor at the College of Engineering, Princess Nourah bint Abdulrahman University, Riyadh, Saudi Arabia. Dr. Urooj is persistently contributing for the technical and professional development of society. She has received the bachelor's degree in electrical engineering and the master's degree in electrical engineering (Instrumentation and Control) from Aligarh Muslim University, India. She obtained her doctorate degree from Jamia Millia Islamia (A Central University), Delhi, India. She has served industry for three years and teaching organizations for over 20 years.

She has authored and co-authored more than 250 research articles, which are published in high-quality international journals, reputed conference proceedings and quality books. She has successfully completed several editorial responsibilities for reputable journals and several quality publishers and proceedings. She is presently contributing as an associate editor in *Frontiers in Energy Research*. She has served as an associate editor of a reputed journal viz. *IEEE Sensors Journal* in the past.

She was a recipient of the Springer's Excellence in Teaching and Research Award, the American Ceramic Society's Young Professional Award, the IEEE's Region 10 Award for outstanding contribution in Educational Activities, Leadership Excellence Women's Award in University Professor category (Middle East), Research Excellence Award for quality publishing/authorship from Princess Nourah University and several other best paper presentation awards.

Dr. Urooj is serving as an active volunteer of Institute of Electrical & Electronics Engineering-IEEE in various capacities. She is the Chairperson of Education Society Chapter of the IEEE Saudi Arabia Section. She has served IEEE Delhi Section, India, in various potential positions for about a decade.

Introduction

Avita Katal

With data analytics, all kinds of information can be worked with in today's world – everything from spotting trends to establishing strategies and making relevant choices. As companies must tackle complex problems and seek to improve their operations while meeting their strategic goals, analytics helps them achieve all of those. With the help of past data and current inputs from businesses, future opportunities can be spotted, results can be predicted and performance can be improved. All these trends from data analytics achieve efficiency and innovation, whether it is for improving utility service in healthcare or coordinating retail supply chains.

From the monitoring of past activities referred to as descriptive analysis to the modern predictive analytics, where the focus is on the predictions of future events, the area has matured into sophisticated data science and analytics. Due to the explosive growth in data from IoT devices, social networks and enterprise systems, it is possible to analyse vast datasets in real-time now with the aid of big data technologies. This advancement allowed the emergence of both artificial intelligence (AI) and machine learning (ML), both of which allowed for the automation of insights and business intelligence (BI). Currently, BI analytics is, for example facilitating predictive maintenance across various industries, personal recommendations in e-commerce, and advanced-level diagnostics in healthcare.

It is quite impressive how data analytics has transformed over the years, specifically by expanding from statistical analysis to big data and ML. Each step in the advancement of technology, data collection and insight generation is marked as an evolution. This emphasizes the importance of statistics as the foundational element in data analytics. Statistics focuses on data and offers analysis to derive insights. This method is deductive in nature and seeks to prove predetermined hypotheses using known data and relationships, using sophisticated mathematical techniques.

Let's take a retail shop, for instance, the traditional approach might use an average monthly sales figure to check whether a yearly advertising campaign had a particular impact on sales revenue by employing methods such as:

- **Descriptive statistics:** Reporting mean sales or listing the best-selling item.
- **Inferential statistics:** Regression analysis to forecast sales figures or determine determinants of customer expenditure.
- **Time series analysis:** Using historical information to establish patterns and estimating sales for the following quarter.

DOI: 10.1201/9781003396772-1

Though this approach is analytical and reveals strong insight, it is inefficient with the existence of large and non-structured data sources as social media trends or customer reviews, which don't fit neatly into rows and columns.

Chapter 1 of this book examines the evolution of data analytics, from classical methods to the combination of big data and data science. It focuses on the transition from descriptive and predictive analytics to ML and AI-powered approaches. Furthermore, this chapter explores how big data analytics has affected the different sectors and investigates where it will be heading in the next several years owing to improvements in IoT, AI and edge computing.

With the increasing digitalization of the world, companies started collecting data from social media, IoT devices and transaction systems which led to the creation of big data. This era is distinguished by the introduction of the "4 Vs":

- **Volume:** The number of customer interactions across multiple platforms reaches into the billions.
- **Velocity:** Data like user activity on mobile applications is received instantaneously.
- **Variety:** The data includes numerous forms, texts, pictures, videos and sensor data.
- **Veracity:** The data is noisy and inconsistent, so it needs to be validated and cleaned.

For example, Amazon has an e-commerce business that handles millions of customer reviews and transactions each day. Understanding this data has moved beyond traditional statistical methods. There is now big data technology like Hadoop and Apache Spark that facilitates distributed storage of data and parallel datasets processing which assists in making sense of large datasets. Patterns such as identifying the top-performing product categories or understanding the customer churn is what big data analytics is aimed towards.

With the coming of analytics of big data, the traditional methods of data analysis and interpretation are becoming obsolete. In their place stepped AI and ML, being trained to look for patterns and make predictions on data without needing explicit coding for every step. The major developments included the following:

- **Supervised Learning:** Useful in prediction as well as classification. For instance banks apply classification methods like logistic regression or decision trees to estimate the likelihood of loan defaults by customers.
- **Unsupervised Learning:** Used to find pre-existing patterns in data. For example, retailers have employed clustering algorithms to segment customers for optimized marketing strategies.
- **Deep Learning:** A type of machine learning that refers to the use of deep neural networks for image recognition (e.g. X-ray analysis for disease diagnosis) and natural language processing (for instance chatbots that evaluate customer sentiment).

Unlike traditional statistics, ML thrives on big, messy and complex datasets, offering scalability and adaptability. For example, Netflix leverages AI to recommend personalized content based on user viewing patterns, improving customer engagement and retention.

Chapter 2 addresses the changing of data processing, analysis and visualization processes across various fields using contemporary technologies in big data. Innovations in Hadoop, for instance HDFS, MapReduce and YARN, have consistently boosted the performance and scalability of data storage and processing. Looking at other frameworks, Apache Storm and Spark provide real-time dynamic analytics, while Tableau and Lumify are the go-to tools for modelling, gaining multimedia insights and collaborating. Splunk distinguishes itself in log management through real-time analytics of IT operations and security. All these technologies give the ability to innovate and increase decision-making processes along with efficiency for actionable insights in healthcare, telecom and government sectors.

Chapter 3 focuses on the statistical approach of data analytics and more particularly talks about ML toolbox. Important sections of data preprocessing, statistical hypothesis testing, regression analysis, classification techniques and advanced statistical methods like Bayesian inference are discussed. Furthermore, this chapter shows how statistical methods can complement ML pipelines.

Chapter 4 primarily studies supervised and unsupervised ML algorithms for data analytics, with an emphasis on clustering, dimensionality reduction and association rule mining. These approaches are critical for evaluating unstructured and unlabelled information, which are becoming more popular these days. In most data analytics applications with structured datasets, supervised ML algorithms such as logistic regression, decision trees and support vector machines provide higher predicted accuracy and interpretability than unsupervised learning approaches. The results show the potential use of unsupervised learning in uncovering hidden patterns and insights that can enhance the decision-making process. With these approaches, readers can better understand the increasing complexity of data and enhance their analytical skills.

Chapter 5 addresses the many possibilities and challenges regarding data analytics and their associations with ML. The potential for data analytics and ML working together is tremendous in routine decision-making, automation and prediction capabilities in a myriad of industries. But at the same time, there are major challenges that come with this integration like high computing power, data quality, how the model is understood, ethics and the lack of straightforward methods of incorporating ML into established data analytics systems. These challenges, if solved, give organizations an opportunity to exploit and have an edge over competitors using the power of ML.

Cloud technology has dramatically transformed data analytics and data science by enabling higher scalability, affordability and flexibility, which was difficult to achieve with conventional infrastructure. Organizations have migrated from on-premises infrastructures to cloud-based systems to improve the way they manage, process and analyse data. This changeover is very prominent in industries which deal with massive amounts of data, where cloud computing has completely changed the rules of the game.

Chapter 6 describes the evolution of cloud computing, its main benefits, and the crucial elements which set it apart from classic information technology systems.

The chapter reviews the cloud computing system, including both the software and hardware components, as well as the important factors involved in the migration to cloud-based infrastructure. The chapter goes on to illustrate how cloud computing enables firms to develop more quickly and with more agility. Finally, we cover upcoming concepts including serverless computing, hybrid clouds and edge-to-cloud interaction.

One of the most significant transformations enabled by cloud computing is the resizing of data storage and processing power in accordance with demand. Traditionally, premised infrastructure made it cost-prohibitive to store and process large amounts of data, causing firms to either pay for excess resources they did not use or be forced to deal with bottlenecks at peak demand times. Companies now have almost unlimited storage and processing power available with the use of the cloud. Amazon S3, Azure blob storage and Google cloud storage are just a few examples of cloud storage services that enable organizations to safely store massive quantities of structured and unstructured data without concern for physical hardware. This fundamental change from on-premise to cloud storage enables companies to pay for only what they use, greatly reducing the arms race spending of pre-cloud computing periods.

Additionally, cloud computing has changed the advancement of the available computational power for data analytics. With the cloud, data scientists and analysts are able to have access to powerful processing capabilities exactly when it is needed, which is extremely important for big data analysis and ML. AWS, Azure, as well as Google Cloud are good examples of cloud services and they provide scalable virtual machines, as well as specialized high computational capacity instances which enable companies to perform complex data modelling, simulations and analyses without incurring extensive costs on on-premise facilities. This on-demand business model enables resources to be dynamically allocated to the workloads, allowing companies to do high-performance computing tasks, such as data processing, deep learning and AI, without underusing resources.

The transformation of information technology has positively impacted cross-functional team collaboration. Traditionally, data science and analytics teams were partitioned along geographical or organizational lines. Now, with the convenience of cloud computing, they are able to communicate and work together no matter where the members are located. These include Jupyter Notebooks and Google Colab, which are cloud-based, and collaborative tools like GitHub or GitLab. These tools can be used by different users at the same time concurrently to modify the same datasets or models. This leads to increased prototyping and effective collaboration. In addition, the cloud infrastructure is built to enhance the management of versions by decreasing the likelihood of erasing or losing critical information.

By enhancing collaboration amongst users, a cloud enables an organization's stakeholders such as business analysts and managers, in addition to the data science team, to work together with improved synergy. Cloud platforms come with embedded BI tools such as Tableau, Power BI and Looker, whereby users without a technical background can access and analyse data with the help of dashboards and reports. This means that business executives can make informed decisions without waiting for periodic updates from their data teams, which is non-time sensitive.

Consequently, the cloud helps to bridge the gap between technical data scientists and business personnel, which ultimately enables decision makers to have more access to relevant and timely data which enhances decision-making processes.

Alongside elasticity, the cost-effectiveness of cloud computing has been another reason for its adoption in data analytics and data science. Traditionally, an organization's infrastructure requires substantial investment in systems, maintenance, hardware and software. Moreover, these systems had to be managed by an IT department which added to the processing cost of data. With the advent of the cloud, companies can do away with these huge initial investments, as well as be subjected to a costs-only incurred model. This enables specialized services to be provided which focus on analytics and ML without the need to develop and sustain one's own infrastructure, particularly for smaller and newer companies.

Cloud computing facilitates the delivery of customized services concentrating on analytics and ML without the requirement to build and maintain one's own infrastructure, especially for small and new businesses. This scalability has promoted more experimentation and quicker adoption of new technologies such as AI, deep learning and big data analytics.

The proliferation of data in the present world of information has called for new means of data analysis which is where cloud computing and ML come in handy. The implications of these advances in data computing and analysis are illustrated in Chapter 7. It starts by looking at contemporary data architecture with a focus on how to handle large and diverse datasets in a scalable and efficient manner. The chapter subsequently investigates the ways ML algorithms are applied within the field of data analytics and how these programs work in extracting priceless information from complex unstructured datasets. More so, the chapter explores the use of serverless data analytics pipelines, which further simplifies the management of workflows dealing with data. In all these strategies, the reader learns how data analytics changes through the use of ML and cloud services to become efficient and intelligent of the most scalable and sophisticated models of making data-driven decisions.

Rapid data development in the digital age has prompted new methods of data analytics, where cloud computing and ML are essential. The revolutionary effects of these developments on data processing and analysis are presented in Chapter 7. To manage big and varied datasets, it starts by examining contemporary data architecture with an emphasis on scalable and adaptable solutions. The chapter then explores how ML is used in data analytics, emphasizing how it may extract valuable insights from complicated and unstructured data. The function of serverless data analytics pipelines is also covered, demonstrating how they simplify data workflow management. Through these advancements, the chapter demonstrates how ML and cloud computing are redefining the field of data analytics, driving more efficient, scalable and intelligent data-driven decision-making. It illustrates how ML, aided by the powerful computing offered by the cloud, is disrupting data analytics as it verticalizes the industry towards greater efficiency, scale and intelligence within the decision-making processes.

Chapter 8 assesses the impact of data analytics, ML and cloud computing on e-commerce as well as on supply chain logistics. In e-commerce, they enable better personalization, inventory control, cover fraud and sentiment analysis, while in logistics, they improve supply chain optimization, predictive maintenance, warehouse management and demand planning.

Dealing with the transformative changes brought by data science, machine learning algorithms and cloud technologies in the health and education industries is becoming increasingly important. In healthcare, cloud technologies enhance early diagnosis, enable personalized treatment plans and help reduce costs. In education, these technologies support personalized learning and data-driven insights to improve teaching and learning outcomes. However, addressing privacy concerns and socio-technical issues such as discrimination in algorithmic systems necessitates solutions such as decentralized AI and AI systems that can explain their decisions. Chapter 9 of this book is wrapped with a forecast on the intelligent systems that aim at enhancing accessibility, effectiveness and personalization in both areas.

Even with the multitude of positive aspects, security and compliance continue to be primary issues when it comes to cloud-based systems for data analytics. Some of the best features offered by cloud service providers include advanced encryption techniques, identity and access management, and multi-factor authentication among many others aimed at ensuring sensitive data is not compromised by careless insiders. Furthermore, several cloud service providers also fulfil various criteria alongside laws governing security such as HIPAA, GDPR and SOC 2 so companies understand that while working with data in the cloud, they will be both compliant and protected. Also, so that data teams can maintain a clear record of who, when and what changes were made to the data, cloud platforms offer wide range audit and monitoring tools which enhance accountability and transparency in the data analytics system.

As a result, more action such as a robust security strategy must be implemented to mitigate such risks. Like many service providers such as Azure, AWS and Google Cloud, they all use a Shared Responsibility Model which means addressing the underlying infrastructure is their responsibility while apps, data and configurations fall to the user. Furthermore, some configurations can allow extreme weaknesses such as allowing insufficient access controls or leaving storage buckets exposed. In order to reduce these vulnerabilities, cloud platforms are equipped with additional essential encrypted components, such as multi-factor authentication, logging tools, and role-based access control (RBAC) which makes it possible to construct secure AI ML workflows.

The AI/ML pipelines encounter different data-related threats which include data breaches, unauthorized access and adversarial attacks. These threats transform into more challenging problems when the data is stored in a distributed manner in the cloud. In order to mitigate these risks, a strong and well-defined security strategy needs to be implemented. AI/ML pipelines undergo several processes such as ingestion, preprocessing, training and deployment, which result in earning unprecedented data. Due to the AI-based models not being too intelligent, it fails to provide a clear separation between the infrastructure and the application, preventing the users from tackling problems. Problems such as exposed storage APIs, including other control parameters, will incline towards serious security threats. To mitigate these risks, cloud-based platforms like AWS, Azure and Google have made it a point to add features like multi-factor authentication, strong encryption, enhanced role-based controls and logging with monitoring features.

Through the steps of ingestion, preprocessing, training and deployment, a tremendous volume of data is handled by AI/ML pipelines which are governed by a series of security challenges like data breaches, unauthorized access and adversarial attacks. These risks are amplified when data is held in a cloud environment because the nature of the environment is distributed, thus an efficient security strategy is needed. AWS, Azure and Google cloud are examples of cloud providers who use a shared responsibility model and secure the underlying framework and users are tasked with protecting their data, applications and configurations. Problems in configuration like exposed storage buckets and access controls that are too lenient could create critical gaps in security. To buttress against these gaps, cloud platforms have built-in features such as encryption, RBAC, multi-factor authentication and logging and monitoring tools to help organizations secure AI/ML workflows.

At the core of AI/ML data pipelines, the first challenge is the protection of data. Model accuracy and other critical decisions are dependent on it. Protecting data must involve encryption, which is one of the essential measures of safety because it ensures that data is safe when not in use as well as in transit. Key management services such as AWS, Azure and Google cloud facilitate better and secure handling of encryption keys by users. Properly crafted Identity and Access Management policies ensure that only authorized people and applications have access to information that is relevant to them, that lowers risks. In addition, masking and tokenization of Personally Identifiable Information data together with the use of cryptographic hashes allow alteration of sensitive data without distortion of the truthfulness of information while ensuring total data security. This, in addition to other best practices, makes it possible for the health and finance sectors to comply with stringent regulations such as HIPAA and GDPR.

Deploying and training ML and AI models must be protected from untrusted access in virtual private clouds, containers and other computing environments. In addition, models should be encrypted and secured with robust API gateways that authenticate and restrict access. It is also necessary to guard against AI adversaries that have malicious intent, such as using expertly engineered inputs designed to manipulate models. Suppressing these attacks is best achieved through strong adversarial suppression methods, including input-filtering and adversarial training, which enhance the models' robustness. With effective logging, unauthorized activities can be detected and removed, thus averting damage. These methods offer a fully integrated solution alongside the rest of the systems provided by the cloud, allowing the protection of AI/ML pipelines to work in tandem with the flexibility and scale of cloud environments. As a result, sensitive information remains safeguarded alongside important workflows, thus enabling constraint-free innovation within the cloud.

In Chapter 10, the attention is drawn towards the problems related to the security of the cloud data analytics pipeline, paying attention to confidentiality, integrity and availability. Among the topics covered are the shared responsibility model, infrastructure security, data protection, multi-tenancy and web application, API and operating system security. Useful intricacies such as data ownership, sharing and governance (including GDPR) are also discussed. The chapter analyses the AWS audit and compliance controls and demonstrates securing AI/ML pipelines with Google's Secure AI Framework and the GAAI Top 10 Controls. Combining AI security with cloud security enables the development of secure and compliant pipelines that safeguard data while enhancing AI/ML analytics.

In the coming years, data analytics will be greatly impacted due to the rising interaction between AI/ML and cloud computing which will innovate and make data more scalable across the globe. Corporations will be able to utilize cloud-based ML to process large amounts of data at an unbelievably fast pace, allowing businesses of all scales to utilize data analytics. With technology like hyper automation, organizations will be able to automate all workflows fully to increase efficiency and make real-time decisions. Cloud computing will be supplemented with Edge AI which will allow real-time data processing within the device itself, which is crucial for IoT networks and self-driving vehicles. Learning that is federated will solve data privacy issues because it allows dispersed ML training to make sure sensitive data is not removed from local systems. This is extremely important for critical industries like healthcare and finance.

As with all cloud computing technologies, Explainable AI will become relevant with pointers focusing on helping streamline the regulatory processes on deploying and utilizing ML models with high trustworthiness metrics especially in finance and healthcare. In addition to these, disruptive technologies such as quantum computing and blockchain will change the landscape of cloud computing analytics. Quantum computers will solve complex optimization problems thousands of times faster than the most powerful supercomputers available, giving rise to significant advancements in drug discovery, logistics and even cryptography. Blockchain will list the above capabilities and add data transparency and security for building the next generation of decentralized AI systems that ensure trustworthy data and models.

Chapter 11 discusses how ML coupled with cloud technology is changing the face of data analytics by enabling organizations to manage huge volumes of data quickly with high return on investment. It analyses the development of ML via the cloud and how it has changed specialization like healthcare, retail and city planning. Further, it highlights hyper automation, AI on the edge, federated AI and explainable AIs as hot topics that will drive analytics in the future.

The book discusses the intersection between data analytics, ML and cloud computing that is transforming industries such as healthcare, education, e-commerce and logistics. It lays out how traditional approaches evolved to AI-powered solutions, detailing the important technologies such as Hadoop, Spark and ML that lie at the heart of their progression. The book also emphasizes cloud computing's pivotal role in driving scalability, flexibility and innovation, with a focus on serverless architecture, hybrid clouds and ML integration. It tackles pressing challenges like data privacy, security and algorithmic bias while offering a forward-looking perspective on emerging trends such as hyperautomation, edge AI and federated learning, all set to redefine the future of data analytics.

1 Data Analytics and Compliance in Cloud-Machine Learning

Seema Rawat and Praveen Kumar

1.1 INTRODUCTION

With the advent of data analytics, it has become one amongst the most prominent fields in contemporary society that directs decision-making algorithms and even deploys across a range of sectors from business to healthcare or government, particularly education. In simple words, data analytics is the process of analysing raw datasets in order to uncover valuable insights which can support decision-making and solving difficult business problems with evidence-based solutions. With technology taking its leap, data analytics has gained prominence as a critical tool for organizations to streamline how they operate and perform while also providing a competitive advantage for them [4].

Data Analytics is such a vast term that includes all the ways and tools used for data processing, analysing, and extracting useful information through processes that do not need intensive human intervention. This domain incorporates descriptive analytics – ensuring that historical data is summarized within the context of operations practices, predictive analytics that uses statistical models and machine learning (ML) algorithms for forecasting future trends (indicators) based on current performance patterns, among others. While each of these may shine for specific use cases, together they cover a broad set of scenarios to analyse structured and unstructured data in this ever-growing landscape that is becoming more-and-more driven by the availability and ease with which one can make sense of diverse types of data [3, 5].

With the growing work in advanced technologies like ML and artificial intelligence (AI), there is a rapid evolution of data analytics from traditional methods which were very descriptive to more dynamic and strategic outputs.

Similar transformation in the domain of cloud computing has also provided scalable and efficient solutions with regard to large datasets. Organizations are now able to deploy scalable complex ML techniques in the market which gives great efficiency and precision in results for real-world problems. As the work in the domain of AI and cloud computing is expanding fast, the new opportunities to work in data analytics are also getting generated.

In this chapter, we are going to particularly talk about the expansion of data analytics because of growing work in AI and cloud computing for future innovations.

DOI: 10.1201/9781003396772-2

We will see the transformation of data analytics from small descriptive techniques to futuristic technology of limitless opportunities.

1.2 THE SHIFT TOWARDS BIG DATA

As the world has moved towards more and more digitalization, vast amounts of data are created every single second all around the globe. This explosion of data, sometimes called "big data", presents new possibilities and challenges for organizations as well as individuals. In big data context, it is characterized by the following four key attributes:

- **Velocity:** Speed at which data is produced and processed
- **Volume:** Sheer scale of data generated
- **Variety:** Diverse types of structured, unstructured and semi-structured data
- **Veracity:** Uncertainty and quality of the data

1.2.1 Challenges of Big Data

The data is so large and numerous that traditional methods of processing the analytics could not handle it. To help with that, new capabilities and methodologies have been developed so companies can process huge amounts of data on the fly [6–8].

1.2.2 Applications of Big Data Analytics

Big data analytics brings the capabilities of these technologies to bear, allowing deeper customer insights into behaviour, operational efficiency and market trends. Big data analytics has empowered many industries such as healthcare, financial services or retail, with its potential of pattern identification and anomaly detection leading to a significant increase in the rate at which innovations occur [3, 8, 9].

Industries like social media have made it important for development of systems which can analyse, process and give meaningful results using big data. Cloud computing in combination with AI has given great results to optimally solve the challenge related to big data.

In today's time, there are various platforms like AWS, MS Azure which make it easy for organizations to effectively store and manage big data without any complex tasks taking place. The same task has been made even easier with the integration of ML techniques. Organizations are now able to get real-time precise insights within limited time on a large set of data. For example, in the stock market industry, tasks like storing past shares data and prediction of new prices have been made easy by ML algorithms that take as little as a few seconds to give reliable results.

One of the most impacted industries which is also getting the most results from this new evolution is the healthcare industry. In healthcare a large set of data is created even for a single patient making it hard to store and manage. Through cloud computing it has become easier to store and manage the same data. Also with the latest advanced ML techniques the operations on data like diagnosis have become very easy and fast.

In conclusion, the cloud computing industry's drastic advancement has made it easier to handle large data and compute them. Further integration with ML techniques has become even more fast, efficient and reliable. This revolution of integration of data analytics with ML and cloud computing will be a great help for future innovations.

1.3 THE EVOLUTION FROM DATA ANALYTICS TO DATA SCIENCE

Data science is a vast field that differs from data analytics for how we use the collected data. Data analytics is in most cases restricted to analysing historical data and then extracting insights, while data science not only goes one step ahead by doing the analysis but also involves various disciplines on a larger scale like statistics, ML, AI, computational algorithms, etc. Data scientists are not only analysing data, but they build models, develop algorithms and tools that can learn from the new/recent data for making predictions or classifying information, or even to generate some necessary knowledge automatically.

1.3.1 Capabilities of Data Science

As data science permeates various industries, it is playing an integral role in shaping the next generation of capabilities – predictive modelling, deep learning and natural language processing. This advancement enables companies to move from a reactive stance with respect to data (i.e. analysing what has occurred) into an approach that is more proactive and predictive. Some examples include companies using data science models in order to predict customer churn, optimize their supply chain, detect fraud or even personalize marketing [4, 10].

1.3.2 Examples of Data Science Applications

Organizations use data science for various purposes, including predicting customer churn, optimizing supply chains, detecting fraud and personalizing marketing efforts. These capabilities demonstrate the transformative potential of data science across industries [1, 9].

1.4 BIG DATA ANALYTICS

Big data analytics, as a specialized branch of data science, specifically focuses on processing and analysing massive datasets to uncover hidden patterns, correlations and other actionable insights. This discipline is fuelled by the availability of large-scale datasets, advancements in cloud computing, and the development of sophisticated algorithms capable of handling complex and varied data types.

1.4.1 Key Technologies

A key component of big data analytics is its ability to transform unstructured data, such as social media posts, videos and sensor data, into structured insights that can drive decision-making. For example organizations can analyse customer sentiments on social media platforms to improve products, or hospitals can use patient data from wearable devices to enhance healthcare outcomes [7, 8].

1.4.2 Applications in Practice

Big data analytics leverages technologies such as Hadoop, Apache Spark and NoSQL databases, which are designed to store, process and analyse large volumes of data efficiently. Furthermore, the integration of ML algorithms with big data analytics enables organizations to identify trends and patterns in real-time, automate decision-making processes and predict future outcomes with high accuracy [2, 5].

There are multiple examples of practical implementation of data analytics with integration of cloud computing and ML. These revolutionizing advancements have helped organizations get faster and better results. Here are some examples of practical implementation:

1. **Smart Traffic management:** Multiple cities globally have implemented a cloud-based ML model to analyse and keep track of traffic data using IoT sensors and cameras. The model provides real-time traffic optimization helping in removing high traffic and congestion.
2. **Energy management:** Cloud platforms are using large datasets to analyse the pattern in energy usage over years for optimal supplies. Machine learning is further giving results like forecasting future energy usage insights where energy can be optimized.

Combination of both cloud computing with ML shows how data analytics can practically be used in practice to address the complex challenges to create solutions in different industries.

1.5 CONCLUSION

As we move further into the digital age, the role of data analytics and big data will continue to evolve. The rise of the Internet of Things (IoT), AI and edge computing will generate even more data which will create both opportunities and challenges for organizations. Companies that can successfully harness the power of data analytics and big data would be able to conquer their sector by being innovators that work through informed decisions [4, 10].

At its core, data analytics and big data are more than a passing technical trend; it is a new model for how business, government and individual thinking will conceptualize problems. This continual transformation towards data science illustrates the significance of comprehending and utilizing data in our progressively connected environment with complex challenges.

REFERENCES

[1] Li Chunquan, Yaqiong Chen, and Yuling Shang. "A Review of Industrial Big Data for Decision Making in Intelligent Manufacturing." *Engineering Science and Technology, an International Journal* 29 (2022): 101021. https://doi.org/10.1016/j.jestch.2021.06.001.

[2] Agostino Marengo. "Navigating the Nexus of AI and IoT: A Comprehensive Review of Data Analytics and Privacy Paradigms." *Internet of Things* 27 (2024): 101318. https://doi.org/10.1016/j.iot.2024.101318.

[3] Riaz Ahmed, Sumayya Shaheen, and Simon P. Philbin. "The Role of Big Data Analytics and Decision-Making in Achieving Project Success." *Journal of Engineering and Technology Management* 65 (2022): 101697. https://doi.org/10.1016/j.jengtecman.2022.101697.

[4] Yaghoob Karimi, Mostafa Haghi Kashani, Mohammad Akbari, and Ebrahim Mahdipour. "Leveraging Big Data in Smart Cities: A Systematic Review." *Concurrency and Computation: Practice and Experience* 33 (2021). https://doi.org/10.1002/cpe.6379.

[5] Justin Zuopeng Zhang, Praveen Ranjan Srivastava, Dheeraj Sharma, and Prajwal Eachempati. "Big Data Analytics and Machine Learning: A Retrospective Overview and Bibliometric Analysis." *Expert Systems with Applications* 184 (2021): 115561. https://doi.org/10.1016/j.eswa.2021.115561.

[6] Magda I. El-Afifi, Bishoy E. Sedhom, Abdelfattah A. Eladl, and Sanjeevikumar Padmanaban. "Survey of Technologies, Techniques, and Applications for Big Data Analytics in Smart Energy Hub." *Energy Strategy Reviews* 56 (2024): 101582. https://doi.org/10.1016/j.esr.2024.101582.

[7] Adilson Carlos Yoshikuni, Rajeev Dwivedi, Marcio Quadros Lopes dos Santos, Feng Liu, and Miguel Mitio Yoshikuni. "Sustainable Environmental Performance: A Cross-Country Fuzzy Set Qualitative Comparative Analysis Empirical Study of Big Data Analytics and Contextual Factors." *Journal of Cleaner Production* 481 (2024): 144040. https://doi.org/10.1016/j.jclepro.2024.144040.

[8] Ao Zan, Yanhong Yao, and Huanhuan Chen. "How Do Big Data Analytics Capabilities and Improvisational Capabilities Shape Firm Innovation?" *Journal of Engineering and Technology Management* 74 (2024): 101842. https://doi.org/10.1016/j.jengtecman.2024.101842.

[9] Yanfang Niu, Limeng Ying, Jie Yang, Mengqi Bao, and C. B. Sivaparthipan. "Organizational Business Intelligence and Decision Making Using Big Data Analytics." *Information Processing & Management* 58, no. 6 (2021): 102725. https://doi.org/10.1016/j.ipm.2021.102725.

[10] Uthayasankar Sivarajah, Sachin Kumar, Vinod Kumar, Sheshadri Chatterjee, and Jing Li. "A Study on Big Data Analytics and Innovation: From Technological and Business Cycle Perspectives." *Technological Forecasting and Social Change* 202 (2024): 123328. https://doi.org/10.1016/j.techfore.2024.123328.

2 Data Analytics
Tools and Technologies

Dr. Neelu Jyothi Ahuja

2.1 INTRODUCTION

Big data analytics (BDA) software is widely utilized by companies that operate Hadoop alongside big data-processing and distribution tools to gather and store data. These solutions often integrate with centralized information distributed platforms, serving as the primary storage hub for an organization's unified data. Big data has become essential for businesses to enhance decision-making and achieve a competitive advantage. Consequently, technologies like Apache Spark and Cassandra are in high demand, with organizations seeking professionals skilled in their use. The importance of big data in driving business decision and maintaining a competitive edge continues to grow. As a result, Big Data technologies like Apache Spark and Cassandra are highly sought after. Organization actively seeks professionals proficient in leveraging these tools to maximize the value of the data generated within the company. These tools play a crucial role in managing massive datasets and identifying patterns and trends within them. If you plan to enter the Big data industry, equipping yourself with these technologies is essential. Let's explore some of the most prominent Big Data technologies (Sandhiya and Prabavathy 2021).

Big data analytics provides significant benefits to organizations such as increased productivity and competitiveness by processing customer-generated data (CGD) in different formats. (Lee et al. 2015) It includes multimedia content, messages, and social media. Companies such as Apple Inc., Google LLC, Meta, eBay Inc. and Amazon.com, Inc., are constantly using digital marketing information to improve their business operations. BDA is gaining importance as it allows organizations to manage their data more effectively. This change increases product performance, operational flexibility and overall business agility. Moreover, it has been instrumental in the rise of cloud computing, where BDA is provided as a service, enabling more adaptable use of information systems (IS). BDA is highly adaptable, enabling decision-makers to evaluate both structured and unstructured data from various sources, including sensor devices, machine logs, mobile communications (MC), geospatial data (GD) and user-generated content (UGC) in the digital economy (Grover and Kar 2017).

The proliferation of big data has made traditional computing infrastructures inadequate for managing and extracting insights from vast datasets. Modern enterprises increasingly turn to cloud platforms and big data tools to implement machine learning (ML) pipelines efficiently. Apache Hadoop, with components like HDFS, MapReduce and YARN, revolutionized data storage and distributed processing.

DOI: 10.1201/9781003396772-3

Parallelly, Apache Spark emerged as a faster alternative with advanced analytics capabilities, particularly through its MLlib library for scalable ML tasks. Apache Storm caters to the needs of real-time stream processing, enabling immediate insights from continuously generated data. Integrating visualization platforms such as Tableau and Lumify simplifies interpreting and presenting data and model predictions. Simultaneously, tools like Splunk improve monitoring and operational analytics by leveraging ML. This chapter explores the convergence of these technologies, specifically examining their compatibility with cloud platforms such as AWS, Azure and GCP. It highlights how cloud-based solutions boost scalability, cost-effectiveness and resource management, making it possible to implement advanced ML workflows across different industries.

2.2 BIG DATA TECHNOLOGIES

This content provides a comprehensive overview of key big data technologies, examining their architectures and applications. It offers a detailed discussion on Apache Hadoop, focusing on its core components: YARN for resource management, MapReduce for parallel computation and HDFS for distributed storage. The content also highlights advancements like HDFS federation and YARN's adaptable execution engine, with a comparison of Hadoop 1 and Hadoop 2. Apache Storm is introduced as a solution for real-time data processing, while Apache Spark is recognized for its advanced analytics capabilities and efficient handling of large datasets. Visualization tools like Tableau and Lumify are highlighted for their strengths in data modelling, geospatial analysis and predictive analytics. Splunk is explored for its data indexing and real-time analytics capabilities, including an overview of its architecture and deployment options. The content emphasizes the scalability, fault tolerance and integration capabilities of these technologies, illustrating their applications in business intelligence, ML and data visualization.

2.2.1 Apache Hadoop

Apache Hadoop is a Java-based open-source framework designed for analysing large datasets through parallel processing and distributed storage. Initially created in 2006 by Doug Cutting and Mike Cafarella to support the Apache Nutch web crawler, it has since become a cornerstone of Big Data analytics (Alexsoft 2022). Hadoop is built to scale from a single server to thousands of machines, each providing local computation and storage. Instead of depending on hardware for high availability, its library is designed to detect and manage failures at the application layer, ensuring reliable service on a cluster of computers, even when individual nodes may fail (https://hadoop.apache.org/)

A study by the Business Application Research Center (BARC) highlights Hadoop's extensive applications, including

- Acting as a test environment (sandbox) for traditional business intelligence (BI), advanced analytics of large datasets, condition-based maintenance (CBM) and data discovery;

- Functioning as a repository for unprocessed data;
- Enabling large-scale data integration (DI); and
- Providing a robust foundation for implementing data lake architectures.

Hadoop's capabilities are utilized across various industries, such as manufacturing, banking and transportation. Furthermore, the adoption of the platform is expected to grow significantly by 2030. According to a recent report by Allied Market Research, the telecommunications, healthcare and government sectors are anticipated to drive the highest growth in Big Data platform adoption.

Figure 2.1 represents a distributed computing architecture commonly used for big data processing, resembling frameworks like Hadoop. At its core, an active metadata manager coordinates the cluster, supported by a standby master for fault tolerance. A cluster manager manages resource allocation, while a task manager is responsible for task scheduling and monitoring. The system comprises multiple data nodes, each equipped with a node manager and map/reduce capabilities for parallel data storage and processing. A workstation serves as the interface for submitting and tracking jobs. This architecture is designed to enable distributed storage and parallel processing, making it well-suited for handling large-scale datasets efficiently.

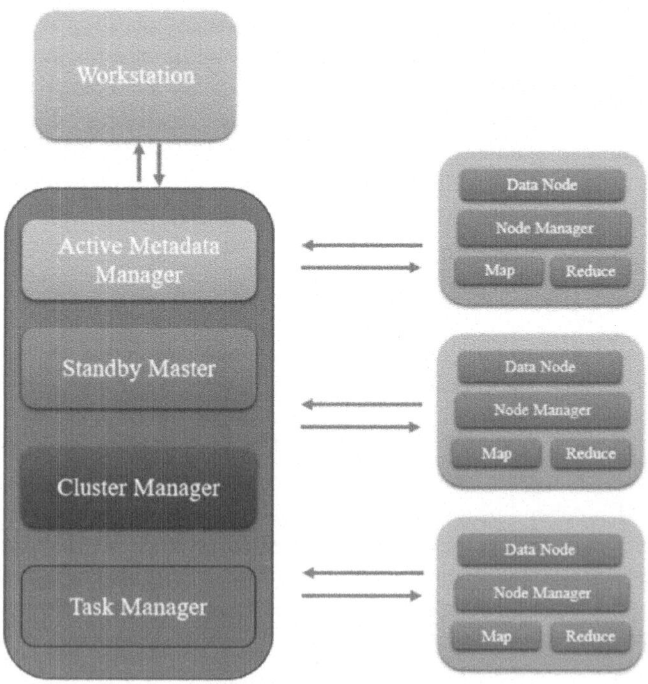

FIGURE 2.1 Hadoop cluster architecture: The diagram illustrates a distributed computing architecture, showing communication between a central management system and distributed data nodes.

Independence among Hadoop nodes does not imply equality, as they are divided into three distinct roles:

- **Master Node:** Handles data and resource allocation while overseeing parallel processing. This function demands the most powerful hardware.
- **Salve or worker node:** Executes tasks assigned by the master node.
- **Client or edge node:** Acts as an interface between the Hadoop cluster and external systems or applications, handling data loading and retrieving processing results without being part of the master-slave hierarchy.

The size of a Hadoop (HDFS) cluster is determined by the amount of incoming data. For example, LinkedIn operates one of the largest clusters with approximately 10,000 nodes. However, smaller setups are possible, starting with just four machines one for all master processes and three for salve tasks with the option to scale up as needed. For testing and evaluation purposes, a single computer is sufficient to deploy Hadoop.

Regardless of its size, each Hadoop cluster comprises three functional layers: Hadoop Distributed File System (HDFS) for storing data, Hadoop MapReduce for data processing, and Hadoop Yet Another Resource Negotiator (YARN) for managing resources (Alexsoft 2022).

2.2.2 Hadoop Distributed File System

The HDFS stores files by dividing them into fixed-size blocks, which are distributed across different nodes in a Hadoop cluster (Figure 2.2). This approach enables HDFS

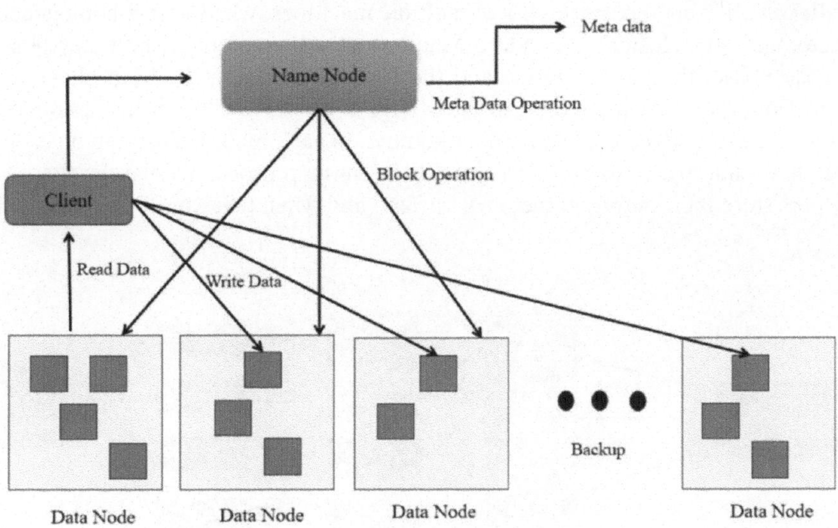

FIGURE 2.2 Architecture of the Hadoop Distributed File System (HDFS): The figure illustrates HDFS architecture consists of the Name Node managing metadata, Data Nodes storing data and handling block operations, and Clients reading/writing data. Replication across Data Nodes ensures fault tolerance and high data availability.

to handle files larger than the disk capacity of any individual node. Files stored in HDFS follow a write-once, read many patterns and cannot be modified after being written. HDFS operates on a master/slave architecture. The NameNode server acts as the master, managing the file system's namespace and regulating client access to files. The DataNodes, functioning as salves, handle data storage and execute the instructions provided by the NameNode. To ensure fault tolerance, HDFS replicates each data blocks across multiple nodes within the cluster (Mavridis and Karatza 2017). A key feature of HDFS is its ability to partition large datasets across multiple machines. The fundamental unit of data in HDFS is a block, which is larger than those used in local files systems. This design minimizes the cost of accessing these blocks (Jain 2017).

Figure 2.2 illustrates the architecture of the HDFS. The **NameNode** serves as the central component, managing file metadata such as file names, locations and permissions, while the actual data is not stored here. Data is stored in blocks across **DataNodes**, which distribute the data throughout the cluster to ensure redundancy. A **Client** communicates with the NameNode to locate specific data and then interacts directly with the DataNodes to read or write data blocks. A **Backup Node**, often referred to as a **Standby NameNode** in modern HDFS implementations, enhances fault tolerance by maintaining a synchronized copy of the NameNode's metadata. This architecture supports scalable, reliable and fault-tolerant storage for processing large datasets.

2.2.3 MapReduce

Hadoop's MapReduce programming model is designed to process large datasets in parallel by utilizing the processors of multiple machines, whether in a homogeneous or heterogeneous cluster. A standard MapReduce job consists of three key phases: the Map phase, the Shuffle phase and the Reduce phase. In the Map phase, each record from the input file stored in the HDFS is processed. To ensure uniqueness, Hadoop adds on offset, often a random number, to each record. The map phase produces key-value pairs, where keys from different map processes may be the same. Mappers store their output in memory buffers, and when these buffers overflow, the

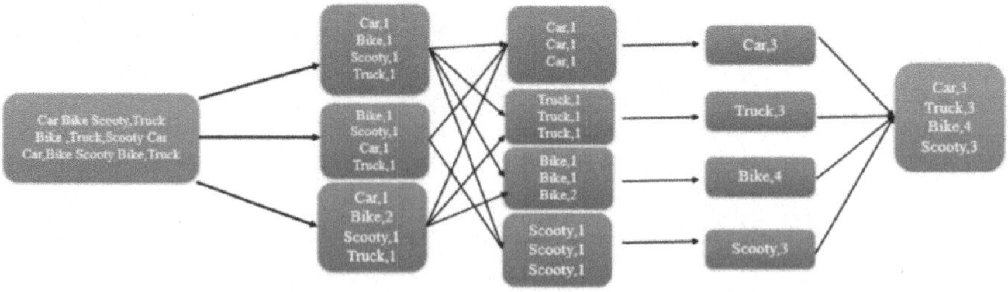

FIGURE 2.3 MapReduce Programming model: The image shows how MapReduce processes data in parallel by splitting it, mapping it to key-value pairs, shuffling and sorting those pairs by key, and then reducing them to produce a final aggregated result.

excess data is written to disk. Excessive spilling can lead to heavy I/O operations that negatively impact performance. Additionally, the mapper performs part of the sorting process. Following the map phase, the shuffle-and-sort phase organizes the map output based on the keys. Once this phase produces a sorted stream of key-value pairs, the reduce phase is triggered. Each Reduce task handles a distinct key along with its associated values. The output from the Reduce phase is subsequently written back to the HDFS. It is crucial to note that while the Map and Reduce phases are executed sequentially, multiple Map and Reduce tasks can run concurrently, depending on the size of the input file (Jain 2017).

This image demonstrates the MapReduce process. Input data, such as a list of vehicles, is divided and transformed into key-value pairs (e.g. "Car, 1") during the **Mapping** phase. In the **Sorting and Shuffling** stage, pairs with the same key are grouped together. The final **Reducing** phase aggregates the values for each key, such as summing up the counts. For example, three instances of "Car, 1" are combined into "Car, 3", representing three occurrences of "Car". This model enables efficient processing of large datasets by parallelizing the mapping and reducing tasks.

2.2.4 YARN (Next-Generation MapReduce)

2.2.4.1 The Tracking of a MapReduce Job Involves Various Components and Sub-Components

Figure 2.4 depicts YARN, the resource management layer of Hadoop. Clients submit jobs to the Resource Manager, which oversees resource allocation across the cluster. Each node runs a Node Manager responsible for managing containers (allocated resources) and reporting their status. For every application, an Application

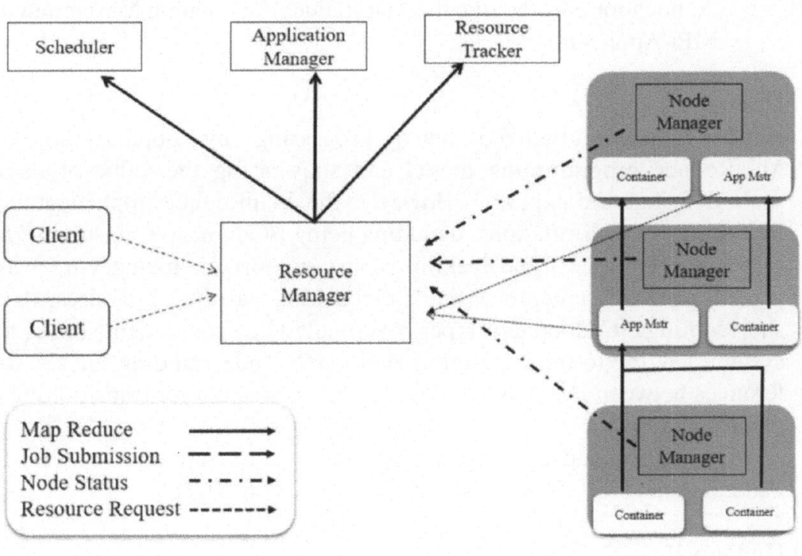

FIGURE 2.4 YARN's architecture: It shows how clients submit jobs to the Resource Manager, which then assigns resources to Node Managers that run containers to execute the applications.

Master coordinates with the Resource Manager to request resources and handles the execution of tasks within containers. The Scheduler, a component of the Resource Manager, determines how resources are allocated on the basis of predefined strategies. This architecture separates resource management from processing frameworks like MapReduce, allowing for diverse workloads to run on a single Hadoop cluster.

(1) **Resource Manager:**
   (a) **Scheduler:** Hierarchical queues can be used, or MapReduce schedulers like the Capacity Scheduler (CS) or Fair Scheduler (FS) can be integrated. Additionally, workflow management tools such as Azkaban or Oozie can be utilized.
   (b) **Application Manager:** The Application Manager handles task submissions, negotiates the initial container to run the Application Master (AM), and restarts the AM container if it fails.
   (c) **Resource Tracker**: Manages settings like the maximum number of retries for the AM, the frequency of container health checks, and the time to wait before considering a Node Manager as dead.
      a. Each hardware node includes a Node Manager (NM) agent tasked with overseeing, tracking and reporting resource "containers" (e.g. CPU, memory, disk and network) to the Resource Manager (RM) or Scheduler. These containers take the place of the fixed Map and Reduce slots found in earlier versions of MapReduce.
      b. The AM is designed for each application and framework, managing the scheduling and execution of application tasks. In a cluster supporting multiple frameworks, such as MapReduce and Message Passing Interface (MPI), each framework has its own dedicated Application Master, like the MapReduce Application Master and the MPI Application Master.

(1) **Hadoop 1:**

Hadoop 1 revolutionized batch processing by popularizing the MapReduce programming model and showcasing the value of large-scale distributed computing. However, the MapReduce implementation in Hadoop 1 had limitations, including being I/O intensive, unsuitable for interactive analytics, and lacking robust support for memory-intensive algorithms like graph processing and machine learning. To address these shortcomings, Hadoop developers overhauled key components of the file system, leading to the creation of Hadoop 2. Understanding the key differences between Hadoop 1 and Hadoop 2 is essential for transitioning to the newer version.

Two significant advancements in Hadoop 2 are the introduction of HDFS Federation and the YARN resource manager (Jain 2017)

(2) **Hadoop 2:**

HDFS has two main components: the namespace Service and the block storage service. The namespace service manages data and directory operations such as creating and modifying, while block storage service manages operations, block operations and replication.

In Hadoop 1, a single NameNode (NN) hosted the entire namespace cluster of Hadoop. With the introduction of HDFS Federation in Hadoop 2, multiple NameNode can manage namespaces, enable horizontal scalability, increase performance and support multiple names. It is worth noting that HDFS Federation is designed to be compatible with existing NameNode configurations without modification.

For Hadoop administrators, transitioning to HDFS Federation requires formatting the NameNodes (NNs), upgrading to the latest version of the Hadoop cluster software and incorporating additional NameNodes into the cluster.

This diagram highlights the differences between Hadoop 1 and Hadoop 2 architectures. In Hadoop 1, the monolithic design relied on MapReduce for both data processing and cluster resource management, which restricted scalability and compatibility with other processing frameworks. Hadoop 2 introduced **YARN** to separate resource management from data processing. YARN now handles resource allocation, enabling multiple data-processing frameworks (such as MapReduce, Spark and others) to run simultaneously. In both versions, **HDFS** serves as the foundational storage layer, ensuring fault-tolerant data storage. This architectural shift in Hadoop 2 enhanced resource efficiency and system flexibility.

(3) Hadoop 2: YARN

The implementation of HDFS Federation greatly improves the scalability and dependability of Hadoop systems while YARN an upgrade, in Hadoop 2 release brings performance improvements for certain applications and enables support, for various processing frameworks with a more flexible execution engine in place of the rigid coupling seen in Hadoop 1. Often

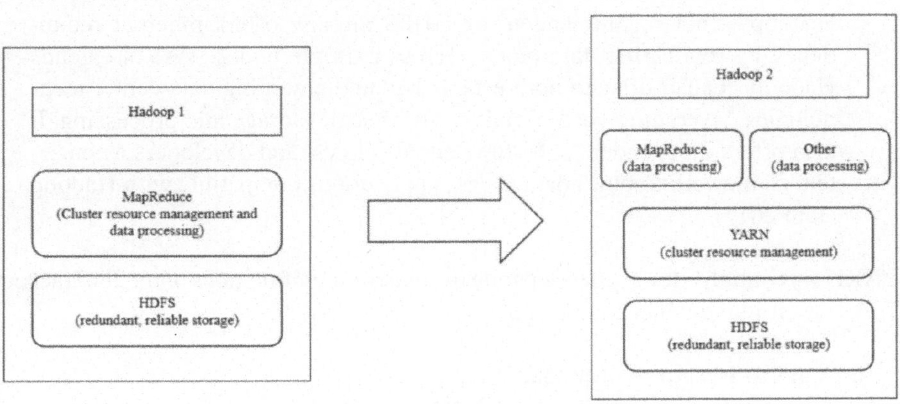

FIGURE 2.5 Hadoop 1 vs. Hadoop 2: The diagram illustrates the differences between Hadoop 1 and Hadoop 2.

referred to as the "brain" of Hadoop system, YARN plays a role in managing tasks by overseeing workloads and maintaining a secure environment for all users while ensuring that high availability features are in place. Like an operating system running on a server, YARN enables a variety of applications to operate on a shared platform designed for user access. In the version of Hadoop 1, users had the flexibility to write MapReduce programs using Java or utilize scripting languages such as Python or Ruby through streaming mechanisms. They also had the option to work with Pig, a language, for data transformation purposes. Regardless of the approach, all relied on the MapReduce framework.

YARN, however, supports multiple processing models beyond MapReduce, reducing reliance on its often I/O-intensive and high-latency framework. This advancement allows Hadoop users to explore alternative processing models, understanding their strengths and limitations to match them with specific use cases.

Key YARN components, such as **Resource Manager**, **Node Manager** and **Application Master**, are integral to its architecture. The Application Master can communicate with multiple hardware nodes and does not need to be replicated on every node. For example nodes may only house containers while the Application Master resides on a nearby node within the same rack, using rack awareness to optimize communication.

Hadoop currently lacks support for IPv6. Organizations operating with IPv6 can use machine names with a DNS server instead of IP addresses for node labelling. IPv6 adoption is gaining traction, particularly in regions like North America, following early adoption in markets like China due to historical IPv4 limitations.

HDFS is built to handle DataNode failures without crashing the entire cluster. When a DataNode fails, the cluster's performance decreases proportionally to the lost storage and processing capacity, as remaining nodes take over the workload. Using RAID (Redundant Array of Independent Disks) for DataNodes or the Linux Logical Volume Manager (LVM) with Hadoop is not recommended, as HDFS already offers inherent redundancy by replicating data blocks across multiple nodes. YARN extends Hadoop's capabilities to both established and emerging data centre technologies, leveraging cost-effective, linear-scale storage and processing. It also offers independent software vendors (ISVs) and developers a consistent framework to build data access applications compatible with Hadoop (Jain 2017)

YARN was initially designed to separate the two primary functions of the JobTracker/TaskTracker into distinct components:

1. A global **Resource Manager**
2. A per-application **Application Master**
3. A per-node **Node Manager** acting as a slave
4. A per-application **Container** running on a NodeManager

2.2.5 Apache Storm

Apache Storm is a distributed, real-time big (RTB) data-processing framework built to manage large data volumes in a fault-tolerant and horizontally scalable way, with high ingestion rates. It utilizes Apache ZooKeeper (ZK) to oversee the distributed system and maintain cluster state. Storm processes raw, real-time data streams by passing them through a series of small processing units, ultimately generating valuable output.

The core components of Apache Storm, as shown in Figure 2.6, illustrate its architecture. A key feature of Apache Storm is its fault tolerance and high speed, with no Single Point of Failure (SPOF) (Basha et al. 2019)

In each Supervisor node, several high-level components play crucial roles:

- **Topology:** Operates across multiple worker processes distributed across several nodes.
- **Spout:** Reads records from a Messaging system and emits them as message streams. It can also connect to APIs, such as Twitter, to emit a stream of tweets.
- **Bolt:** Represents the smallest unit of processing logic within a topology. A bolt's output can serve as the input for another bolt, enabling a sequential data-processing flow within the topology.

This image illustrates a Storm topology, a graph designed for real-time data processing. Spouts act as data sources, emitting data in the form of tuples (units of data). Bolts process these tuples by applying operations such as filtering, aggregation or

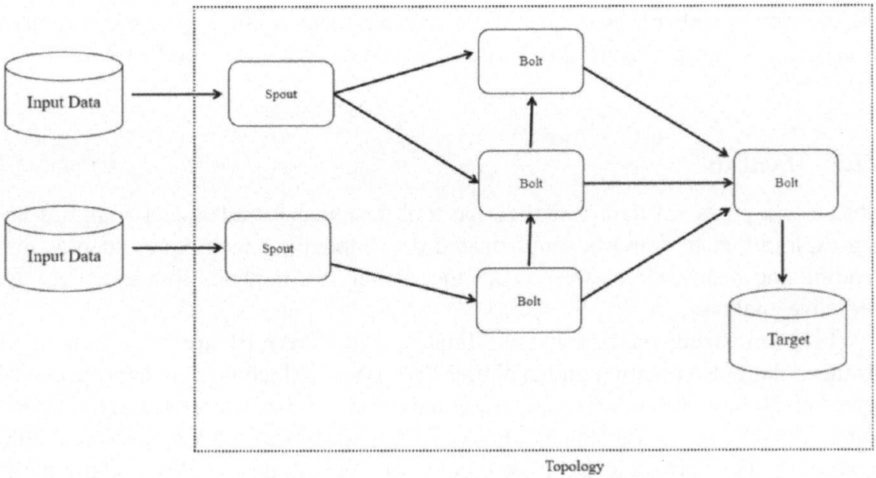

FIGURE 2.6 Storm topology: Where Spouts generate data streams that are processed by Bolts. Bolts handle transformations and computations, producing results that are sent to a target data store, thereby establishing a real-time data-processing pipeline.

transformations. Tuples move through the topology along directed edges, forming the data flow. The entire processing structure is referred to as the Topology. Data from input sources enters through spouts, and is processed by interconnected bolts, and the results are sent to the target destination. This architecture supports continuous data flow, enabling real-time analytics and stream processing.

Features:

- Capable of transmitting one million 100-byte messages per second for each node.
- Ensures data processing occurs at least once.
- Offers excellent horizontal scalability.
- Includes built-in fault tolerance.
- Automatically restarts in case of crashes.
- Developed using Clojure.
- Operates with a topology structured as a directed acyclic graph (DAG).
- Produces output files in JSON (JavaScript Object Notation) format.
- Supports diverse use cases, such as real-time analytics, log analysis, ETL (Extract, Transform, Load), continuous computing, distributed RPC (Remote Procedure Call) and deep learning.

2.2.6 Spark Framework Environment

Apache Spark is highly efficient for data engineering, capable of handling large datasets with minimal reliance on the underlying infrastructure. It supports data ingestion, processing, ML and model refinement, while also providing a framework for developing distributed systems. One of the main strengths of big data technologies is their rapid data access and transfer, achieved by utilizing MapReduce to keep data in memory rather than on disk. Furthermore, these technologies offer extensive library support for programming languages such as Java, Scala and Python (Basha et al. 2019)

2.2.7 Tableau

Tableau is a powerful data visualization tool designed for advanced analytics and data exploration. It supports sophisticated data modelling techniques such as data blending and reshaping, as well as advanced analytics methods like statistical and predictive analysis.

When comparing methodologies, Tableau and Power BI are better suited for advanced data visualization and analytics than Excel, which is more appropriate for basic data manipulation and analysis. For handling large datasets or integrating data from multiple sources, Tableau and Power BI provide more advanced data modelling capabilities. They also enable the use of advanced techniques like ML and predictive analytics to derive insights and forecast outcomes from data.

The choice of methodology ultimately depends on the user's needs and preferences. While Excel is suitable for simpler tasks, Tableau and Power BI excel in scenarios requiring complex data modelling and sophisticated analytics, especially when dealing with extensive datasets or diverse data sources (Tripathi et al. 2023)

2.2.8 Lumify

Lumify, developed by Altamira, is a free and open-source tool designed for large-scale data (Benlachmi and Hasnaoui 2021) integration, analysis and visualization, created to address challenges associated with managing vast amounts of data.

Key features of Lumify include search indexing, data mapping, automated pattern recognition, network analysis, spatial data integration, location analysis, multimedia content review and real-time collaboration through shared projects or workspaces (Sandhiya and Prabavathy 2021).

Advantages:

- Highly scalable
- Ensures robust security
- Backed by specialized development team
- Compatible with cloud-based environments and integrates seamlessly with Amazon AWS

2.2.9 Splunk

Splunk is a powerful tool designed to search and index log files, helping Institutions gain useful findings from their data. One of its primary benefits is its use of indexing to store data, which eliminates the need for an external database to manage the information. Splunk is extensively used for monitoring and querying large-scale data. It indexes and correlates data to make it easily searchable, enabling the creation of alerts, reports and visualizations. It can detect data patterns, generate metrics and aid in troubleshooting, helping to resolve business issues such as IT management, security and compliance (https://cloudian.com/guides/splunk-big-data/splunk-data-analytics-splunk-enterprise-or-splunk-hunk/).

2.2.10 Splunk Architecture

Splunk's architecture consists of components responsible for data collection, indexing and analytics (Figure 2.7).

The foundational level of Splunk architecture outlines the various methods for data input that Splunk supports. These data input methods can be set up to send information to Splunk indexers, where it may be parsed or sanitized before indexing, if required. Once the data is indexed, the subsequent step involves querying and analysing the log data.

Splunk provides two deployment models: stand-alone and distributed deployment. Searches are conducted on the basis of the chosen model. The Splunk engine also includes other components such as the Knowledge Manager, reporting and scheduling features, and alerting capabilities. Users can interact with the full Splunk

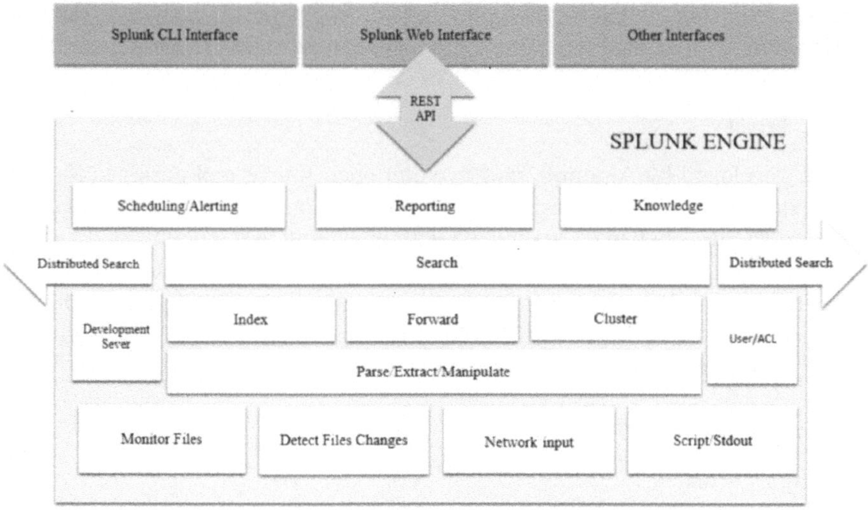

FIGURE 2.7 Splunk's structure: The image shows the structure of Splunk, emphasizing its data ingestion capabilities, data-processing pipeline, indexing mechanism, search functionality and various user interfaces. It highlights Splunk's ability to handle large volumes of machine-generated data and provide powerful tools for searching, monitoring and analysis.

engine via the Splunk Command-Line Interface (CLI), web dashboard and Software Development Kit (SDK), which are compatible with most programming languages. Splunk deploys a distributed server process on the host machine called "splunkd", which is responsible for indexing and processing large volumes of data from multiple sources. This process can manage high data streams and index them for real-time analytics (RTA) across one or more data streams (Kumar and Yadav n.d.)

2.2.11 Integration of Big Data Tools with ML on Cloud Platforms

The processing and analysis of large datasets have been completely transformed by the combination of ML in cloud computing environments with big data frameworks like Apache Hadoop, HDFS, MapReduce, YARN, Apache Storm and Spark, as well as analytics tool like Tableau, Lumify and Splunk. The basis for training sophisticated ML algorithms is provided by HDFS, which provides distributed, scalable and fault-tolerant storage for a variety of datasets. Large-scale clusters can process data in parallel thanks to MapReduce, which guarantees speed and efficiency when managing heavy workloads. In the meantime, Hadoop 2's YARN further expands these capabilities through better cluster management and dynamic resource allocation, guaranteeing that ML models run smoothly on cloud infrastructures.

Real-time analytics makes use of frameworks such as Apache Storm together with Hadoop which facilitate stream processing. This is important for applications such as sentiment extraction from social media and sensor data analysis, on which dynamic applications rely. Furthermore, Apache Spark supports in-memory data processing, which is important for some of the iterative ML techniques such as gradient boosting and all the deep learning models. In this regard, it is important to recognize that these frameworks are complementary, each addressing some parts of the batch, stream and iterative processes, which is why cloud platforms are best suited for those workloads.

Here, monitoring and visualization are found alongside each other. For example Tableau provides the ability to display complex ML output in a more User-Friendly manner, along with exposure of their patterns and insights interactively through dashboards to coordinate via stakeholders. In addition, Lumify integrates connection mapping and data fusion, enabling applications like threat intelligence or fraud detection. Finally, Splunk has strong monitoring and analytics capabilities enabling organizations to have higher-level situational awareness so potential problems can be identified and resolved.

These technologies offer exceptional scalability and more flexibility, allowing organizations to run different workloads on the cloud without needing to make hardware purchases upfront. Such an AI and 5G network synergy is opening doors of use cases such as real-time fraud detection, AI-powered medical diagnostics, intelligent transportation systems, retail personalization, supply chain optimization that are stimulating innovation in sectors as diverse as healthcare, retail and finance. Armed now with big data technology, ML algorithms and cloud platforms, organizations can take this data and transform them into timely and accurate insights which will facilitate quicker and smarter strategic decisions than ever before.

2.3 CONCLUSION

Big data technologies like Apache Hadoop, Apache Storm, Apache Spark, Tableau, Lumify and Splunk have revolutionized the way the data is processed, analysed, and visualized. Google Cloud Dataflow has a distributed model that enables users to build data pipelines in a general way. Performance and Scalability As you can imagine, Hadoop 2 comes with many performance and scalability improvements. Tools such as Apache Storm and (up-to-date Spark) are for real-time data processing and advanced analytics and are inherent to dynamic big data applications.

Visualization tools such as Tableau, and Lumify provide interactive ways of representing data. Lumify harnesses geospatial and multimedia analytics, complementing the statistical analysis provided by Tableau, for an all-inclusive view of data that encourages collaboration. A leader in log management, Splunk delivers real-time analytics and monitoring to support IT operations, security and compliance.

These tools enable industries such as healthcare and telecommunications to extract actionable insights, boosting innovation and operational efficiency. By ensuring scalability, fault tolerance and advanced analytics, they transform raw data into meaningful insights that support informed decision-making.

The integration of ML capabilities on a cloud platform with Hadoop, Spark and Storm offers high efficiency and scalability. Real-time analytics is supported by Storm, scalable ML is improved by Spark, and distributed computing is mastered by Hadoop. Other technologies such as Splunk, Lumify and Tableau offer useful information and insights. Cloud systems help companies cut expenses, simplify data dissemination, and scale their resources. This method speeds up and simplifies complicated tasks like model prediction and anomaly identification. Operational transformation, data-driven decision-making and the potential of analytics and ML will all be facilitated by developments in big data and cloud-based integration.

REFERENCES

Alexsoft. 2022. "The Good and the Bad of Hadoop Big Data Framework." *Alexsoft Software R&d Engineering*, July 29.

Basha, Shaik Abdul Khalandar, Syed Muzamil Basha, Durai Raj Vincent, and Dharmendra Singh Rajput. 2019. "Challenges in Storing and Processing Big Data Using Hadoop and Spark." In *Deep Learning and Parallel Computing Environment for Bioengineering Systems*, 179–187. Elsevier. https://doi.org/10.1016/B978-0-12-816718-2.00018-X.

Benlachmi, Yassine, and Moulay Lahcen Hasnaoui. 2021. "Open Source Big Data Platforms and Tools: An Analysis." *Indonesian Journal of Electrical Engineering and Informatics (IJEEI)* 9 (3). https://doi.org/10.52549/.v9i3.3170.

Grover, Purva, and Arpan Kumar Kar. 2017. "Big Data Analytics: A Review on Theoretical Contributions and Tools Used in Literature." *Global Journal of Flexible Systems Management* 18 (3): 203–229. https://doi.org/10.1007/s40171-017-0159-3.

Jain, Vijay Kumar. 2017. *Big Data and Hadoop*. Khanna Publishing.

Kumar, Ashish, and Tulsiram Yadav. n.d. *Advanced Splunk: Master the Art of Getting the Maximum Out of Your Machine Data Using Splunk*. 2016th ed. Birmingham: Packt Publishing Ltd.

Lee, Won Sang, Eun Jin Han, and So Young Sohn. 2015. "Predicting the Pattern of Technology Convergence Using Big-Data Technology on Large-Scale Triadic Patents." *Technological Forecasting and Social Change* 100 (November): 317–329. https://doi.org/10.1016/j.techfore.2015.07.022.

Mavridis, Ilias, and Helen Karatza. 2017. "Performance Evaluation of Cloud-Based Log File Analysis with Apache Hadoop and Apache Spark." *Journal of Systems and Software* 125 (March): 133–151. https://doi.org/10.1016/j.jss.2016.11.037.

Sandhiya, Ramasamy, and Perumal Prabavathy. 2021. "A Review on Software and Tools for Massive Big Data Processing." *Journal of Information Technology and Society* 1 (1–7).

Tripathi, Prince, Chetan Bajaj, Meet Bhanvadia, Vaishnavi Parsekar, and Vikas Magar. 2023. "Comparative Study of Data Analytics Tools for Effective Business Decision." *An International Multidisciplinary Peer-Reviewed E-Journal* 8 (7 May): 461–486.

3 Data Analytics
Statistical Approach

Seema Rawat and Praveen Kumar

3.1 INTRODUCTION

Over the years, statistical methods have been at the very heart of the evolution of data analytics, acting as scaffolding for learning and making inferences from raw datasets. Although statistics have since been revolutionized by the rise of machine learning (ML) and artificial intelligence (AI), basic statistical methods are still important in performing data preprocessing, analysis and interpretation. Statistics is perfectly fit not only for summarizing large datasets in the form of descriptive statistics but also for inferring relationships with regression models.

ML algorithms are capable of learning from data and using feedback to retrain themselves is a bonus point for data analytics. Applying ML algorithms, work of a data analyst can be minimized to a great extent as an ML model can easily and in less time point patterns and makes a decision with high precision. This chapter will talk about the usage of ML in statistical data analytics by examining methods like classification, clustering and regression to work on complex large datasets. By combining data analytics and ML, these students aim to show how evolution of data analysis has taken place making it even more futuristic for innovation.

This chapter also delves into the statistical underpinnings of data analytics also highlighting how traditional statistical techniques fit together with ML pipelines. When these approaches are combined, organizations can effectively handle data complexity, ensure model transparency and derive meaningful insights [1].

3.2 THE ML TOOLCHAIN IN DATA ANALYTICS

An ML toolchain offers a disciplined process using which you can convert raw data all the way to meaningful insights. Statistical methods underpin all phases of this toolchain, providing data quality controls from end-to-end. The following sections delve into the core aspects [1].

3.2.1 Data Collection

Data collection is the first step in any analytical pipeline. This data collection effort can include the retrieval of raw or unstructured data from diverse sources such as databases, APIs, IoT devices, surveys, etc. Statistical sampling methods, such as random sampling or stratified sampling, ensure representativeness and reduce bias during this phase [2].

DOI: 10.1201/9781003396772-4

3.2.2 Data Preparation

Data Extraction and Validation: It is very important to extract proper data and validate its quality. To determine and thus address this, outlier detection techniques like Z-scores or interquartile ranges (IQR) are implemented.

Data Labelling: As we know, accurate labelling of the data is a must in cases where you are going for supervised learning. Commonly, statistical agreement measures such as Cohen's kappa are used to evaluate the inter-annotator consistency during labelling.

3.2.3 Featurization

Statistical methods, such as principal component analysis (PCA) and t-SNE, help reduce dimensionality and identify the most critical features in datasets. Feature scaling methods, like standardization and normalization, are applied to ensure model compatibility [2].

3.2.4 Model Development

Training and Testing: Data is broken into training and testing sets, using statistical techniques such as k-fold cross-validation that allow objective evaluation of model performance and prevention of overfitting.
Hyperparameter Tuning: It is a process to set up the different parameters of the model. Grid search, random search which is often supported by Bayesian optimization are common ways to optimize model parameters.
Model Tracking: Statistical Metrics such as Precision, Recall, F1-score and ROC-AUC score are calculated to understand the model's precision and reliability.

3.2.5 Deployment and Monitoring

Once trained, ML models are deployed into production. Monitoring involves statistical control charts, anomaly detection techniques, and drift detection methods to ensure models remain accurate over time.

3.2.6 Model Explainability

The statistical approach like SHAP (Shapley Additive Explanations) and LIME (Local Interpretable Model agnostic Explanation) add more insights to the model providing an ethical and explainable AI.

3.3 STATISTICAL METHODS IN DATA ANALYTICS

Statistical methods are the backbone of data analytics, and they give you many ways to summarize your data, detecting patterns in it and predict what will be like next. This section will take a closer look at all the basic and advanced techniques used in data analytics.

3.3.1 Descriptive Statistics

Descriptive statistics summarize the dataset to give you a big picture of the trends and distributions in the data which makes it easy to understand by any analyst.

- **Measures of Central Tendency:**
  - **Mean (Arithmetic Average):** The mean provides a quick summary indication of the central value from its surrounding numbers and is, however, affected by outliers.

$$\text{Mean}(\mu) = \frac{\sum_{i=1}^{n} x_i}{n}$$

    where x_i represents the data points and n is the total number of data points.
  - **Median:** The central value (less sensitive to extreme data points and therefore robust with presence of skewed data distributions).
    For sorted data:

$$\text{Median} = \{x_{\frac{n+1}{2}} \quad \textit{if n is odd} \frac{x_{\frac{n}{2}} + x_{\frac{n}{2}+1}}{2} \quad \textit{if n is even}$$

  - **Mode:** Tells you the value that appears most frequently in a distribution and is useful for categorical data.
    The mode is the value x that appears most frequently in the dataset.
- **Measures of Dispersion:**
  - **Variance and Standard Deviation:** Quantify how much individual data points deviate from the mean. High variance suggests data points are spread out while low variance indicates clustering around the mean.

$$\text{Variance}(\sigma^2) = \frac{\sum_{i=1}^{n} (x_i - \mu)^2}{n}$$

$$\text{Standard Deviation}(\sigma) = \sqrt{\frac{\sum_{i=1}^{n} (x_i - \mu)^2}{n}}$$

  - **Range:** Basic measure of spread, calculated as difference between max and min values.

$$\text{Range} = \text{Max}(x_i) - \text{Min}(x_i)$$

- **Interquartile Range (IQR):** Measures data spread by determining the variance between quartiles, and thereby handling outliers.

$$\text{IQR} = Q3 - Q1$$

- **Visualization Techniques:** Graphical tools improve the understandability of information.
  - Box Plots: Represents the median, quartiles and potential outliers.
  - Histograms: Histograms display the distribution of frequencies.
  - Heatmaps: Show relationship between variables in a dataset.

3.3.2 Inferential Statistics

Inferential statistics allow us to make assumptions about a population using data collected from the sample.

- **Hypothesis Testing:**
  - ***t*-Test Formula:**

$$t = \frac{\underline{x} - \mu}{\frac{s}{\sqrt{n}}}$$

  where $\underline{x}$ is the sample mean, μ is the population mean, s is the sample standard deviation and n is the sample size.
  - **Chi-Square Test Formula:**

$$\chi^2 = \sum \frac{(O_i - E_i)^2}{E_i}$$

  where O_i is the observed frequency and E_i is the expected frequency.
  - **Null Hypothesis (H_0):** Assumes no effect or relationship exists.
  - **Alternative Hypothesis (H_1):** States that there is an effect or relationship.
  - Statistical tests like *t*-tests, chi-square tests and *F*-tests evaluate the likelihood of observed results under H_0.
  - ***P*-value:** Quantifies the evidence against H_0. A smaller *P*-value indicates stronger evidence to reject H_0.
- **Confidence Intervals (CIs):** Provide a range of plausible values for population parameters, aiding decision-making under uncertainty

$$\text{CI} = \underline{x} \pm Z \cdot \frac{s}{\sqrt{n}}$$

where Z is the z-value corresponding to the confidence level, $\underline{x}$ is the sample mean and s is the standard deviation.

3.3.3 ML Statistics

ML uses a combination of multiple statistical methods to get improved prediction and recognize patterns from data. These statistical techniques are a very important part of the ML algorithm, as it makes them understand the relationship of data efficiently. Unlike traditional methods, ML techniques like classification directly analyse data for patterns. The combination of these fields makes an even more accurate prediction and decision for outputs. Here are the ML approaches for statistics.

3.3.3.1 Regression Analysis

Regression is an ML algorithm used for the prediction of continuous output on the basis of input variable. Regression techniques model relationships between independent and dependent variables, predicting outcomes and quantifying effects.

- **Simple Linear Regression:** Models the relationship between a single predictor and response variable.
  Example: Predicting house prices based on size.

$$y = \beta_0 + \beta_1 x + \epsilon$$

  where
  - y is the dependent variable,
  - x is the independent variable,
  - β_0 is the intercept,
  - β_1 is the slope and
  - ϵ is the error term.

- **Multiple Linear Regression:** Incorporates multiple predictors to handle more complex scenarios.

$$y = \beta_0 + \beta_1 x_1 + \beta_2 x_2 + \ldots + \beta_k x_k + \epsilon$$

- **Polynomial Regression:** Captures nonlinear relationships by fitting polynomial curves.
- **Logistic Regression:** Used for classification tasks, such as predicting the likelihood of an event.

$$P(y=1) = \frac{1}{1 + e^{-(\beta_0 + \beta_1 x)}}$$

Regression is mostly used in models giving prediction as output, like prediction of stock price and estimating its cost.

3.3.3.2 Classification and Clustering

Classification and clustering are methods of ML used to solve problems with categorical data [3]. These methods classify data into categories or group similar data points:

- **Classification Techniques:** Classification is a supervised ML technique used to assign input into different classes. For example classification of email as spam or not spam uses regression to analyse the result.
  - **Decision Trees:** Hierarchical models that split data based on features.
  - **Naïve Bayes:** A probabilistic approach using Bayes' theorem.
  - **Support Vector Machines (SVM):** Find the optimal hyperplane for data separation.
- **Clustering Techniques:** Clustering is another ML algorithm but it falls under the unsupervised learning domain where grouping of similar data together takes place. This model is great as it discovers pattern automatically and forms clusters.
  - **k-Means Clustering:** Partitions data into k clusters using distance measures.

    $$J = \sum_{i=1}^{k} \sum_{j=1}^{n} |\left| x_j^{(i)} - c_i \right||^2$$

    where $x_j^{(i)}$ is a data point assigned to cluster i and c_i is the cluster centroid.
  - **Hierarchical Clustering:** Groups data into nested clusters, visualized through dendrograms.
- **DBSCAN:** A density-based method identifying clusters of arbitrary shape [4].

These algorithms are used in multiple real-world applications like market segmentation, sentiments analysis.

3.3.3.3 Bayesian Statistics

Bayesian is a statistical approach that takes probability in account for precision. In the ML domain, Bayesian statistics is a dynamic modelling method which updates its hypothesis with updates in data. Bayesian methods offer a probabilistic framework for updating beliefs with new evidence.

- **Bayesian Networks:** Graphical models representing variables and their conditional dependencies [4].
  Example: Diagnosing diseases based on symptoms.
- **Markov Chain Monte Carlo (MCMC):** Simulates complex probability distributions to estimate parameters.

Bayesian statistics follows Bayes theorem of probability to give the probability of an event taking place when another dependent event has already taken place. In scientific language, it gives the probability of hypothesis as per the given prior data knowledge.

Mathematically, it can be expressed as:

$$P(H \mid D) = P(D \mid H)P(H)/P(D)$$

where P(H|D) is the posterior probability of the hypotheses after analysis of the given past data. P(D|H) is the likelihood of observing the data. P(H) is the prior probability of the hypothesis before observing the data. P(D) is marginal likelihood of the data.

Bayesian method of statistical analysis is useful in problems involving uncertainty and where prior knowledge is given. It gives a probabilistic solution making it highly usable in industries like healthcare, stock market.

3.4 APPLICATIONS OF STATISTICAL APPROACHES IN DATA ANALYTICS

The broad applicability of statistical techniques can be seen in their use in many different industries. Expanded applications are discussed next.

3.4.1 Healthcare

- **Predictive Analytics:**
  - Regression models are used to predict patient outcomes and hospital readmission rates.
  - Time-series analysis predicts disease outbreaks and trends in patient volume.
  - Cloud-based ML algorithms like ResNet help in processing and predicting patient datasets increasing the hospital overall efficiency. For example using an AWS-based ML model that predicts future health problems for a patient based on past records.
- **Diagnostics:**
  - ML algorithms using statistical principles enhance disease detection accuracy.
  - Bayesian networks combine symptoms and test results for probabilistic diagnosis.
  - Using Cloud computing services like MS Azure to deploy an ML model for example a brain tumour diagnosis application based on previous datasets of brain tumour diagnosed patients.
- **Personalized Medicine:**
  - Clustering algorithms group patients with similar conditions for tailored treatments [5].
  - Drug creation is a very complex lab work especially a personalized system to create drugs which only help a specific group of people. Using an ML model which can directly analyse user needs as per the details given can give efficient and fast results. It can further be hosted on the cloud for mass use so most people can get benefit through it.

3.4.2 Finance

- **Fraud Detection:**
  - Anomaly detection techniques flag suspicious transactions.
  - Logistic regression models classify high-risk activities.
  - Real-time fraud detection models can be installed by organization using ML algorithms like clustering which can be deployed online for other uses too.
- **Portfolio Optimization:**
  - Statistical methods like Monte Carlo simulations predict investment risks and returns.
  - Time-series forecasting aids in stock price predictions [5].

3.4.3 Retail and E-Commerce

- **Demand Forecasting:**
  - Regression models predict seasonal trends and inventory needs.
  - Retailers can use a cloud-based ML model to predict seasonality in the dataset and offer season-specific demand to customers.
- **Customer Segmentation:**
  - Clustering divides customers into actionable groups for marketing campaigns.
  - Product management teams can use ML-based customer segmentation models to create segments of target marketing campaigns, making customer-specific marketing.
- **Recommendation Systems:**
  - Bayesian statistics improve personalized recommendations [5].
  - An ML model can be created to analyse user preferences and recommend future material based on it. It can further be deployed on online cloud-based platforms like AWS.

3.4.4 Education

- **Student Performance Analytics:**
  - Regression models predict outcomes based on attendance, grades and participation.
  - Education institutes use a regression model to predict student future scores and betterment. It can be further used by multichain schools using a cloud-based model.
- **Curriculum Effectiveness:**
  - Statistical hypothesis testing evaluates the impact of new teaching methods.
  - ML can be used to evaluate the curriculum of a specific college/school to facilitate students with the best syllabus.

3.4.5 Environmental Monitoring

- **Climate Modelling:**
  - Regression and time-series analysis model temperature trends and greenhouse gas effects.

    - Cloud-based models using ML can be implemented to create models which can predict climate trends and other environmental monitoring.
- **Wildlife Tracking:**
    - Bayesian methods analyse animal movement patterns for conservation efforts.
    - Models can be created to analyse animal movement and patterns for prediction of wildlife animal life tracking and get regular insights into their health.

3.5 ADVANCEMENTS IN STATISTICAL METHODS FOR BIG DATA

As data grows in volume, velocity and variety, statistical methods have evolved to address new challenges:

3.5.1 High-Dimensional Data Analysis

Traditional methods struggle with datasets where features vastly outnumber observations. Solutions include [6]:

- **Regularization Techniques:**
    - LASSO and Ridge Regression reduce overfitting by penalizing model complexity.
- **Dimensionality Reduction:**
    - PCA and t-SNE condense data while preserving critical information. PCA reduced dimensionality by transforming the data to a new basis:

$$Z = XW$$

where W is the matrix of eigenvectors of the covariance matrix of X.

3.5.2 Real-Time Analytics

Streaming data requires efficient statistical processing:

- **Sliding Window Analysis:** Processes data in small, overlapping windows for real-time trend detection. If t is the current time, the data window contains values from $t - w$ to t, where w is the window size.
- **Online Learning Algorithms:** Update models incrementally as new data arrives.

3.5.3 Distributed Computing

Big data frameworks like Hadoop and Spark integrate statistical methods for scalable analysis:

- **MapReduce for Statistics:** Parallel computation of metrics like mean, median and variance.

- **MLlib in Spark:** Provides scalable implementations of clustering, regression and classification algorithms [6].

3.5.4 Bayesian Methods in Big Data

Bayesian inference has adapted to big data:

- **Variational Inference:** An alternative to MCMC, offering faster approximations for complex distributions.
- **Hierarchical Bayesian Models:** Handle multi-level data structures effectively [7].

3.5.5 Statistical Learning with AI

Statistical learning as an intermediate between traditional statistics and AI, offers models that are interpretable:

- **Tree-Based Methods:** Random forests and gradient boosting improve accuracy while retaining interpretability [8].
  Random Forest: The prediction is an average (regression) or majority vote (classification):

  $$\hat{y} = \frac{1}{T}\sum_{t=1}^{T}\hat{y}_t$$

  where T is the number of trees and $\hat{y}_t$ is the prediction from the t-th tree.
- **Kernel Methods:** SVMs with kernel functions capture nonlinear patterns in data.
  Kernel Function for SVM:

  $$K(x,x') = \phi(x)\cdot\phi(x')$$

  where K is the kernel function and $\phi(x)$ maps the data to a higher-dimensional space.

3.5.6 Ethical Considerations

Ethical issues from big data analytics improvements:

- **Data-Driven Bias Detection:** Automated statistical tools help you to validate datasets for bias.
- **Tools for Explainability:** Techniques such as SHAP and LIME to make sure that the statistical models follow the ethical lines.

3.6 CHALLENGES AND FUTURE DIRECTIONS

3.6.1 Challenges

- **Traditional Methods:** Traditional ways of carrying out text analysis often struggle with big unstructured data.
- **Interpretability:** This is particularly tricky as we need to strike a balance between model complexity and interpretability.
- **Data Quality** – Accurate and complete data is everything when it comes to stopping bad determination.

3.6.2 Future Directions

- **Integrating AI:** Merging of statistical approaches with AI for more insightful decisions.
- **Edge Computing:** Running models on edge devices for real-time analytics.
- **Robotics Process:** To automate the process of statistics and analytics development so that no human intervention is required.

3.7 CONCLUSION

Statistical methods continue to be an indispensable part of modern data analytics as they support the new era of ML and AI models. Such methods and approaches can be effectively used by organizations to gain insights, predict future trends and decisions. Statistical methods combined with big data, IoT and AI in this era of technology landscape will change the accuracy of analytics as technology transformation technology from statistical methods to a different level [9].

REFERENCES

[1] Bishop, C. M. (2006). *Pattern Recognition and Machine Learning*. Springer. A comprehensive text on statistical learning and machine learning foundations, covering Bayesian methods, regression, and classification techniques. https://link.springer.com/book/9780387310732

[2] Hastie, T., Tibshirani, R., & Friedman, J. (2009). *The Elements of Statistical Learning: Data Mining, Inference, and Prediction*. Springer. https://link.springer.com/book/10.1007/978-0-387-84858-7

[3] Pedregosa, F., Varoquaux, G., Gramfort, A., Michel, V., Thirion, B., Grisel, O., . . . & Duchesnay, E. (2011). Scikit-learn: Machine Learning in Python. *Journal of Machine Learning Research*, 12, 2825–2830. www.researchgate.net/publication/51969319_Scikit-learn_Machine_Learning_in_Python

[4] Murphy, K. P. (2012). *Machine Learning: A Probabilistic Perspective*. MIT Press. https://books.google.co.in/books?hl=en&lr=&id=RC43AgAAQBAJ&oi=fnd&pg=PR7&dq=Murphy,+K.+P.+(2012).+Machine+Learning:+A+Probabilistic+Perspective.+MIT+Press.&ots=unixcESp17&sig=t8zmIUjN4mMXl0HVyPKOYYuAt_Y#v=onepage&q&f=false

[5] Wasserman, L. (2010). *All of Statistics: A Concise Course in Statistical Inference.* Springer. https://link.springer.com/book/10.1007/978-0-387-21736-9
[6] Lundberg, S. M., & Lee, S. I. (2017). A Unified Approach to Interpreting Model Predictions. *Advances in Neural Information Processing Systems (NeurIPS).* https://papers.nips.cc/paper_files/paper/2017/hash/8a20a8621978632d76c43dfd28b67767-Abstract.html
[7] Gelman, A., Carlin, J. B., Stern, H. S., Dunson, D. B., Vehtari, A., & Rubin, D. B. (2013). *Bayesian Data Analysis.* CRC Press. www.taylorfrancis.com/books/mono/10.1201/b16018/bayesian-data-analysis-david-dunson-donald-rubin-john-carlin-andrew-gelman-hal-stern-aki-vehtari
[8] Chen, T., & Guestrin, C. (2016). XGBoost: A Scalable Tree Boosting System. *Proceedings of the 22nd ACM SIGKDD International Conference on Knowledge Discovery and Data Mining.* https://dl.acm.org/doi/10.1145/2939672.2939785
[9] Aggarwal, C. C. (2018). *Neural Networks and Deep Learning: A Textbook.* Springer. https://link.springer.com/book/10.1007/978-3-031-29642-0

4 Supervised and Unsupervised Methods of Machine Learning Used in Data Analytics

Shabana Urooj

4.1 INTRODUCTION

Machine learning (ML) is a subset of artificial intelligence (AI) that allows systems to automatically acquire from data and improvise the performance without exclusive programming. It is crucial to data analytics due to its capacity to process massive data, recognition of patterns and provide correct predictions or decisions. ML enables organizations in finance, healthcare, marketing and manufacturing to ease complex decision-making tasks and attain valuable insights. Common real-world applications include predicting customer behaviour, detecting anomalies in cybersecurity, enhancing healthcare diagnostics and optimizing supply chains.

The three main core forms of ML techniques: Supervised learning, where models are trained on labelled data to forecast outcomes (e.g. decision trees, neural networks); unsupervised learning, which reveals hidden patterns in unlabelled data (e.g. clustering algorithms like k-means) and reinforcement learning, where models learn by interacting with environments and obtaining feedback (used in robotics and gaming).

Research on ML is growing, and it could improve our knowledge of how to describe, forecast and handle a wide range of applications. For humans, the decision-making process is largely opaque. Especially when it comes to making decisions in extremely delicate areas, ML algorithms have recently begun to solve problems and make decisions while they are being developed. When it comes to solving problems that conventional statistical methods are not well equipped for, ML provides new tools. With an emphasis on supervised learning techniques intended to predict or categorize a result of interest, this chapter offers an overview of supervised and unsupervised methods of ML used in data analytics.

4.2 SUPERVISED METHODS OF ML

This section describes the supervised methods of ML used in data analytics and explores their advantages and applications. The goal of supervised ML classification algorithms is to classify information or data based on present knowledge. Data

DOI: 10.1201/9781003396772-5

science problems include classification quite a bit. Since computers need to be able to learn and analyse data without explicit programming, learning occurs when data and mathematical models are joined. One of the most difficult issues with supervised learning is that it needs labelled data. The model must be trained using both the inputs and the corresponding outputs to generate a function that is sufficiently close to being able to predict outputs for new inputs when they are introduced. Regression problems and classification challenges are two categories of supervised learning problems.

The major challenge for humans is to forecast the inputs and outputs of the data analysis each time. Regression problems occur when the outputs are continuous, whereas classification problems occur when the outputs are categorical. This section tries to compare different types of classification algorithms in supervised ML that are used in data analytics and to explain its concept. The volume and complexity of data are growing exponentially, indicating that most datasets are unlabelled as wide arrays become the norm rather than the exception.

Even though ML is an area of computer science that strives to identify patterns in data to boost performance on a variety of tasks. Furthermore, the development of algorithms that preserve to generate extensive patterns and hypotheses by utilizing instances that are provided by outside sources to anticipate the outcomes of subsequent instances is known as supervised ML. Figure 4.1 depicts a typical working style of supervised learning. Supervised learning focuses on teaching machines to learn patterns from labelled examples to generalize to unseen data.

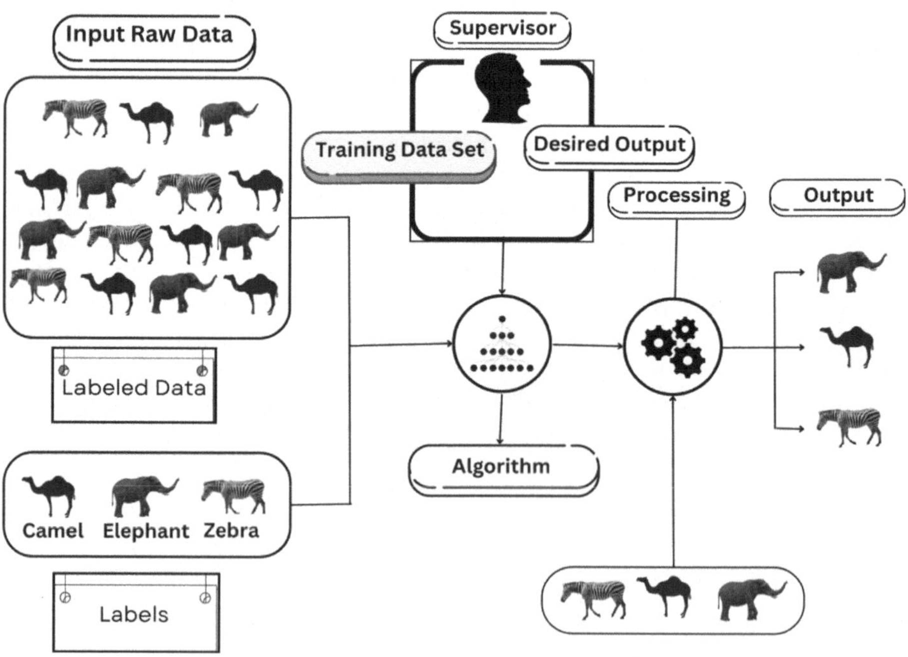

FIGURE 4.1 Working of supervised learning.

Precisely, supervised learning is an ML approach that relies on marked data, where each data point is marked with the right answer or classification. The algorithm is learned by analysing this labelled data and then applies the learned relationships to make predictions on new, unlabelled data. For example a dataset of animal images might have each image labelled as "Elephant", "Camel", or "Cow". The algorithm uses this information to classify new images.

The key points are as follows:

- **Labelled Data:** Data with predefined answers or categories.
- **Training:** The machine learns the relationship between inputs (e.g. images) and outputs (e.g. labels).
- **Prediction:** Once trained, the model can classify or predict outcomes for new data.

4.2.1 Regression and Classification

Supervised learnings are further bifurcated into two classes: Regression and Classification Regression predicts continuous outcomes (e.g. house prices, weights). The common algorithms are Linear Regression, Decision Tree Regression, Random Forest Regression. Classification predicts categorical outcomes (e.g. "spam" or "not spam"). Common algorithms of classification are Logistic Regression, Support Vector Machines, Naïve Bayes, Random Forests, etc. Figure 4.2 shows the various techniques for regression and classification of supervised learning.

Regression is a type of supervised learning which is used to forecast continuous estimates, such as house prices, stock prices or consumer churn. Regression algorithms acquire a function that derives from the input features to the output value.

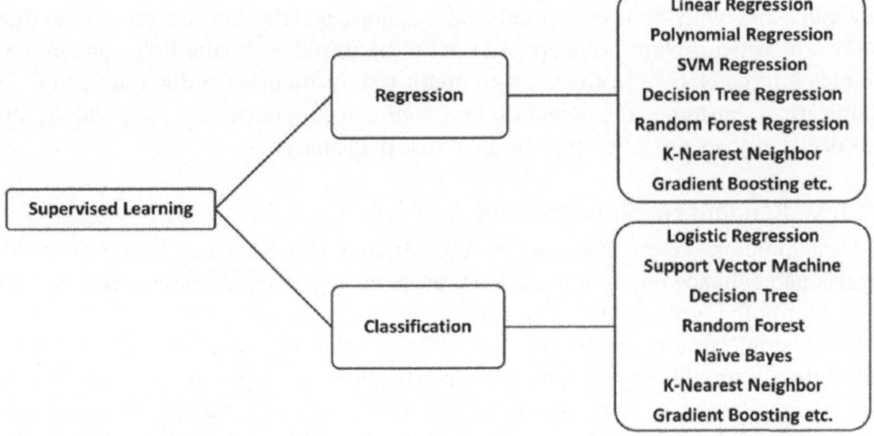

FIGURE 4.2 Chart describing various techniques for regression and classification.

Some common algorithms include

- Linear Regression
- Decision Tree Regression
- Random Forest Regression
- Logistic Regression
- Support Vector Machines
- K-Nearest Neighbour
- Naïve Bayes
- Gradient Boosting

4.2.1.1 Linear Regression

Linear regression is one of the easiest supervised learning algorithms for predicting continuous numeric outcomes. It represents the relationship relating to output (dependent variable) and inputs (one or more independent features/variables) as a linear equation. It has an underlying algorithm that minimizes the mean squared error (MSE) to get the best fit line, showing the relationship between variables. Thanks to its simplicity in implementation and ease of interpretation, linear regression is among the most widely applicable for tasks such as time-series forecasting, sales study and financial modelling. But it assumes a very linear relation which can be false most of the time and is also very dependent on outliers, will greatly affect predictions. Although not without limitations, it is still a fundamental algorithm for regression tasks due to its ease of understanding and interpretability.

4.2.1.2 Decision Tree Regression

Decision trees are one of the most versatile supervised learning models that can be used for both regression and classification tasks. They divide the dataset into branches, creating a tree structure based on feature conditions with leaves representing final predictions. Important splits are determined by Gini impurity or entropy type criteria. Decision trees are interpretable and do not require preprocessing, as they can work with both numerical and categorical data. On the downside, they can overfit when grown too deep and tend to be unstable as small changes in data produce a large change in trees. From credit risk in finance, to diagnostic tools in healthcare, to customer segmentation in e-commerce, applications vary widely, and thus decision trees are a flexible option across data analytics.

4.2.1.3 Random Forest Regression

The Random Forest technique is a vigorous ML approach used to reduce the overlifting risk and enhance prediction accuracy by using a group of decision trees, making it ideal for both regression tasks and classification.

Every single tree is trained with a different arbitrary sample from the dataset and outputs a prediction. During the classification, the algorithm determines the final label by taking a "vote" among trees, but it averages the outputs for regression. Having the ability to assess feature importance is one of Random Forest's strengths, it measures each feature's impact on the decision paths which helps to determine which variables have the most predictive power.

Although its benefits, when more trees are added the model can become computationally intensive, leading to slow down the predictions, especially with large datasets. Overall, Random Forest is special for its capacity to manage large datasets effectively, flexibility and resilience to noisy data.

4.2.1.4 Logistic Regression

Logistic regression is a supervised learning algorithm applied in binary classification problems, where only two classes exist for the target variable (e.g. 0/1 or yes/no). It uses the sigmoid function to predict probabilities that are always in the range [0,1]. Then a threshold (usually 0.5) is applied to categorize the observations into one of the two categories. Logistic regression is computationally inexpensive and works great on datasets with linear decision boundaries. However, it has difficulty capturing non-linear patterns unless additional transformations are performed. Some common applications are spam detection, customer churn prediction and medical diagnosis. It is a preferred choice for classification problems because it outputs probabilities, which provides additional information regarding each prediction of confidence.

4.2.1.5 Support Vector Machines

Support vector machines (SVM) are the commonly used supervised learning models for regression and classification purposes. It majorly deals with high-dimensional complex data. SVM works very well in high-dimensional data and clears class margins. It finds the hyperplane with maximum margin between classes. It uses the "kernel trick" to map it to a higher-dimensional space for the data which is not linearly separable.

SVM transforms data into a high-dimensional space for categorization, even if it isn't linearly separable. It finds a hyperplane as a separator so that predictions can be made for new records based on their features. Referring to Figure 4.3, (a) which contains data points in two classes, (b) reveals a curve separates them. A hyperplane is defined as the boundary after transformation into (c). The main concept of SVM is finding an optimal hyperplane which is a boundary that separates classes of data points with maximum margin between them. Support vectors are the data points close to the hyperplane and critical to the margin orientation to define it. With the ability to be applicable to both linear and non-linear kernel functions, SVMs map the data into higher-dimensional spaces to be easily separated. Although having the power to classify tasks, SVMs can become expensive with large datasets.

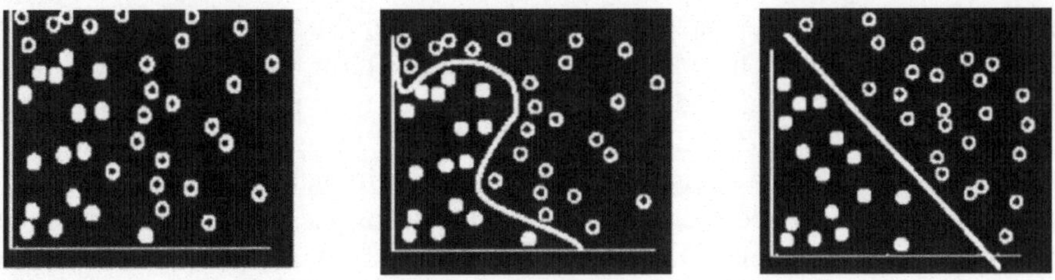

FIGURE 4.3 (a) Original dataset, (b) data with separator added and (c) transformed data.

4.2.1.6 K-Nearest Neighbour

The K-nearest neighbours (KNN) algorithm is straight forward versatile method of ML which is widely used for regression and classification. By examining the "k" closest points in the dataset, KNN classifies new data. Defining the label due to the majority class among neighbours for classification, or averaging values for regression. Due to the reliance on data proximity, KNN can manage non-linear, complex data structures with minimal training. Moreover, it becomes computationally expensive with large datasets, as it calculates distances for all points, affecting efficiency and requiring careful selection of the "k" parameter. On the other hand, KNN is sensitive to the scale of data and performs poorly if irrelevant features are included.

4.2.1.7 Naïve Bayes

Naïve Bayes is a powerful probabilistic classifying approach which is based on Bayes' theorem. It assumes that the features are conditionally independent in a given class label. Its computational efficiency is a major benefit, making it perfect for handling large datasets and real-time applications. Text classification, including spam detection, sentiment analysis and document categorization is one of the most known applications of Naïve Bayes. It's also used in medical diagnostics to calculate the probability of diseases based on symptoms.

The algorithm's predictive accuracy is generally good for tasks where the independence assumption is approximately held, such as classifying documents where the occurrence of words can be treated independently. Yet, it faces complex datasets with significant relationships between features, as presuming simplicity would undervalue real-life correlations. For example Naïve Bayes is less effective for image recognition tasks because of the strong correlation among pixel values.

Naïve Bayes thrives in interpretability because of its simplicity. It lets users examine how characteristics affect predictions by providing them with explicit probabilistic outputs for every class. For instance, it is clear and easy to see how particular keywords contribute to the categorization in email spam detection. Naïve Bayes offers a direct mapping between input characteristics and predictions, which makes it more usable in jobs requiring explicit explanations than unsupervised techniques viz. dimensionality reduction (e.g. PCA) or K-means clustering (e.g. K-means), which decrease dimensions or group data.

4.2.1.8 Gradient Boosting

Gradient boosting approach of ML is based on boosting or improvising in a functional space, targeting pseudo-residuals rather than the traditional residuals. This technique falls under the category of ensemble supervised ML algorithms, effective for both classification and regression tasks. The term "ensemble" refers to the process of creating a final model that combines predictions from multiple individual models. Essentially, it constructs a prediction model by aggregating several weak models, typically simple decision trees that make minimal assumptions about the underlying data. Each tree fixes the error of the previous ones, improving a loss function using gradient descent. This algorithm is widely used in applications like fraud detection, credit scoring and churn prediction. Gradient Boosting's ability to model non-linear relations and interactions between features makes it a powerful tool for handling structured data in both classification and regression problems.

Its predictive accuracy is often superior to simpler models like Naïve Bayes, especially in complex datasets with intricate feature interactions. For example Gradient Boosting can identify complex trends in financial information to forecast stock prices or identify fraudulent activity in transactions where the connection between different attributes is crucial. Nevertheless, computational complexity poses a disadvantage, as it necessitates extensive resources and tuning of hyperparameters for optimal performance.

In contrast to Naïve Bayes, Gradient Boosting's interpretability is lower. As an ensemble of hundreds or thousands of trees, it is considered a "black box" model. While tools like SHAP and feature importance metrics provide insights into feature contributions, they do not offer the simplicity of Naïve Bayes' probabilities. Gradient Boosting's lack of transparency contrasts sharply with unsupervised methods like PCA, which can clearly highlight feature importance through variance explanations but do not provide predictive capabilities.

The demand for advanced data analytics leads to the utilization of ML. This is essential to emphasize the importance of supervised ML algorithms in data analytics, showing their superiority over unsupervised learning methods to assure better predictive accuracy and interpretability in most of the applications of data analytics with structured datasets. This also shows the supervised methods, including Linear Regression and Naïve Bayes which are simple and widely applicable. Logistic Regression is inexpensive and works great on datasets. Random Forest enhances prediction accuracy. SVM is commonly used on complex, high-dimensional data. Gradient Boosting's accuracy is superior. This section underlines the necessity of selecting algorithms aligned with the dataset's characteristics and depending on the learning tasks, enabling effective decision-making and innovative applications in data science.

4.3 UNSUPERVISED METHODS OF ML

Unsupervised learning is a class of ML that investigates and clusters unlabelled data accordingly. It operates on ML algorithms to explore the possibility of clustering unlabelled datasets. These algorithms can discover the unseen or hidden patterns within data without any human intervention. Over the last decade, improvements in hierarchical learning, clustering algorithms and outlier detection have been able to achieve improvements in the state of the art of unsupervised ML techniques. Therefore, this section explores unsupervised ML for data analytics.

Clustering, dimensionality reduction and association are the key components of unsupervised learning techniques. Clustering groups' unlabelled data is based on likenesses or distinctions, such as in K-means, where data points are divided into clusters. It's useful for tasks like market segmentation and image compression. Association identifies relationships between variables in a dataset, frequently applied in market basket analysis and recommendation systems (e.g. "Customers who bought this also bought that"). Dimensionality reduces the number of attributes in a dataset while retaining essential information, commonly used in preprocessing to simplify data or remove noise (e.g. autoencoders enhancing image quality).

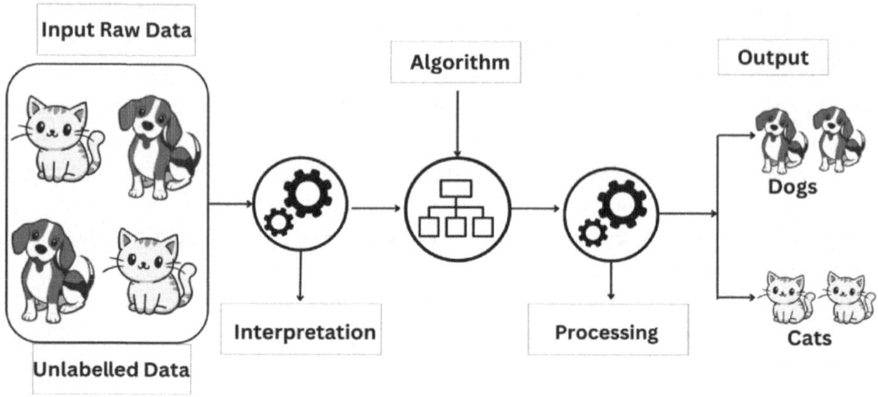

FIGURE 4.4 Working of unsupervised learning.

These methods are majorly used to analyse unstructured data. This section describes that these techniques can detect important trends, latent structures and relationships in unstructured raw data, they also constitute powerful means to extract actionable insights. This hypothesis will be tested through an exploration of relevant algorithms and will be concluded with evidence supporting the proposed hypothesis.

Unsupervised ML is an important part of the general data analytics framework that allows observation and understanding of datasets by means of extraction of hidden structures. Figure 4.4 illustrates the working of an unsupervised learning. Unsupervised learning methods do not have any labelled data or explicit instructions [1]. This feature makes it easier to explore and analyse complicated datasets and is relevant for many applications, where it is not feasible to collect labelled data. Furthermore, it eliminates the requirement for labelled data and manual feature extraction, thus enabling greater flexibility and automation in ML methods. Unsupervised learning solves the problems with rich unlabelled data that needs a lot of work to tag manually. Automated pattern detection and analysis facilitate data processing and exploration of unstructured datasets [2].

Clustering and dimensionality reduction are two main areas of unsupervised learning. Clustering algorithms back down to the similarities between data points and segregate a set of data points according to their similarity which helps in identifying the natural clusters in the datasets. It includes the arrangement of data in natural meaningful groupings, based on the similar characteristics between features to discover its structure. There are three major types of clustering, including partitional clustering, hierarchical clustering and Bayesian clustering [3].

4.3.1 Partitional Clustering

Partitional clustering is a specific division of clustering algorithms. Partitional clustering is further divided into K-means clustering and mixture models which break the observed data into a set of exclusive clusters [4]. K-means splitting of the dataset into a defined quantity of clusters to minimize the variance of each cluster. The algorithm initializes k centroids randomly, and then assigns each data point to its closest centroid according to some distance metric. Clusters are then the mean of all data points within a cluster, and finally cluster assignments and the cluster centroids are updated iteratively until convergence [5]. When assigning observations to a cluster, this is done by assigning based on the cluster's mean. It has been shown through the results of experiments and analysis on the K-means set of rules is able to search the cluster globally better [6]. Mixture models are probabilistic models that represent a dataset as a combination of multiple Gaussian distributions. They estimate the likelihood of each data point fitting to each cluster, allowing for soft clustering without hard boundaries. Finite mixture models have a finite number of data-generating sources, allowing parameter inference for data clustering [4].

4.3.2 Hierarchical Clustering

Hierarchical clustering is characterized by the establishment of a tree-like structure of clusters. An important part of the method is selecting a suitable distance measure (e.g. Manhattan or Euclidean). Manhattan distance aggregates the absolute differences between the coordinates, whereas Euclidean distance approximates the in-line distance between points in a multi-dimensional space [2]. The hierarchical clustering technique has a major disadvantage that it is not flexible; after merging or splitting up the clusters, we cannot go back. Yet, such a rigidity may result in employment of lesser computational cost absent choice combinatorial explosion. Hierarchical clustering types are of two types: Agglomerative clustering that is a bottom-up approach, gives each data point as a separate cluster [1] and BIRCH that builds a tree of cluster summaries. Balanced iterative reducing and clustering using hierarchies (BIRCH) is one of the commonly used unsupervised algorithms for data mining. It is used to perform hierarchical clustering over exceptionally large datasets. It incrementally merges with the closest clusters until only one remains. This is a great method but can be computationally slightly expensive with large datasets. Yet, divisive clustering uses this top-down approach where all the data points begin in one cluster, and it recursively splits clusters by using a flat clustering algorithm until each data point is a singleton cluster [7]. Although divisive clustering has greater conceptual complexity, it can be more efficient, particularly when a full hierarchy all the way down to individual clusters is not required.

4.3.3 Density-Based Spatial Clustering of Applications with Noise

Density-based spatial clustering of applications with noise (DBSCAN) that recognizes clusters based on the density of data points in particular regions. One of the advantages of this method is that it scales well to larger datasets with noise and can identify clusters of any shape. The basic idea of DBSCAN is that we say a point is a portion of a cluster if in the neighbourhood there are at least MinPts points. High-density regions imply clusters, while low-density areas are regarded as noise. The advantages of DBSCAN are its competence to identify data clusters that are not necessarily convex, its robustness inputting noise without requiring a predetermined cluster number [8].

4.3.4 K-Means Clustering

K-means is a prevalent unsupervised learning method used to partition data into clusters. It works by initializing a predefined number of cluster centres and then iteratively assigning data points to the closest cluster centre, followed by adjusting the centres based on the meaning of the assigned points. This process repeats until the clusters stabilize. K-Means is effective for finding patterns where data points within a cluster are more like each other than those in different clusters.

4.4 DIMENSIONALITY REDUCTION

Dimensionality reduction is one of the key unsupervised learning tasks that refers to the process of lowering the dimensionality of a dataset while retaining its intrinsic structure. Datasets from real-life applications tend to be high-dimensional, containing many correlated features. However, the intrinsic dimensionality of the number of important underlying parameters that govern the system is usually much smaller. This intrinsic dimension extraction is the heart of dimensionality reduction, which is important due to issues like "curse of dimensionality", wherein properties that can be seen in high-dimensional spaces may be lost in low-dimensional manifolds [9]. While feature selection is a supervised method that selects significant features, dimensionality reduction is unsupervised, generating new features which can improve visualization, also modelling and subsequently compression of data by reducing redundancies and drawing attention to relevant patterns [10].

Important techniques are projection, which maps high-dimensional points to lower dimensions, independent representation, which defines statistically independent dimensions, and sparse representation, which combines data into fewer basis vectors [11]. PCA and ICA are some of the most used linear methods, but their underlying assumption is that the data lie on linear subspaces, ignoring otherwise possibly important non-linear structures [9]. Non-linear methods like ISOMAP, GTM, LLE, Principal Curves, NMDS and t-SNE address these limitations by extracting more complex patterns and optimizing the configuration of points in low-dimensional space. For example ISOMAP integrates PCA and MDS to find geodesic distance and facilitate nonlinear manifold representation, whereas in t-SNE, probability distributions are built to visualize clusters [10–12]. They are crucial for dimensionality reduction, visualization and analysis of complex high-dimensional datasets and are a necessity in each modern analytics and ML tasks [9, 11].

4.5 ASSOCIATION RULE MINING

Association Rule Mining (ARM), a powerful procedure in data analytics. This data analytics technique discovers potential relations between variables in big databases and provides potential mining patterns that can help decisions. Frequent itemset mining is a data mining technique to find frequent itemset (which is a set of one or more items) in a transaction or event-based data. Many algorithms are developed for ARM with Apriori and FP-Growth being the most important. These algorithms have different methods to find frequent itemsets and generate association rules [13].

4.5.1 Apriori Algorithm

Apriori Algorithm is the most used algorithm for ARM. Its approach is based on depth-first search algorithm to identify the common item sets. It works in two main steps: first, it finds all recurrent item sets by minimum support threshold for the data; second, it generates strong association rules from the frequent item sets using a minimum confidence threshold. Apriori algorithm is simple and easy to implement, which is a major advantage of it. This helps to effectively chiseling down the search space by eliminating those infrequent item sets which become quite handy in manipulating the algorithm. Its main drawback, however, is the high computational cost, as it would need to scan the database several times, which can be quite long and resource-consuming [13].

4.5.1.1 Strengths and Limitations of Apriori Algorithm

- **Strengths:** It works with unlabelled data, excellent for discovering hidden patterns, often used for exploratory data analysis.
- **Limitations:** Results are harder to interpret, choosing the right model or number of clusters can be challenging and it is sensitive to noise.

4.5.2 Frequent Pattern Growth Algorithm

FP-Growth or Frequent Pattern Growth steps is an efficient approach for frequent itemset mining, and it can be considered as an improvement over the Apriori algorithm using the approach of divide-and-conquer. FP-Growth does not generate a candidate set like Apriori, rather it first compresses the database into the valuable structure. The generated tree allows direct extraction of frequent itemsets from the tree, eliminating the need for multiple passes through the database. Compared to the Apriori algorithm, FP-Growth can do all the above with a single scan of the database without generating all the candidates, making it more efficient. Yet, the building and navigation of the FP-tree leads to a more challenging to elaborate and grasp algorithm than Apriori [14].

Apriori and FP-Growth algorithms are the two algorithms which form the backbone of Association Rule Mining and have their own merits and demerits. Apriori is simple, easy to implement, and serves well for smaller datasets and less complex applications, whereas FP-Growth is typically better for larger datasets, as it reduces the number of times the database needs to be scanned.

4.5.3 Anomaly Detection

Deep anomaly detection is an important aspect of ML, where deep learning frameworks are adopted to detect anomalies in the data. This may involve feature extraction, learning normality representations or even anomaly scoring integrated end-to-end. These include Feature extraction; generic normality feature learning; anomaly measure dependent feature learning; and end-to-end anomaly score learning. These approaches deal with problems viz. adaptability and scalability, which are difficult to solve. The proposed approaches establish a hierarchy confirming the flexibility of deep anomaly detection technology that guarantees more precision and adaptation to dynamic data [15].

4.6 SEMI-SUPERVISED LEARNING: A BLEND OF SUPERVISED AND UNSUPERVISED APPROACHES

Semi-supervised learning is an interesting ML technique that associates the attributes of both supervised and unsupervised learning. It employs labelled and unlabelled data to train models for tasks like classification and regression. While it serves similar purposes to supervised learning, it stands out by incorporating unlabelled data into the training process alongside labelled data, which traditional supervised methods require exclusively. The mixed use of labelled and unlabelled data in the training process, making it a great option when labelled data is limited or feature extraction is challenging. It is especially effective for handling large datasets with only a small portion of labelled examples. This approach is particularly valuable in fields like medical imaging. For instance, a radiologist may label a few CT scans to diagnose tumours, enabling the algorithm to improve its accuracy in identifying patients who may need further medical evaluation.

This technique is particularly useful when labelled data is insufficient or expensive to obtain, and unlabelled data is abundant and accessible. In such cases, semi-supervised learning offers a more effective solution than relying solely on supervised or unsupervised methods.

4.7 NEURAL NETWORK ALGORITHMS FOR DATA ANALYTICS

Different neural network algorithms outdo data analytics tasks depending on the nature of the dataset and the task needs. Majorly, there are three types of Deep Neural Networks (DNNs) and deep learning fundamentals. DNNs have recently demonstrated remarkable performance in complex ML tasks such as image classification, image processing, text and speech recognition. Multi-layer perceptrons (MLPs), convolutional neural networks (CNNs) and recurrent neural networks (RNNs) are majorly covered in this section.

MLPs will perform better in applications involving simpler structured data, RNNs in sequential data, and CNNs in image-based analytics. Neural network algorithms have become important tools in data analytics, enabling the extraction of insights from complex datasets across multiple domains. These algorithms, which draw inspiration from the structure of the human brain, excel in processing unstructured data, including text, photos and time series. CNNs, RNNs and deep belief networks (DBNs) are some of the most well-known varieties of neural networks. Each has special qualities suited to analytical tasks. CNNs use layers of filters to record spatial patterns and hierarchies, which helps them perform well in tasks like object detection and picture classification [16]. RNNs process sequential input, they are perfect for speech recognition and natural language processing (NLP). The problems with long-term reliance are addressed by long short-term memory (LSTM) variations [17]. DBNs, which are composed of stacked restricted Boltzmann machines (RBMs), have applications in speech and picture recognition and are useful for unsupervised learning, feature extraction and dimensionality reduction [18]. These three neural network techniques will be examined in subsequent sections along with their applications, architecture and unique benefits in the data analytics space. We can more effectively utilize their potential to spur insights and innovation across a range of fields if we are aware of their advantages and disadvantages.

4.7.1 Conventional Neural Networks

Convolutional Neural Networks (CNNs) are a kind of deep learning model that are mostly used to interpret photos and other structured grid data. A CNN is a deep learning architecture designed to learn directly from data. CNNs excel at recognizing patterns in images, making them highly effective for object recognition. Beyond images, CNNs can also classify other data types, such as audio, time series and signal data. CNNs' remarkable capacity to identify temporal and geographical relationships in data has contributed to their rise in popularity. They are now the preferred architecture for applications like natural language processing, object identification and image classification.

The following are the key concepts in CNNs.

- **Kernel (Filter) or Feature Detector:** In CNNs, a kernel (or filter) extracts features from input images. It processes the image to identify patterns such as edges or textures. The size of the output feature map is calculated as,

$$\text{Output size in kernel} = (i - k) + 1.$$

- **Stride:** The stride determines how far the kernel moves over the image. For example a stride of 1 process the image pixel by pixel, while a stride of 2 skips every other pixel. The formula for the output size when using stride is

$$\text{Output size in stride} = \frac{i-k}{s} + 1.$$

- **Padding:** Padding refers to adding extra pixels around the edges of an image to prevent the size from shrinking during convolution. For example with zero-padding, added pixels have a value of zero. Padding is critical for preserving the original dimensions and retaining low-level features. The formula for calculating the output size with padding is:

$$\text{Output size in padding} = \frac{i-k+2p}{s} + 1$$

where i is size of the input; k is size of the kernel; s is the stride.

- **Pooling:** Pooling reduces the size of feature maps, generalizing the features extracted by the convolutional layers. This helps the network recognize patterns regardless of their position. Common pooling methods include max pooling and average pooling.
- **Flattening:** Flattening converts 2D feature maps into a single continuous linear vector, which is then fed into the fully connected layers for classification tasks.

4.7.1.1 Architecture of CNNs

CNNs are highly effective for processing image, audio and speech data due to their layered structure. The main layers of CNN are convolution layers, pooling layers and Fully Connected (FC) layers. They use filters (or kernels) to apply convolution operations on the input data. To create feature maps that capture the spatial characteristics of the data, including edges, textures and forms, these filters move over the input. The convolution layer is the first layer of CNN which is responsible for extracting features from the input image using kernels. The pooling layer reduces the spatial size of feature maps to minimize computation. It operates independently on each feature map, and common techniques include max pooling and average pooling. By minimizing the spatial dimensions of feature maps, pooling layers lower the chance of overfitting and computational complexity. The two most popular methods are max pooling and average pooling. While average pooling calculates the average value, max pooling chooses the largest value within an area. The FC layer connects neurons across different layers using weights and biases. It is typically placed before the output layer and is crucial for the final classification. A typical CNN is shown in Figure 4.5. Fully connected layers establish connections between each neuron in one layer and every neuron in the subsequent layer. These layers are employed towards the conclusion of the CNN to integrate the features acquired in the preceding layers and to generate predictions. The final layer generally utilizes a softmax activation function for tasks related to classification [19].

One of the additional features of CNNs is dropout. The Dropout layer randomly disables a subset of neurons during training to prevent overfitting and improve generalization. The activation functions in CNNs decide whether a neuron should be activated, influencing the network's predictions. Commonly used activation functions include Sigmoid; used for binary classification, outputs values between 0 and 1, Tanh; like sigmoid but symmetric around the origin, with outputs ranging from –1 to 1, Softmax; normalizes outputs into probabilities, often used for multiclass classification, ReLU; activates neurons selectively, improving efficiency by not activating all neurons simultaneously.

CNNs combine all these layers and concepts to effectively process complex data, achieving remarkable results in tasks such as image recognition, object detection and signal processing.

CNNs are trained using supervised learning techniques. Figure 4.5 demonstrated the key stages of a CNN. The process involves minimizing a loss function using an optimization algorithm like Stochastic Gradient Descent (SGD) or Adam. Backpropagation is used to compute gradients, which are then used to update the

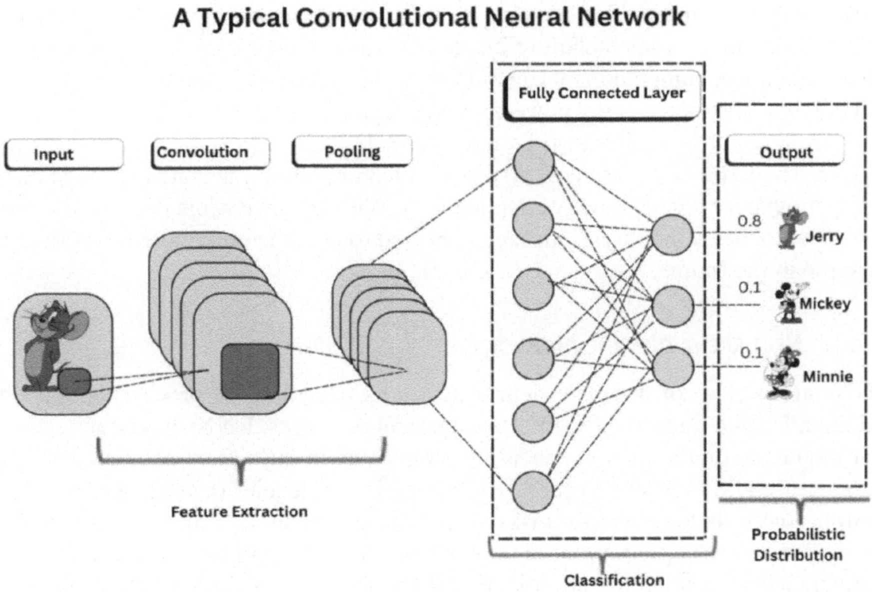

FIGURE 4.5 Convolution neural networks.

model parameters. Regularization techniques like dropout and data augmentation are often employed to improve the model's generalization ability [20].

CNNs are a class of deep learning models primarily designed for processing structured grid data, such as images. CNNs have gained popularity due to their exceptional ability to capture spatial and temporal dependencies in data. They have become the go-to architecture for tasks such as image classification, object detection and natural language processing. The architecture of CNNs includes an input layer that typically consists of image data represented as a multidimensional array [21]. Convolutional layers, the core building blocks of CNNs, perform convolution operations on the input data using filters to produce feature maps that capture spatial features like edges, textures and shapes. An activation function, commonly ReLU is applied to the output of the convolutional layer to introduce non-linearity, helping to prevent the vanishing gradient problem and accelerate convergence. Pooling layers the spatial dimensions of feature maps can be reduced to lower computational complexity and mitigate the risk of overfitting, with max pooling and average pooling being the most prevalent methods. Fully connected layers establish connections between every neuron in one layer and every neuron in the subsequent layer, integrating features acquired in earlier layers to facilitate predictions. The final layer typically employs a softmax activation function for classification purposes. CNNs are trained through supervised learning methods, focusing on minimizing a loss function via optimization algorithms such as SGD or Adam, while backpropagation is utilized to calculate gradients for the adjustment of model parameters [22]. To enhance the model's generalization capabilities, regularization techniques like dropout and data augmentation are frequently applied. CNNs are extensively utilized across various domains due to their proficiency in processing visual and spatial data, with common uses including image and video recognition. With the ongoing advancements in computational capabilities and data accessibility, CNNs are anticipated to become increasingly powerful and adaptable in the future [23].

Convolutional Neural Networks have revolutionized the field of deep learning and AI. Their ability to automatically extract features from raw data has made them indispensable for a wide range of applications. With advancements in computational power and data availability, CNNs are expected to become even more powerful and versatile in the future.

4.7.2 Recurrent Neural Networks

RNNs are a class of artificial neural networks designed for processing sequential data. Unlike traditional feedforward neural networks, RNNs have connections that loop back on themselves, enabling them to maintain a form of memory. This architecture allows RNNs to capture temporal dependencies in sequences, making them particularly effective for tasks such as language modelling, speech recognition and time series prediction. In an RNN, each input is processed in a sequential manner, with the hidden state updated at each time step. This hidden state carries information from previous inputs, allowing the network to learn patterns over time. However, standard RNNs can struggle with long-range dependencies due to issues like vanishing gradients. To address this, more advanced architectures like LSTM and Gated Recurrent Units (GRU) have been developed. These variations introduce mechanisms to better manage memory and control the flow of information, significantly improving performance on complex tasks. RNNs have gained popularity due to their ability to handle diverse applications, from generating text and music to analysing financial trends, making them a vital tool in the field of deep learning.

4.7.3 Deep Belief Networks

DBNs introduced in the year 2006 by Geoffrey Hinton et al. are a class of neural network algorithms that play a significant role in data analytics, particularly in unsupervised learning and feature extraction. Each layer of DBN is connected only to the one above it, with no connections within the same layer. Structurally, they resemble MLPs, but their connections are strictly inter-layer. Each layer functions as an independent model, training on the output of the previous layer. This makes a DBN a stack of networks, with each layer capturing different features and patterns from the raw input data.

4.7.3.1 Architecture of DBNs

DBNs are composed of multiple layers of stochastic, latent variables, typically binary and are used to model complex distributions over high-dimensional data. DBNs are primarily used for pre-training DNNs, helping them to achieve better performance on tasks such as classification, regression and clustering. The layered architecture enables DBNs to handle both supervised and unsupervised tasks effectively. Their ability to extract and understand complex data patterns also

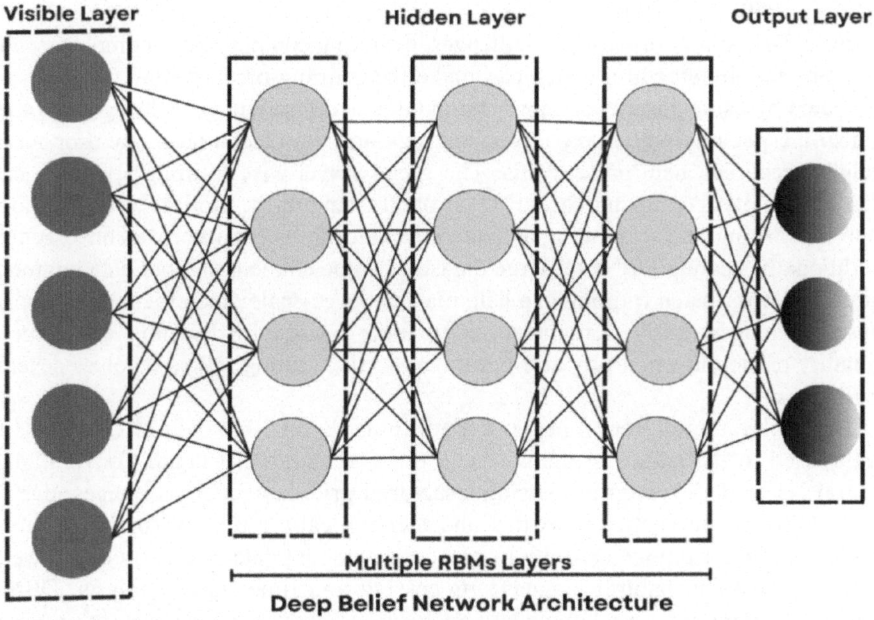

FIGURE 4.6 Deep belief networks.

makes them ideal for generative applications. Broadly, they have a visible layer, hidden layers and an output layer as represented in Figure 4.6. Let's explore their architecture in more detail.

- **Layered Structure:** DBNs consist of multiple layers of RBMs, which are simple, two-layer neural networks used for unsupervised learning.
- **Greedy Layer-Wise Training:** Each layer of a DBN is trained separately, using the output of the previous layer as input. This is known as greedy layer-wise training.
- **Top Layer (Visible Units):** The top layer of a DBN is composed of visible units that directly interact with the input data.
- **Hidden Layers:** Each hidden layer learns to capture higher-order correlations in the data by adjusting the weights between visible and hidden units.
- **Energy-Based Model:** DBNs are energy-based models where the goal is to minimize the energy function, which represents the negative log probability of the data given the model parameters.
- **Weight Sharing:** DBNs utilize shared weights between layers, meaning the weights learned at each layer are used for both upward and downward passes through the network.
- **Probabilistic Generative Models:** They can generate new samples from the learned distribution, making them useful for data generation tasks.
- **Fine-Tuning:** After pre-training the layers individually, the entire network is typically fine-tuned using backpropagation to improve its performance on specific tasks [24].

4.7.3.2 Training DBNs

Training DBNs involves several challenges, including computational complexity due to their deep architecture, which can make the training process slow. This can be mitigated by using parallel computing and GPU acceleration. Overfitting is another concern, especially with many layers, but regularization techniques like dropout or weight decay can help prevent this. The greedy layer-wise training approach can also be complex, requiring careful hyperparameter tuning. Optimization methods such as learning rate scheduling and adaptive algorithms can improve convergence. Additionally, scaling DBNs for large datasets can be challenging, but data augmentation and mini-batch training can help manage large-scale data efficiently. Despite these challenges, DBNs remain powerful tools for feature learning and dimensionality reduction when properly optimized [25]. Training DBNs involves several challenges.

The exploration of neural network algorithms reveals that their effectiveness is deeply tied to the nature of the data and the specific task at hand. Convolutional Neural Networks excel in processing structured grid data, such as images, due to their ability to automatically extract and hierarchically represent spatial features. RNNs, with their unique capacity to process sequential data, are particularly well-suited for tasks in natural language processing and time series analysis. DBNs, though less commonly used in modern applications, showcase the power of unsupervised learning by discovering meaningful patterns in complex datasets.

Each of these architectures has unique strengths and limitations, making them indispensable tools in the realm of data analytics. By understanding their differences and capabilities, researchers and practitioners can choose the most suitable neural network for a given task, maximizing accuracy and efficiency. As advancements in computational power and algorithm design continue, the potential applications of neural networks are expected to expand further, driving innovation across fields like AI, healthcare and autonomous systems. Ultimately, this underscores the importance of a nuanced approach to leveraging neural networks, tailored to the specific demands of each problem domain.

4.7.4 Key Points of DBNs

DBNs have played a significant role in the evolution of deep learning. The key points to remember about DBNs are as follows:

- DBNs are built by stacking multiple RBMs.
- Each RBM in the stack is trained independently using greedy learning techniques.
- DBN training involves two phases: unsupervised pre-training followed by supervised fine-tuning.
- They excel at understanding latent data representations and generating new data samples.
- DBNs have been applied in areas like classification, motion capture and speech recognition.

However, DBNs have fallen out of favour in recent years, largely replaced by more advanced deep learning models such as CNNs and RNNs.

REFERENCES

[1] Eckhardt, C. M., Madjarova, S. J., Williams, R. J., Ollivier, M., Karlsson, J., Pareek, A., & Nwachukwu, B. U. (2023). Unsupervised machine learning methods and emerging applications in healthcare. *Knee Surgery, Sports Traumatology, Arthroscopy*, 31(2), 376–381.

[2] Naeem, S., Ali, A., Anam, S., & Ahmed, M. M. (2023). An unsupervised machine learning algorithm: Comprehensive review. *International Journal of Computing and Digital Systems,* 13(1), 911–921.

[3] Usama, M., Qadir, J., Raza, A., Arif, H., Yau, K.-L., Elkhatib, Y., Hussain, A., & Al-Fuqaha, A. (2017). Unsupervised machine learning for networking: Techniques, applications and research challenges. *IEEE Access*. https://doi.org/10.1109/ACCESS.2019.2916648.

[4] Jin, X., & Han, J. (2010). Partitional clustering. In *Encyclopedia of Machine Learning*. Boston, MA: Springer, p. 766.

[5] Jianliang, M., Haikun, S., & Ling, B. (2009). The application on intrusion detection based on k- means cluster algorithm. In *Proceedings of the International Forum on Information Technology and Applications (IFITA)*, vol. 1, 2009, pp. 150–152. https://doi.org/10.1109/IFITA.2009.34

[6] Chitrakar, R., & Chuanhe, H. (2012). Anomaly detection using support vector machine classification with k-medoids clustering. In *Proceedings of the 3rd Asian Himalayas International Conference on Internet (AH-ICI)*, pp. 1–5. https://doi.org/10.1109/AHICI.2012.6408446

[7] Shetty, P., & Singh, S. (2021). Hierarchical clustering: A survey. *International Journal of Applied Research*, 7(4), 178–181. https://doi.org/10.22271/allresearch.2021.v7.i4c.8484

[8] Madhulatha, T. S. (2012). An overview on clustering methods. *arXiv preprint arXiv:1205.1117.*

[9] Usama, M., Qadir, J., Raza, A., Arif, H., Yau, K. L. A., Elkhatib, Y., . . . & Al-Fuqaha, A. (2019). Unsupervised machine learning for networking: Techniques, applications, and research challenges. *IEEE Access*, 7, 65579–65615.

[10] Xie, H., Li, J., & Xue, H. (2017). A survey of dimensionality reduction techniques based on random projection. *arXiv preprint arXiv:1706.04371.*

[11] Van Der Maaten, L., Postma, E. O., & Van Den Herik, H. J. (2009). Dimensionality reduction: A comparative review. *Journal of Machine Learning Research*, 10(66–71), 13.

[12] Khalid, S., Khalil, T., & Nasreen, S. (2014, August). A survey of feature selection and feature extraction techniques in machine learning. In *2014 Science and Information Conference* (pp. 372–378). IEEE.

[13] Santoso, M. H. (2021). Application of association rule method using apriori algorithm to find sales patterns case study of indomaret tanjung anom. *Brilliance: Research of Artificial Intelligence*, 1(2), 54–66.

[14] Senthilkumar, A., & Hari Prasad, D. (2020). An efficient FP-Growth based association rule mining algorithm using Hadoop MapReduce. *Indian Journal of Science & Technology*, 13(34), 3561–3571.

[15] Pang, G., Shen, C., Cao, L., & Hengel, A. V. D. (2021). Deep learning for anomaly detection: A review. *ACM Computing Surveys (CSUR)*, 54(2), 1–38.

[16] Analytics Vidhya. (2021, September). *Introduction to Artificial Neural Networks*. Retrieved from www.analyticsvidhya.com/blog/2021/09/introduction-to-artificial-neural-networks/
[17] Simplilearn. (n.d.). *Deep Learning Algorithm: Everything You Need to Know*. Retrieved November 25, 2024, from www.simplilearn.com/tutorials/deep-learning-tutorial/deep-learning-algorithm
[18] Analytics Vidhya. (2021, July). *Understanding the Basics of Artificial Neural Network (ANN)*. Retrieved from www.analyticsvidhya.com/blog/2021/07/understanding-the-basics-of-artificial-neural-network-ann/
[19] Wikipedia. (n.d.). Convolutional neural network. In *Wikipedia*. Retrieved November 25, 2024, from https://en.wikipedia.org/wiki/Convolutional_neural_network
[20] arXiv. (n.d.). Convolutional neural networks. *arXiv:1511.08458*. Retrieved November 25, 2024, from https://arxiv.org/abs/1511.08458
[21] IBM. (n.d.). Convolutional neural networks. *IBM*. Retrieved November 25, 2024, from www.ibm.com/topics/convolutional-neural-networks
[22] LearnOpenCV. (n.d.). *Understanding Convolutional Neural Networks (CNN)*. Retrieved November 25, 2024, from https://learnopencv.com/understanding-convolutional-neural-networks-cnn/
[23] SpringerLink. (n.d.). *Convolutional Neural Networks*. Retrieved November 25, 2024, from https://link.springer.com/chapter/10.1007/978-3-031-24349-3_
[24] Deep Belief Network. (2024, August 13). In *Wikipedia*. Retrieved from https://en.wikipedia.org/w/index.php?title=Deep_belief_network&oldid=1240122786
[25] Kalita, D. (2022, March). *An Overview of Deep Belief Network (DBN) in Deep Learning*. Retrieved from https://www.analyticsvidhya.com/blog/2022/03/an-overview-of-deep-belief-network-dbn-in-deep-learning/

5 Opportunities and Challenges for Data Analytics Integrated with Machine Learning

Shabana Urooj

5.1 INTRODUCTION

In the new era, we use data analytics to support smart decisions, as data provides abundant data, and they thrive as a prominent pillar. Machine learning (ML), a branch of artificial intelligence (AI) – takes this one step further by utilizing algorithms to learn from data, recognize patterns and predict outcomes. While data analytics serves as an initial step of understanding, ML takes it a step further by providing predictive and prescriptive capabilities, thus offering a powerful combination that is applicable in various domains including, but not limited to, healthcare, finance and autonomous systems.

Modelling will ideally be created for each kind of analytics that is valuable to the business which includes correlation analysis, predictive analytics, diagnostic Analytics, etc. However, this convergence brings with it specific challenges such as the interpretability of models, data security and computational resources to implement on a wide scale, among others. On the one hand, the integration of ML into data analytics unlocks opportunities for automation, efficiency and precision. However, this integration is not without its challenges. This chapter explores the prospects and perils of merging data analytics with ML, examining its exponential power and the fundamental challenges that must be addressed.

5.2 FUNDAMENTALS OF DATA ANALYTICS AND ML

Data analytics is primarily about interpreting and understanding data to derive actionable insights through methods like visualization, statistical analysis and trend identification. On the other hand, ML enhances this process by automating tasks such as pattern recognition, prediction and prescription. While analytics answers "what" and "why", ML focuses on "what will happen" and "what should be done". Together, they enable comprehensive data-driven decision-making.

DOI: 10.1201/9781003396772-6

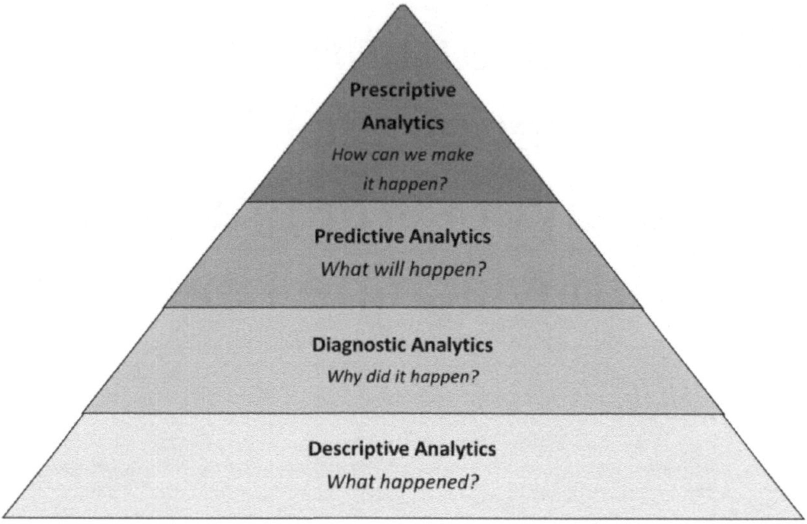

FIGURE 5.1 Types of data analytics.

5.2.1 Data Analytics

Data analytics is a computer science field that focuses on extracting insights from raw data. Data analysts use statistical techniques and programming languages to uncover patterns, trends and relationships inside large datasets. Data analytics is important for many industries, where many business leaders use data to inform decision-making. The types of data analytics are shown in Figure 5.1.

5.2.2 Machine Learning

ML techniques are essential for data analytics, extracting insights from large datasets. They include supervised learning, which uses labelled data to predict outcomes (e.g. linear regression, decision trees); unsupervised learning, which finds patterns in unlabelled data (e.g. k-means clustering); semi-supervised learning, which combines labelled and unlabelled data, useful when labelled data is scarce; reinforcement learning, which trains models to make decisions by rewarding desired actions, often used in robotics and games; and deep learning, which uses multi-layer neural networks to model complex patterns (e.g. convolutional and recurrent neural networks). These methods are applied in fields like healthcare, finance and e-commerce.

ML techniques were categorized into five main groups:

- **Supervised Learning:** Involves training models on labelled data, with key algorithms like linear regression, decision trees and neural networks.
- **Unsupervised Learning:** Focuses on finding patterns in unlabelled data, featuring methods such as k-means and hierarchical clustering for exploration data analysis.

- **Semi-Supervised Learning:** Combines labelled and unlabelled data, particularly useful when obtaining labels is costly.
- **Reinforcement Learning:** Trains agents through feedback (rewards and penalties) and discusses its applications in decision-making.
- **Deep Learning:** Examines complex neural network architectures, including CNNs and RNNs, and their effectiveness in handling intricate data types.

5.2.3 Relationship between Data Analytics and ML

The relationship between data analytics and ML is symbiotic, with each discipline enhancing the capabilities of the other which is clear in Figure 5.2. Together, they provide powerful tools for extracting actionable insights and automating decision-making processes.

5.2.3.1 Complementary Roles

Data analytics primarily focuses on the interpretation and understanding of data through methods like visualization, statistical analysis and trend identification. It answers questions such as "what happened?" and "why did it happen?" ML, on the other hand, extends this capability by automating tasks like prediction and prescription. By analysing patterns in historical and real-time data, ML models can forecast future trends, recommend actions and uncover hidden relationships. While analytics lays the groundwork for data comprehension, ML builds upon it to deliver enhanced predictive and prescriptive capabilities.

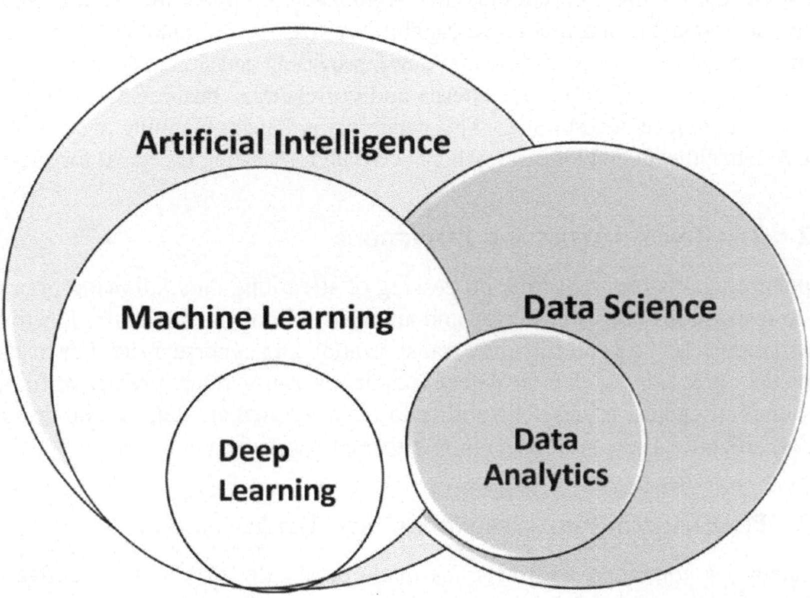

FIGURE 5.2 Relationship between data analytics and machine learning.

5.2.3.2 Feedback Loop

The interplay between data analytics and ML is iterative and mutually reinforcing. ML models rely on high-quality, well-prepared datasets, which are generated through data analytics processes such as cleaning, transformation and feature engineering. In turn, ML enriches data analytics by generating more accurate predictions, which can then be used to refine data preparation and modelling processes. This feedback loop ensures continuous improvement in both analytics and ML applications.

5.3 OPPORTUNITIES OF DATA ANALYTICS WITH ML

In today's era of big data, organizations are harnessing the power of data analytics and ML to uncover actionable insights and drive smarter decision-making. This dynamic combination enables businesses to go beyond traditional analytical methods, leveraging advanced algorithms to extract deeper patterns, automate processes and predict outcomes with remarkable precision. ML amplifies the potential of data analytics by enabling real-time processing, personalized solutions and groundbreaking innovations across diverse industries. From healthcare and finance to retail and beyond, this transformative synergy offers unprecedented opportunities for growth, efficiency and competitive advantage, reshaping the way organizations operate and innovate. The integration of data analytics with ML has unlocked significant opportunities across industries, transforming how data is processed, interpreted and utilized for various applications. An in-depth discussion of these opportunities is provided in the following sections.

5.3.1 Enhanced Decision-Making

The combination of data analytics and ML significantly improves decision making by offering deep insights and predictive capabilities. ML models analyse historical and real-time data to forecast trends and outcomes, providing decision makers with actionable intelligence. By identifying patterns and correlations, businesses can optimize strategies and reduce uncertainties. This capability enhances planning in sectors such as finance, healthcare and logistics, where accurate forecasting is crucial for success.

5.3.2 Real-Time Analytics and Predictions

The integration enables real-time processing of streaming data, allowing organizations to respond instantly to changes and anomalies. Real-time analytics has revolutionized industries like e-commerce, transportation and cybersecurity. For instance, ML models process live data to detect fraudulent transactions, predict traffic flow or dynamically adjust prices. The ability to make immediate data-driven decisions helps organizations stay agile and competitive in fast-paced environments.

5.3.3 Personalized Recommendations and User Experiences

Data analytics combined with ML has made personalization more effective than ever. By analysing user behaviour, preferences and past interactions, businesses can create tailored experiences that enhance customer satisfaction and engagement. This is evident in recommendation systems used by streaming platforms, online retailers and digital marketers. These systems adapt dynamically, ensuring that each user receives content, products or services aligned with their specific needs and interests, fostering long-term loyalty.

5.4 BIG DATA IN ML

The use of advanced technologies and techniques to analyse complex large datasets is referred to as big data analytics (BDA). By analysing these data, businesses are allowed to uncover hidden patterns, trends and insights. Therefore, businesses are enabled to make data-driven decisions, find new market opportunities, have more optimized processes, and enhance customer experiences. As technology continues to enhance and data becomes more available, BDA is expected to play a crucial role in shaping the future of business operations. BDA has significantly transformed the world of business. By providing valuable insights that aid in making informed decisions, it has optimized organizations; operations in a remarkably impactful way, leading to improved decision-making and high efficiency.

5.4.1 Advancing Scientific Research and Discovery

The integration of ML and data analytics plays a transformative role in scientific research. Researchers can analyse large, complex datasets to uncover insights that were previously unattainable. ML models enable the identification of hidden patterns, simulate complex systems, and predict outcomes in areas like climate science, drug discovery and material science. This automation accelerates research processes, allowing scientists to focus on innovation and hypothesis testing while minimizing the time spent on data processing.

5.4.2 Automation and Cost Reduction in Businesses

The synergy between ML and data analytics drives automation, reducing operational costs and enhancing efficiency. Tasks such as inventory management, predictive maintenance and quality assurance are streamlined, allowing businesses to allocate resources effectively. Automated processes minimize human error, increase productivity and improve decision-making. This integration is especially beneficial in manufacturing, supply chain management and customer support, where operational efficiency directly impacts profitability.

5.5 CHALLENGES OF DATA ANALYTICS WITH ML

The integration of data analytics and ML has revolutionized industries, enabling data-driven insights and predictive capabilities. However, this integration is not without its challenges, which range from managing data quality to addressing ethical concerns. Issues such as data quality, model interpretability and ethical concerns present significant obstacles. The effectiveness of ML models heavily depends on the availability of high-quality, representative data, which is often scarce or plagued by biases. Organizations often struggle with scalability, computational complexity and the interpretability of ML models, making adoption and implementation difficult. Evolving data streams and privacy issues further complicate the landscape, demanding innovative solutions. Addressing these challenges is essential for unlocking the full potential of these technologies. Some key challenges associated with the integration of data analytics and ML are discussed next.

5.5.1 Computational Demands

Incorporating ML into data analytics is resource-intensive, especially for large-scale datasets, where it requires a lot of computing power. The training of sophisticated architectures such as GPT-4 or GANs has a considerable energy cost, which can provoke environmental sustainability issues. ML, in addition to being data-hungry, is also frequently concerned with real-time analytics, interactive applications and systematic optimization; thus, infrastructure demands often require high-performance computing (HPC) systems that can be prohibitively expensive for smaller enterprises. Cloud-based solutions are a practical alternative for minimizing infrastructure usage-related expenses, but they also heighten exposure to data protection regulatory compliance challenges – exacerbating accessibility issues for cash-strapped organizations.

5.5.2 Data Quality and Availability

Your ML models highly depend on data, and data comes with availability and accuracy issues, to mention a few. Data labelling which is done manually takes a long time and is expensive, particularly for large datasets and inconsistent or incomplete data can lead to biased models and inaccurate analytics. These problems need progress in the automated data labelling and augmentation methods. Approaches such as transfer learning and synthetic data generation are being investigated to overcome these challenges, especially in sensitive fields such as medicine and self-driving vehicles.

5.5.3 Model Interpretability

ML models, especially deep learning architectures, are often criticized for their inability to be interpreted. The highly non-linear nature of neural networks, which are often viewed as black box models, makes them especially difficult to understand in terms of how a prediction was made. The inability to explain the decision made is particularly an issue in healthcare and law, where accountability is paramount, and this can lead to limited adoption. Although predictive models can be useful in criminal justice, the lack of transparency in what informs their decisions could create mistrust and scepticism in their outcomes. In response to these issues, the rise of Explainable AI (XAI) has attempted to make algorithms transparent and understandable while maintaining performance.

5.5.4 Ethics and Control Issues

ML and data analytics Collective use of both ML and data analytics has enormous promise but raises serious ethical and legal issues such as algorithmic bias, privacy and security concerns. ML models can amplify and keep biases found in training data, which can consequently lead to inequitable results like excluding qualified under-represented candidates in a hiring process if not managed properly. Moreover, sensitive data should require strict protection to avoid unauthorized access. And while regulations such as the GDPR in Europe and CCPA in California have led some companies to work towards these privacy and ethical implications, complying with all of them across the world is a moving target and an incredibly complicated task.

5.5.5 Complexity of Integration

However, these analytics systems were not prepared for the ML revolution that approached and have been co-evolving, introducing technical and search system challenges (e.g. ML compatibility with old analytics systems, skill gaps) as well as organizational barriers. ML tools often have a huge gap to fill to align with legacy infrastructures, and there are also not enough people who have the ability to work in both data analytics and ML. These challenges can be met by deploying employee development workforce training programs. Other development of easy-to-use ML platforms with simple user interfaces will also help minimize the skill gap and drive adoption and integration.

5.6 APPLICATIONS IN BIG DATA ENVIRONMENTS

The hybrid quantum-classical algorithm, GPU acceleration and ML techniques find their practical applications across different industries:

- **Finance:** These techniques can help optimize trading strategies through real-time analysis of huge amounts of market data to be processed with high speed. Quantum algorithms show promises in portfolio optimization and risk assessment tasks.
- **Healthcare:** By analysing patient records, genetic information and data from clinical trials at scale, healthcare providers can increasingly personalize treatment regimens, potentially improving patient outcomes. Quantum computing may enhance the existing methodologies for drug discovery processes by simulating molecular interactions faster.
- **Logistics and Supply Chain Management:** ML models can help predict demand and optimize inventory management throughout complex supply chains.
- **Scientific Research:** In astronomy, particle physics and climate science, these techniques can help process and analyse massive datasets produced

by scientific instruments and simulations. Quantum algorithms show potential in simulating quantum systems and could lead to many advances in materials science and chemistry.

5.7 CHALLENGES AND FUTURE DIRECTIONS

Although hybrid approaches show much promise in improving the scalability of classical algorithms for big data applications, it pose many challenges:

- **Quantum Decoherence:** It is important to maintain a certain level of quantum coherence for a reasonably long duration to ensure the accuracy of quantum computation. Environmental disturbances interfere with correct calculations, introducing errors. Development of robust quantum hardware and error correction is crucial.
- **Scalability of Quantum Systems:** The major challenge is to scale up quantum systems while maintaining their coherence and error rates.
- **Algorithm Design:** The complex algorithm design requires experts in both quantum computing and classical algorithm design as well as a great understanding of the problem domain.
- **Integration with existing infrastructure:** Organizations will have to train their staff and upgrade their infrastructures to support new technologies such as quantum processors or GPU clusters. This has been shown to be difficult to adopt, especially for smaller organizations.
- **Data Privacy and Security:** With growing complexity and distribution, ensuring data privacy and security is an increasing challenge, especially in healthcare and finance, where data breaches pose a great concern.
- **Energy Efficiency:** As data centres cater to big data, energy consumption is raising concern. Development of energy-efficient hardware and algorithms is important to sustain big data analytics.

Future research directions to tackle the issues include the following:

- Development of more robust and scalable quantum hardware.
- Creation of new hybrid algorithms that optimally balance quantum and classical resources.
- Enhancements in error-correcting techniques relative to quantum systems.
- Improving GPU architecture and programming models for big data tasks.
- Engineering energy-efficient computing technologies.
- Ensuring explainable AI and interpretable ML models.
- Progressing secure multi-party computation and homomorphic encryption for privacy-preserving data analytics.

It can be believed that classical algorithms have the potential to resolve scalability issues posed on big data processing by strategic integration with cutting-edge computational techniques, such as hybrid quantum-classical approaches, GPU acceleration and ML models. These methods can greatly improve performance as well as inspire the development of efficient solutions for larger datasets

The combination of classical algorithms with innovative technologies allows the possibility of extracting value from big data. By leveraging the strengths of each approach – the reliability and versatility of classical algorithms, the parallelism of GPUs, the adaptive capabilities of ML, and the unique computational properties of quantum systems – a powerful hybrid solution can be developed. Research and technology development should offer more efficient and innovative solutions to handle large data environments in various domains. The future of BDA does not suggest abandoning classical algorithms but enhancing and intermixing with new computational paradigms to enable the full potential of our data resources.

6 Cloud Computing
A Change in the IT Infrastructure Landscape

Seema Rawat and Praveen Kumar

6.1 INTRODUCTION

The adoption of cloud computing is a game-changer. It signifies a departure from tangible asset (physical hardware) ownership and maintenance to on-demand computing solutions provided over the Internet. Cloud computing meets the dynamic needs of every industry by providing scalable and even economical access to computing power, storage and software.

In this chapter, we discuss the development of cloud computing, basic ideas about how it works and the impact of cloud in enterprises. This chapter discusses its architecture, features and how it allows for stream processing and better operational efficiency. The chapter also explores how it allows for global collaborations and innovations in our digital-first world [1].

6.2 HISTORY OF CLOUD COMPUTING

Many cloud computing concepts were developed over several decades tracing back to the 1960s when mainframe computers were introduced that enabled multiple users to share access to the same centralized computing resource. The evolution of cloud computing has gone through the following major milestones:

- **1960s:** The Age of Mainframes and Time-Sharing Systems: Because mainframes were very expensive in relation to the budget of an Institute or a university, time-sharing systems came into the picture in order to take advantage of real-time interactive access to a single computer by multiple users. And thus was resource virtualization, boundary and context switching, and shared computing.
- **1990s:** Grid Computing and SaaS: Grid computing, in which the power of many computers is pooled together for a goal – for example scientific research. This was also the decade in which the first Software-as-a-Service (SaaS) applications such as Salesforce began to take off – proving that software served via the Internet was viable [2].

DOI: 10.1201/9781003396772-7

- **2000s:** Commercial Cloud Services: The simple virtualization was revolutionary and in 2006, Amazon Web Services (AWS) released its Elastic Compute Cloud (EC2) enabling users to gain scalable and flexible computing power. That marked the beginning of commercial cloud services, closely followed by platforms from Microsoft Azure and Google Cloud Platform.
- **2010s:** The Rise of Cloud Models and Multi-Cloud Strategies: The variety of cloud models: IaaS, PaaS and SaaS changed how IT infrastructure was managed in a big way. In response to this, hybrid and multi-cloud strategies were born; allowing organizations to tap into the strengths of various cloud ecosystems while minimizing vendor lock-in concerns.
- **Current Era:** Machine learning (ML) integration with cloud services has made cloud platforms essential for predictive analytics and large data processing.

These are just a few of the accomplishments that illustrate the evolution of cloud computing from the beginning to the present day, and its role in modern IT.

6.3 CLOUD COMPUTING CONCEPTS

Cloud computing is the delivery of computing services – servers, storage, databases, networking, software and analytics – over the Internet. Here are some of the core service models:

1. **Infrastructure as a Service (IaaS):** IaaS provides virtualized computing resources over the Internet, such as servers, storage and networking. It allows companies to eliminate the need for purchasing and maintaining physical hardware while being able to scale resources as needed. This incorporates AWS EC2, Microsoft Azure Virtual Machines, Google Compute Engine and so on [3].
2. **Platform as a Service (PaaS):** PaaS is a cloud-based platform used for application development and deployment. This allows developers to create, test and deploy applications without the need to manage or worry about the underlying infrastructure. Examples include Heroku, Google App Engine and AWS Elastic Beanstalk [3].
3. **Software as a Service (SaaS):** SaaS is a technology delivery model that allows users to access software applications through the Internet. No installation, no maintenance, everything from the cloud. Some typical examples are Google Workspace, Microsoft 365 and Dropbox [3].
4. **Deployment Models:** Public Cloud: Solutions that are hosted by third-party providers and available to anyone over the Internet. Scalable and cost-effective. Private Cloud: Infrastructure is on dedicated hardware for one organization. Hybrid Cloud: Spread over both private and public cloud environments to run multiple applications and services for data and app portability

These models vary in cost and availability of features, catering to everything from startups in need of an affordable product to enterprises looking for customized and secure cloud environments.

6.4 CLOUD COMPUTING CHARACTERISTICS

Cloud Computing has different features such as:

- **On-Demand Self-Service:** Users can provision and manage resources as they need without the intervention of people
- **Broad Network Access:** Cloud services can be accessed over the Internet and on devices like laptops, smartphones and tablets.
- **Resource Pooling:** Resources are pooled and shared among multiple users who access a multi-tenant environment.
- **Rapid Elasticity:** The cloud can be appropriated and released in high amounts, giving the right number of assets to handle or be accessible at any one minute in time.
- **Usage:** Resources are monitored and charged based on usage, which provides transparency and allows for cost control.

These features distinguish cloud computing from old IT frameworks disconnected, permitting unrivalled adaptability and efficiency [4].

6.5 CLOUD COMPUTING ARCHITECTURE

The architecture of cloud computing is built on two core components:

6.5.1 Software Architecture

- **Virtualization:** Provides a way to set up virtual machines, allowing physical machines to run multiple operating systems on it. This leads to using resources efficiently and minimizes costs [5, 6].
- **Middleware:** It connects various apps and services, enabling communication between them in the cloud [5, 6].
- **APIs:** They allow for the integration and interaction between cloud services and applications, promoting interoperability [6].

6.5.2 Hardware Architecture

- **Data Centres:** The backbone of cloud computing, they contain servers, storage systems and any other networking equipment.
- **Load Balancers:** It spreads the workload across multiple servers to ensure that they are always available and performing [5].
- **Edge Devices:** Bring computational power closer to users by reducing latency and enhancing real-time data processing.

A robust architecture is thus vital to allow services to run smoothly, each addressing different business needs [6].

6.6 CLOUD APPROACH CONSIDERATIONS

Cloud is not a switch that can be turned on or off with one go, rather it requires multifaceted planning before adoption, whether it is technical, financial or operational. Here's a closer look at some of those considerations:

6.6.1 Security and Compliance

Security continues to be the main worry for companies moving to the cloud. Organizations must ensure that any cloud service provider used does its share in complying with certain industry standards such as GDPR, HIPAA and ISO 27001. Data encryption at rest and in transit, frequent security audits and identity management systems (such as IAM) are all must-have features [7].

Healthcare companies, for example that use the cloud to store electronic medical records have to abide by HIPAA rules to ensure sensitive patient data is secure.

6.6.2 Cost Analysis

While cloud computing cuts costs relating to initial infrastructure investments, the operational costs may soar high when a data-hungry ML workload is run on-demand. The organizations hence make a thorough comparison of the total cost of owning (TCO) along with expenses incurred by data storage, model training, processing power (like GPU/TPU use), in addition to bandwidth utilization to avert unexpected increases in expenditure.

For instance, a business training ML models via the pay-as-you-go model may see costs going up if the system is unverifiable for resource allocation. Some suggestions for optimizing cloud use and actively preventing over-allocation of ML resources include auto-scaling training clusters, monitoring resource use, and again relying on spare instances wherever possible for non-critical ML work.

6.6.3 Integration with the Existing Systems

Integrating cloud solutions with legacy systems is often challenging but crucial for seamless operations. Assume you have existing legacy systems that need to integrate with the new cloud-based solution. APIs and middleware can fill those gaps, but they add even more complexity and cost. For example retail organizations that combine local inventory systems with cloud-based customer management platforms need to ensure data consistency [8].

6.6.4 Scalability and Performance

Imagining the future of cloud platforms, Reducibility is one of the most exciting advantages of using the cloud. You have the flexibility to increase or decrease your resources based on the workloads, and this does not affect performance. Organizations need to perform scalability testing scenarios under peak usage. Cloud scalability is a must for e-commerce Platforms such as Black Friday sales.

6.6.5 Reliability and Support of Vendor

Choosing a dependable vendor ensures consistent service levels. Evaluating SLAs (service level agreements), uptime guarantees and customer reviews can help businesses make informed decisions [7].

Example: Companies often consider AWS, Microsoft Azure or Google Cloud because of their proven track record in reliability and global infrastructure.

6.7 CLOUD COMPUTING AND BUSINESS TRANSFORMATION

Cloud computing has become a cornerstone of business innovation, efficiency and new-age technology potential. In this section, there are some transformative effects specifically pertaining to data analytics and ML.

6.7.1 Speeding Up the Application Development

Cloud platforms give the cloud-native DevOps tools like Docker, Kubernetes and CI/CD pipelines that make the application development and deployment simpler. These tools have distinct advantages for modelling lifecycle management, through which data scientists are enabled to deploy models faster and iterate quickly.

For example Google AI Platform provides out-of-the-box configurations for quick training and deployment of ML models. Likewise, Spotify applies Google Cloud Platform to rapidly develop and deploy new features for a wide audience base around the world.

6.7.2 Improving the Agility of Business

Cloud platforms offer real-time data processing through their global distributed ML pipelines. For instance, Netflix uses AWS streaming, providing hand-picked personalized video content through an ML model that recommends shows and movies based on the user preferences, with localized servers cutting down on latency [9]. This means that businesses across the globe can build and deploy any model on ML almost instantly based on infrastructure scalability, such as AWS, Google Cloud, Microsoft Azure, etc. Example: Companies use the cloud to build and benchmark ML models that guests can apply throughout their customer journeys, allowing for a quick roll-out of directed solutions.

6.7.3 Expanding Global Reach

Cloud computing provides the platforms to improve global reach by ensuring low latency and high performance for delivery to customers all over the globe. Content delivery networks (CDNs) integrated with other ML tools, the user experience is significantly enhanced during data and personalized content delivery. By hosting globally distributed ML pipelines, cloud platforms allow real-time data processing. Example: Netflix uses AWS streaming to deliver personalized video content through the ML model, recommending shows and movies on the basis of user preferences, with provided localized servers reducing latency [9].

6.7.4 Operating Expenses Decrease

Transitioning to a cloud-based infrastructure removes hardware maintenance, power and cooling costs from the equation for businesses. Instead, they only pay per resource consumed.

For example: Non-profit organizations rely on Google Cloud's free tier to perform business-critical operations on tight budgets.

6.8 WHAT ARE THE TRENDS EMERGING IN CLOUD COMPUTING

Cloud computing is not static and continuously incorporates new technologies and fulfils emerging needs. Here are some key trends.

6.8.1 Serverless Computing

Serverless architecture lets developers write code without concern about the management of infrastructure. This model lowers costs and operational complexity. AWS Lambda, for instance, allows companies to execute code based on events, billing them only for the amount of time the code is being executed [9].

6.8.2 Hybrid and Multi-Cloud Strategies

Hybrid models have begun to gain traction within organizations. In turn, public and private clouds are being mixed for cost and security optimization. Multi-cloud strategies are adopted to avoid vendor lock-in and also for resilience. For example financial institutions use hybrid clouds to run private environments for sensitive data but complementary public clouds for customer-facing applications [10].

6.8.3 Edge-to-Cloud Integration

Edge computing refers to processing data nearer to where it is generated, minimizing latency and bandwidth. The cloud allows for centralized management and long-term storage. Example: Autonomous vehicles use edge computing for real-time decision-making and at the same time upload some processed data to the cloud for analytics [10].

6.8.4 Cloud Computing with AI and ML

AI examples: Cloud platforms provide AI services such as natural language processing (NLP), computer vision and predictive analytics to democratize access to cutting-edge capabilities [9, 10].

For example, with Amazon SageMaker, data scientists can purpose-built ML models at scale without managing any of the infrastructure beneath them.

Cloud platforms have turned into major facilitators of the implementation and scaling up of AI and ML models. They offer services such as NLP, computer vision and predictive analytics which democratize access to advanced capabilities for enterprises of all sizes.

AI SERVICES ON CLOUD PLATFORMS

The cloud platforms provide AI-enabled tools and frameworks that help in speeding up model development:

- **Amazon SageMaker:** Enables the data scientist to construct, train and deploy ML models at scale with infrastructure management.
- **Google Vertex AI:** Streamlines end-to-end ML workflows including data ingestion and model deployment.
- **Microsoft Azure AI:** Offers speech recognition, image classification and translation APIs as part of its cognitive services.

These instruments enable organizations to apply artificial intelligence in problem-solving at the workday level and cloud scalability ensures the effective management of even resource-intensive models.

Key Advantages

- **Mass Automation:** AI services in the cloud automate tasks that involve data processing on a repetitive basis and leave resources for high-value analytics.
- **World Reach:** AI capability becomes virtually available in every nook and corner because cloud platforms support remote teams as well as applications distributed across different locations.
- **The driver of Innovation:** Organizations can bring forth innovative solutions by merging AI with other new technologies, examples being fraud detection in real-time or supply chain optimization influenced by the environment.

Cloud computing has transcended the mere role of hosting AI; it now plays a pivotal part as a platform for future innovations by converging AI with other upcoming technologies to address the intricacies of problems and the new frontiers opened by data discovery.

6.8.5 Sustainability under the Cloud

As environmental issues take centre stage, cloud providers are moving towards energy-efficient practices, like harnessing renewable energy for their data centres and enhancing hardware utilization rates [10].

For instance, Microsoft Azure plans to be carbon negative by 2030 and begin purchasing wind and solar energy projects.

TABLE 6.1
Comparative Analysis: Traditional IT versus Cloud Computing

Aspect	Traditional IT	Cloud Computing
Ownership	Full ownership of hardware	Shared infrastructure
Scalability	Limited	On-demand and virtually unlimited
Cost Structure	High upfront capital expenditures	Pay-as-you-go
Maintenance	Managed in-house	Managed by service providers

Table 6.1 compares Traditional IT (owned hardware, limited scalability, high upfront costs) with Cloud Computing (shared, on-demand scaling, pay-per-use, provider-managed), highlighting key operational differences with benefits of using cloud.

6.9 CONCLUSION

There is no doubt that cloud computing has revolutionized the way organizations view and approach their IT infrastructure, heralding principles of new-age agility, scalability, and such innovation. As one of the most engaged AI ecosystems, you are working on a response to all of that and more. This is not merely the adoption of new technology; it represents a transformation in how companies operate, innovate and provide value to their customers and employees.

One of the biggest advantages of a cloud computing is the scalability of it because organizations can instantly ramp up or down resources according to their needs. As a result, organizations of all sizes can take advantage of advanced computation, storage and software without the associated large incremental capital outlay. Cloud platforms offer a pay-as-you-go model that bills far less than traditional IT models would, levelling the field for even startups with small budgets. Additionally, by outsourcing hardware upkeep and infrastructure management to cloud service providers, companies can shift their attention towards core operations and innovation.

With increasing levels of abstraction from the user to the provider, different service models are available: IaaS, PaaS and last but not least, SaaS.

Plus, the cloud's power to facilitate collaboration and global distribution has changed everything. Now companies can cross boundaries with ease and can access resources as well as applications in real time. For example companies can save their data and have applications running from anywhere in the world, aiding in better collaboration of remote teams which is the need of the hour in the global economy today. Cloud computing provides broad network access: Mobile devices are ubiquitous and need constant, seamless access to data for the business to remain agile.

But, of course, there are challenges to adopting cloud computing. Migrating to the cloud requires organizations to evaluate security, costs, compatibility with legacy systems, vendor reliability and other factors. Strong data protection by encryption, industry compliance, robust identity management systems, among others, is an utmost important security measures one must take to ensure the integrity and privacy of data on cloud. Besides, it is important for organizations to evaluate the Total Cost of Ownership (TCO) and Operational Expenditure (OPEX) over the long term to ensure that the costs do not outweigh what they initially invested in terms of bandwidth, processing and storage costs. Integration with existing systems can be tricky, as can scaling cloud resources to support performance requirements.

In the future, cloud computing will also evolve with trends like serverless computing, hybrid cloud models and edge computing. Serverless offers the promise of taking things even further: you will no longer have to manage infrastructure, while both hybrid and multi-cloud strategies enable the end user to take advantage of what multiple cloud providers can offer while reducing the risks of vendor lock-in. The move towards edge computing, which allows information to be processed near the data source, will help reduce latency and enable quicker, real-time decision making and more efficient operations. In summary, cloud computing is a paradigm shift in technology usage that would breach business growth and innovation crusade rather than a buzz word. As organizations continue migrating to the cloud, they discover more ways to consolidate operations, scale and pivot efficiently. Along with the prevailing focus on AI, ML and sustainability, the worth of the cloud will only continue to grow, and it will remain as an essential enabler of the digital transformation journey spanning vertically into industries. Even so, companies that can leverage cloud computing strategically will be optimally positioned to thrive amid an ever-evolving technology landscape [1, 5].

REFERENCES

[1] Armbrust, M., Fox, A., Griffith, R., Joseph, A. D., Katz, R., Konwinski, A., . . . & Zaharia, M. (2010). A View of Cloud Computing. *Communications of the ACM*, 53(4), 50–58. https://dl.acm.org/doi/10.1145/1721654.1721672

[2] Buyya, R., Yeo, C. S., & Venugopal, S. (2008). Market-Oriented Cloud Computing: Vision, Hype, and Reality for Delivering IT Services as Computing Utilities. *IEEE International Conference on High Performance Computing and Communications*. https://ieeexplore.ieee.org/document/4637675

[3] Mell, P., & Grance, T. (2011). The NIST Definition of Cloud Computing. *National Institute of Standards and Technology, Special Publication 800–145*. https://csrc.nist.gov/pubs/sp/800/145/final

[4] Marinescu, D. C. (2013). *Cloud Computing: Theory and Practice*. Morgan Kaufmann. https://books.google.co.in/books?id=XOBWEAAAQBAJ

[5] Rittinghouse, J. W., & Ransome, J. F. (2017). *Cloud Computing: Implementation, Management, and Security*. CRC Press. www.taylorfrancis.com/books/mono/10.1201/9781439806814/cloud-computing-james-ransome-john-rittinghouse

[6] Kratzke, N., & Quint, P. C. (2017). Understanding Cloud-Native Applications After 10 Years of Cloud Computing – A Systematic Mapping Study. *Journal of Systems and Software*, 126, 1–16. www.researchgate.net/publication/312045183_Understanding_Cloud-native_Applications_after_10_Years_of_Cloud_Computing_-_A_Systematic_Mapping_Study

[7] Microsoft Azure Documentation. *Azure Architecture Guide*. https://learn.microsoft.com/en-us/azure/?product=popular

[8] Amazon Web Services (AWS) Documentation. *Overview of Amazon Web Services*. https://aws.amazon.com/free/

[9] Fox, G. C., & Chang, G. (2014). *Big Data and Cloud Computing: Current State and Future Opportunities*. Springer. www.researchgate.net/publication/221103048_Big_Data_and_Cloud_Computing_Current_State_and_Future_Opportunities
[10] Hashem, I. A. T., Yaqoob, I., Anuar, N. B., Mokhtar, S., Gani, A., & Khan, S. U. (2015). The Rise of "Big Data" on Cloud Computing: Review and Open Research Issues. *Information Systems*, 47, 98–115. www.sciencedirect.com/science/article/abs/pii/S0306437914001288

7 Redefining Data Analytics with ML and Cloud

Avita Katal

7.1 INTRODUCTION

The emergence of new technologies in data analytics, machine learning (ML) and cloud computing is facilitating dramatic changes in the world. The integration of these powerful approaches has begun this era of data analytics which is not only informative but also scalable, economical and versatile. This exploitive development merges data analytics with ML and cloud computing, illustrating what's possible, the concepts and their advantages, and what case studies are supporting the transformation of environments, fostering new ideas and speeding up the decision-making process based on data (Medvedev & Kurasova, 2016).

This development and its implications of using cloud computing have changed the narrative about how business processes and data are gathered. It offers an easy-to-use resource that is readily available over the Internet such as storage, computing power and software applications among many others. This kind of model does away with the requirement of investing in cost-expensive physical infrastructures, thus permitting organizations to exploit operations that are cloud-based, cost-effective, flexible and scalable. Cloud computing and data analytics are bound and complementary. It gives companies the ability to cost-effectively and easily store, process and analyse large amounts of data efficiently.

Integrating ML in a cloud environment allows organizations to unlock synergies between the two technologies harnessing ML algorithms which can take advantage of the cloud's distributed costs and allow algorithms to be trained and deployed at lower incredible cost.

The amount of data created each day increases at an alarming rate. On-premises models have limited capacity for such data which makes them expensive, congested and ineffective. The elasticity associated with cloud computing is a revolution, allowing organizations to scale their services up and down as their data requires. The conventional process of obtaining, supporting and upgrading on-site computer systems components and programs is quite costly. Instead with cloud services, organizations' expenses are reasonably reduced since they only spend on assets they use (Manekar & Pradeepini, 2015). A cloud solution now has the benefit of mobility. Cloud-based data analytics and ML software are accessible from any part of the world, and this enhances teamwork and remote working which is greatly needed in today's world of globalization. ML algorithms operating in the cloud, which processes large amounts of data, enable businesses to minimize risks while making

 DOI: 10.1201/9781003396772-8

crucial decisions during critical operations. Real-time insights can be crucial and game-changing, whether it be in e-commerce for dynamic pricing, in the supply chain to enhance routing in real time, or in healthcare for example in assisting in early disease outbreaks.

With further acceptance of cloud to drive data analytics and ML, hybrid and multi-cloud have been adopted as reasonable alternatives. These include incorporating both the private and public clouds or several cloud providers. They allow more flexibility, resilience and provide cost optimizations. From IoT to financial markets, data is developed within organizations at the highest order ever. Most businesses rely on cloud-based data analytics coupled with machine-learning solutions to such a great extent that this technology now enables organizations to respond and make instant decisions (Darwish, 2024).

As information becomes a very valuable element to assisting in decision making, businesses and individuals are finding it stimulating and easy to operate in such a world which is surrounded by data. Provided with the correct methods, tools, strategies and moral aspects to such data, we can be assured of a world with data analytic techniques and ML that is effective and innovative.

This chapter develops the field of data analytics as it looks at a couple of the core concepts. It commences with presenting the new data architecture, stressing the importance of elastic and scalable systems that support high volumes of heterogeneous data. The chapter then continues with the incorporation of ML into data analytics which demonstrates how ML algorithms have increased the capability to extract and interpret information from intricate datasets. It further discusses the different categories of ML services that are offered in the cloud environment and how they assist in the automated and efficient execution of data analyses and other related activities. Lastly, the chapter considers the AWS serverless data analytics pipeline reference architecture with an emphasis on how serverless technologies transform data processes and enhance efficiency through minimal management, and thus, allow organizations to create powerful and scalable analytics platforms.

7.2 TRANSITION TO MODERN DATA ARCHITECTURE

The transition from conventional to contemporary data architecture has been brought about due to many reasons, but the most notable has to do with the shortfalls of traditional systems and the needs of the current business world which is data-rich. In order to execute reports and queries on data, ETL (Extract, Transform, Load) involves obtaining data from a data source, doing any necessary transformations, and then loading the data into a data warehouse. This technique or paradigm's drawback is that it involves a lot of data parsing, variable modification, string processing and I/O activity (Berisha et al., 2022). The goal of ELT (Extract, Load, Transform) is to move the most computationally demanding task – transformation – to the cloud rather than to an on-premise service, which is already under strain from handling transactions on a regular basis (Berisha et al., 2022). This indicates that when data warehousing solutions are utilized for various kinds of data, data staging is not necessary. The data encompassing raw, semi-structured, unstructured and structured data, this strategy makes advantage of the idea of "data lakes", which vary from OLAP (Online Analytical Processing) data warehouses in that they don't need data transformation prior to loading. The principles justifying this change are as follows.

- **Volume and Variety of Data:** Older architectural frameworks were more focused on structured data which in most instances was kept in relational databases. However, due to the continuous increase of Internet and its applications, more types of data such as unstructured, semi-structured, from sources like IoTs and social media have been integrated; traditional systems faced tough challenges, and managing this complexity required substantial growth. However, contemporary data architecture like a data lake for example allows for seamless capturing and storing large volumes of different data more efficiently and quickly.
- **Scalability:** On-premise server-based traditional data architecture systems have been known to have their own shortcomings with regard to scaling. The deployment of these systems must be supported and controlled by a significant amount of hardware as the quantity of data increases, which is what makes managing this type of infrastructure complicated. Today's modern architectures, though, especially those that are hosted in the cloud provide organizations the opportunity to inevitably shape their resources as per their needs without the constraint of the physical equipment infrastructure limitations.
- **Real-Time Data Processing:** In earlier systems, batch processing techniques were commonly used which resulted in windows of time before any data or insights could be made available. In today's enterprise, there is an increasing need to enable as data-driven decisions as possible in real-time or almost in real time. With the help of stream processing and serverless companies' models, data can be immediately ingested, transformed and analysed when needed, allowing for faster, more reliable decisions.
- **Cost Efficiency:** Outdated data architecture and structure came with expensive costs associated with hardware and capital. Similarly expensive continuing and operational costs came with maintenance. By using modern day architecture, cloud businesses have a larger clientele as they instantiate pay as you use architecture which cuts costs. This is advantageous as it solves several issues such as management and maintenance as well.
- **Flexibility and Agility:** With modern architectures, organizations are now able to be enabled to add new data, analytics and ML models without having to face strong head winds. Business systems in earlier times were normally fixed and required time to affect changes, which was a hurdle in meeting changing business or tech requirements.
- **Advanced Analytics and ML:** The growing demand for advanced analytics, ML and AI has led to the adoption of modern data architectures. These architectures enable seamless embedding of ML platforms and analytics tools to allow execution of complex data models, predictive analytics and data visualizations efficiently by businesses.
- **Data Governance and Security:** Compliance with regulatory requirements is steadily becoming another feature of architecture as well, which is

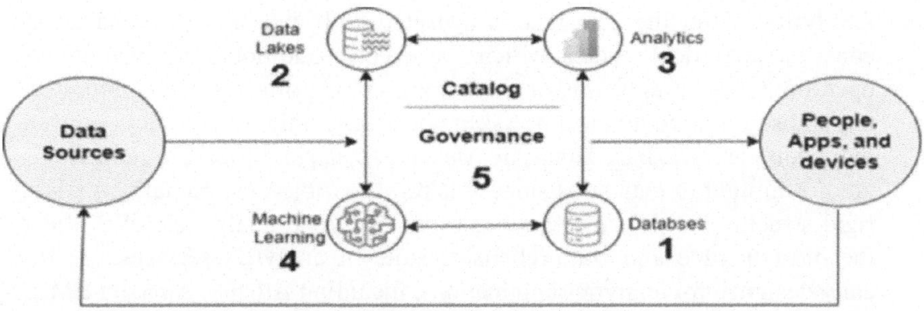

FIGURE 7.1 Core components of modern data architecture.

concerned with data governance and security. A centralized access control is provided by tools like AWS Lake Formation to ensure that sensitive data is in the right hands and is accessible to the right people. Manual security management is an inherent weakness of traditional systems, and this level of governance is very difficult to achieve.

If you are an application developer, self-service modern BI solution user or someone coping with high-volume data processing, a modern data architecture on AWS provides a fast data lake as well as a comprehensive range of analytics data services that include low latency, high interactivity, log data analysis, big data analytics or data warehousing. It efficiently transfers information between an S3 data lake and purpose-oriented data services in a flexible and smart way. It also assists in establishing policies and compliance in a holistic manner to control, audit and manage data access. AWS calls this architecture of data analysis which runs on cloud resources the modern data architecture as schematically illustrated in the figure.

The present-day data architecture (*What Is a Modern Data Architecture? – Build Modern Data Streaming Architectures on AWS*, n.d.) has these core components at its setting (refer Figure 7.1).

a) **Databases:** Data can be stored in databases that are built for modern applications and their different features. This database does not have to be a single type anymore because of the newer applications that are being developed. It could be a NoSQL database, cache store or anything else that works for the application. AWS has more than 15 engines that are purpose-built towards different data models such as: Relational databases, Key-value database, Document databases, In-memory databases, Graph databases, Time-series databases, Wide-column databases and Ledger databases.
b) **Data lakes:** It follows that one can use a data lake on a storage service such as Amazon S3 to provide storage to data created by those purpose-built databases, preferably in its native format or in an open file format. Built on AWS-powered data lakes, utilizing the unmatched availability of Amazon S3, they are scalable, agile and flexible enough to combine different data and analytics approaches.

c) **Analytics:** After the data lake is hydrated with data, it will be easier to construct analytical models, which may involve traditional data warehouse operations, batch reporting, or even complex real-time reporting, monitoring and so on. It could even be asking questions only once on data or even more complex ML-based analytic use case scenarios. Today, organizations are not limited to data silos since it is now possible to store data on a less rigid structure, which allows more room for broad analytics. AWS offers the most flexible and comprehensive suite of analytics services specifically designed for analytics applications, including Athena, Amazon EMR, OpenSearch Service, Kinesis, Amazon MSK and Amazon Redshift.
d) **Machine Learning:** AI and ML are also necessary to treat modern data strategy, as it allows organizations to foretell future occurrences and add intelligence to their systems and applications. Few providers, including AWS, offer the broadest and deepest set of ML services and support cloud infrastructure, enabling ML to be accessible for every developer, data scientist and expert practitioner. The AWS platform provides three distinct tiers of AWS in building an ML-based workload in AWS which provides varying levels of ML services to enable speed-to-market while considering your level of customization and competence in ML: AI services, ML services and ML frameworks and infrastructure.
e) **Data governance:** Last but not least, there is data governance which is an important factor in the integration and dissemination of data from different spheres such that the data is made available to all the people within the organization. Data management and data governance go hand in hand. There is also the AWS Glue Data Catalog which can also serve as a centralized marketplace for storing and selling metadata. It is the primary objective of the data catalog to serve as a central repository for metadata which makes it possible for different systems to create, locate and utilize that metadata to query and manipulate data. Serving and building productive databases and ensuring their interoperability with external functional clients being the source or endpoint for any data processing or data flow is one other critical feature for this level of Data governance. However, due to the advancement of data or datasets because of various use cases, particularly streaming use cases, there should be a standard agreement between the various data producers and consumers to enhance the level of governance as well as enable any modifications to the schemas. The AWS Glue Data Catalog is built around the concept of centralized governance and provides a means to manage schema within data streaming applications using Apache Kafka, Amazon Managed Streaming for Apache Kafka, Amazon Kinesis Data Streams, Apache Flink, Amazon Managed Service for Apache Flink and Lambda.

In its aim of providing an end-to-end data analytics application within a modern architecture approach, AWS and other cloud platforms offers a broad managed services platform. No hardware needs to be purchased, or infrastructure maintained, only offered services to collect, store, process and analyse the data. As the need for giving a lot of data increases, AWS provides analytical solutions fitting for this need and business intelligence purposes.

7.3 ML IN CLOUD

Cloud-based ML provides many benefits when analysing data – it is more cost-effective, scalable and offers ease of use. As data continues to increase, cloud platforms offer expandable infrastructure options based on a pay-as-you-go basis, making sure there are no upfront expenditures. These platforms come with built ML and specialized packages, making the process of creating, managing and implementing ML solutions effortless. ML systems incorporate easily into big data environments, which allow performing special and advanced analysis on vast datasets. Even promethean-based ML systems provide data-centric and even pattern-centric automated forecasting solutions to the users which help organizations to make timely decisions that are backed up by sophisticated analytics procedures. The speedy nature of the format automation facilitates efficiency in the selection of the ML pipelines, where every decision is based on the application of adequate algorithms. Not everything remains unlocked, compliances and security policies are in place to lock the data along with the models. Additionally, built-in security features and compliance certifications ensure that data and models are secure (Rajan & Vetriselvi, 2023). Cloud platforms also foster collaboration by centralizing access to datasets, models and results, empowering teams to work more effectively. Ultimately, cloud-based ML enables organizations to leverage advanced analytics and AI at scale, driving better business insights and decisions.

ML is a huge component of cloud platforms. It investigates the data for patterns and uses the found patterns for building the models. The model would make sense of new data points that have not been seen before and would provide insights based on those data points. Given below are a few of the many applications of ML services in different sectors and use cases:

a) **Fraud Identification and Avoidance:** By reporting questionable transactions or seeing irregularities in account activity, such as illegal login attempts or sudden changes, ML may be used to identify fraudulent activity. By proactively addressing possible risks, it improves security.
b) **Demand Prediction and Forecasting:** By examining past order data, ML helps companies estimate product demand and aid in efficient inventory management. By predicting consumption patterns and lowering utility and smart grid expenses, it may also optimize energy use.
c) **Intelligence in Media and Content:** By enhancing search and discovery, automating content translation, guaranteeing compliance and bolstering monetization tactics, ML may optimize value for media and content operations. By automatically detecting offensive or unnecessary information in photos, it may help improve platform security.
d) **Customization and User Interface:** By anticipating user preferences and providing real-time recommendations within apps, ML makes customization easier. It also aids user activity analysis for website customization, enhancing user engagement and overall experience.

e) **Sentiment analysis and social media:** Businesses may use ML to consume and analyse social media feeds in order to find patterns and actionable insights. Sentiment analysis drives changes in goods and services by gaining insight into consumer sentiment via reviews, comments and support issues.
f) **Customer Service and Communication:** Personalized interactions, lower operating costs and improved customer service can all result from integrating ML into customer support systems like intelligent contact centres.

The infrastructure, tools and services provided by cloud computing have changed the entire approach to ML as well as data science, by making the development, training and deployment of ML models much more scalable. When an organization moves to the cloud, it can benefit from enormous computing power and high-capacity storage as well as specialized ML services without the costs of on-premises infrastructure. Moreover, cloud-based ML allows data scientists to concentrate on model design and data analysis, instead of hardware and software management. Various cloud service providers have different offerings for ML and other analytic services, aligned to the various business needs. These services enable the ingestion, transformation and storage of data in a highly scalable architecture, and include data storage and pre-processing tools. Furthermore, numerous cloud providers offer model development frameworks and ML algorithms as templates to expedite the process of model development. Some services include automated model training, hyperparameter optimization and model evaluation to ensure the best performance with minimal human intervention. For streaming analytics, cloud services enable analytics on interactive and visualization data queries so that corporations obtain live information from large data files, enabling faster decision-making and innovation. These integrated solutions enhance these organization's ability to deploy and scale ML models in a cost-effective and efficient manner, achieving the needed business outcomes.

7.3.1 Key ML and Analytics Services in AWS

With the most extensive collection of ML services, infrastructure and deployment tools, AWS enables them to innovate with ML at scale. More than 100,000 clients have selected AWS ML services to address business challenges and spur innovation, ranging from the biggest corporations in the world to up-and-coming startups. With infrastructure and tools designed specifically for each stage of the ML lifecycle, Amazon SageMaker enables the client to develop, train and implement foundation and ML models at scale. In this section, we discuss various data analytics and ML services provided by AWS (*Machine Learning (ML) on AWS – ML Models and Tools – AWS*, n.d.).

a) **AWS Sagemaker:** A single platform for data, analytics and AI is Amazon SageMaker. With unified access to all of your data, Amazon SageMaker offers an integrated analytics and AI experience by combining the extensively used AWS ML and analytics capabilities. With Amazon Q Developer, the most powerful generative AI assistant for software development, you can work together and produce more quickly from a single studio (preview) utilizing well-known AWS resources for model creation, generative AI, data processing and SQL analytics. Access all of your data, whether it is kept in federated, third-party, data lakes or warehouses, with governance integrated to satisfy business security requirements.

Key Features

- **Use a single data and AI development platform to collaborate and create more quickly:** The trial version of Amazon SageMaker Unified Studio offers an integrated experience for using all data analytics and artificial intelligence capabilities.

  With a full suite of AI development tools that are safe by design, it's possible to speed up AI with Amazon SageMaker. ML and foundation models (FMs) may be trained, customized and deployed on a very efficient and economical infrastructure.
- **Create and expand AI use cases using a variety of technologies:** It's possible to make use of specially designed tools that cover every stage of the AI lifecycle, from distributed training and high-performance IDEs to inference, AI operations, governance and observability. Amazon Q Developer speeds up AI development by making it easier to find data, design and train ML models, perform SQL queries and create and execute data pipeline operations using natural language.
- **To consolidate all of your data, employ an open lakehouse to reduce data silos:** It's possible to use Amazon SageMaker Lakehouse to consolidate all data across Amazon Redshift data warehouses and Amazon Simple Storage Service (Amazon S3) data lakes. It provides you the freedom to use any tools or engines that are compatible with Apache Iceberg to access and query your data on a single copy of analytics data. It's also possible to create fine-grained permissions for all of your analytics and artificial intelligence technologies in Lakehouse to protect your data. With zero-ETL connectors, it's possible to bring data from running databases and apps into lakehouse very instantly.
- **Use end-to-end data and AI governance to meet your company security requirements:** With integrated governance throughout the whole data and AI lifecycle, it guarantees business security. With Amazon SageMaker, it's possible to manage who has access to what data, models and development artefacts for what purposes. Using a single permission model and fine-grained access restrictions with Amazon SageMaker Catalog, build and implement access policies consistently. It provides the support to use data classification, toxicity detection, guardrails and responsible AI regulations to safeguard and defend your AI models. You can detect sensitive data, automate data-quality monitoring, and trace data and ML to build trust throughout your company.

7.3.1.1 Use Case with SageMaker

The Amazon SageMaker makes ML more accessible by providing a variety of tools, including integrated development environments for data scientists and ML engineers and visual interfaces that don't require any coding for business analysts. This allows more people to create with ML. In order to prepare data on a wide scale for ML, Amazon SageMaker facilitates the access, labelling and processing of vast volumes of structured (tabular) and unstructured (photo, video and audio) data. With its optimized infrastructure, Amazon SageMaker helps cut down training time from hours to minutes. With its specially designed tools, it accelerates ML development and increases team productivity by up to ten times. Amazon SageMaker facilitates the automation and standardization of MLOps procedures throughout the company in order to develop, train, implement and oversee ML models at a larger scale.

- **Provides one-click Jupyter Notebooks –** Additionally, because the underlying computing resources are completely elastic, a user may simply adjust the resources that are available, and the adjustments will be made automatically in the background without interfering with your work. One-click notebook sharing is also made possible by Amazon SageMaker. Because all code dependencies are automatically recorded, working with others is simple, and everyone will have access to the same notebook, saved in the same location.
- **Provides RStudio Interface –** Existing RStudio licenses may be transferred to Amazon SageMaker, and RStudio installations can be safely and simply lifted and moved to the platform. With RStudio on Amazon SageMaker, customers may use on-demand cloud computing resources in a familiar RStudio IDE. Because it is completely managed, users may run RStudio from Amazon SageMaker with just one click, and R developers can dial-up compute from inside the same interface, minimizing work interruptions and increasing productivity.
- **Provides AutoML –** While giving customers complete control and visibility, Amazon SageMaker autopilot automatically creates, trains and fine-tunes the optimal ML models depending on the data. After that, users may iterate to enhance the model's quality or simply deploy the model to production with a single click.
- **Provides Pre-built Solutions for the Open-Source Models –** Using pre-built solutions that can be deployed with a few clicks, Amazon SageMaker JumpStart assists customers in getting started with ML rapidly. Additionally, SageMaker JumpStart allows for the fine-tuning and one-click deployment of over 150 well-known open-source models.
- **Provides Local mode –** Amazon SageMaker enables users to test and prototype locally. The Apache MXNet and TensorFlow Docker containers used in the AWS SageMaker are available on GitHub. Users can download these containers and use the Python SDK to the test scripts before deploying to training or hosting.

b) AWS Deep Learning AMIs

To speed up deep learning on Amazon EC2, ML researchers and practitioners may use a well-selected and secure collection of frameworks, dependencies and tools from AWS Deep Learning AMIs (DLAMI). It is easy to deploy and execute these frameworks and technologies at scale with Amazon Machine Images (AMIs), which are built for Amazon Linux and Ubuntu and preloaded with TensorFlow, PyTorch, NVIDIA CUDA drivers and libraries,

Intel MKL, Elastic Fabric Adapter (EFA) and the AWS OFI NCCL plugin. It is used for the development of autonomous vehicles, processing natural language, analysis of healthcare data and quicker training of models

c) **AWS Deep Learning Containers**
Docker images containing the most recent iterations of well-known deep learning frameworks preconfigured and tested are called WS Deep Learning Containers. With Deep Learning Containers, it's easy to implement bespoke ML environments without having to start from scratch with environment creation and optimization.

d) **Amazon Rekognition**
It uses ML to automate and reduce the cost of video and image analysis.

Key features:

- **Add APIs quickly:** It easily includes customized or pre-trained computer vision APIs into apps without having to start from scratch with ML infrastructure and models.
- **Analyse in a matter of seconds:** It uses AI to supplement human review activities and analyse millions of photos, video streams and saved videos in a matter of seconds.
- **Scale easily:** With fully managed AI capabilities, it can scale up or down according to company needs and only pay for the photos and videos you analyse.
- **Liveness of the face:** In only a few seconds, employ spoofs to identify legitimate users and discourage malicious actors during face verification.
- **Identification and evaluation of faces:** Identify faces in pictures and videos and identify characteristics of each face, including open eyes, spectacles and facial hair.
- **Personalized labels:** With just ten photos, you can train your models to recognize unique things, such as company logos, using automated ML (AutoML).
- **Text recognition:** Extract twisted and skewed text from videos and pictures of product packaging, social media postings and street signs.
- **Comparing and searching faces:** Assess a face's resemblance to another image or to your personal image collection.

Amazon Rekognition is used in multiple ways described below:

- **Identify offensive material:** It identifies unsuitable or dangerous information in picture and video assets quickly and correctly using generic or company-specific rules and procedures.
- **Online identity verification:** It remotely confirms the identification of opted-in users, incorporates facial analysis and comparison into user onboarding and authentication processes.
- **Simplify media analysis:** It reduces the time, effort and expenses associated with video ad insertion, content operations and content creation by automatically identifying important video portions.

- **Send smart notifications to your connected home:** When a desirable object is identified in live video broadcasts, send out prompt, useful notifications. It creates experiences using home automation, like a light that turns on by itself when a person is spotted.

e) **Amazon Redshift**

Redshift is a data warehousing software developed by Amazon Web Services (AWS) as a fully fledged managed service. It is suited for petabyte-scale data, and its architecture and implementation are designed to ensure high speed of query and analysis of substantial amounts of data. It is quick and can be scaled easily, an attribute that has made Redshift to be highly regarded in terms of data warehousing and analytics application.

Key Features and Capabilities:

- **Columnar Storage:** Redshift has a columnar storage architecture which is optimal for analytical queries. This architecture minimizes the number of I/O requests and speeds up the response time since only the relevant columns for the query will be accessed.
- **MPP:** Redshift is based on MPP architecture. This allows multiple nodes to process various queries concurrently, allowing rapid responses in queries, even in large datasets.
- **Expansion:** Redshift does have the ability to scale from several hundred gigabytes to a few petabytes with exceptional ease. This flexibility allows organizations to develop their data warehouses as their needs dictate.
- **Integration:** It also has the capability of connecting other AWS services such as Amazon S3, Lambda and Data Pipeline.

7.3.1.1.1 Use Cases

Amazon Redshift can be used to quickly and easily analyse and visualize data for a specific set of use cases, including:

- **Business Intelligence (BI):** Companies deploy Redshift to enhance their existing BI applications which help in making interactive dashboards and reports.
- **Data Discovery:** A vaguely defined area is where data analysts and even data scientists can use Redshift to perform bulk data loading as well as complex data-processing tasks.
- **Log Analysis:** The analysis of log data is performed frequently using Redshift to determine the usage of a system as well as the performance and security of applications.
- **Marketing Analytics:** It gives marketing teams the ability to study consumer trends, campaign results and target markets in order to prepare marketing plans.
- **Financial Analytics:** Redshift is referenced in case of risk management, detection of fraudulent cases as well as preparation of reports of compliance to regulations within the financial sectors.

f) **Amazon EMR (Elastic MapReduce)**
EMR is a big data-processing cloud. This means that it allows users to process vast amounts of data easily and is built on Apache Hadoop, Spark or Hive for easy and cost-effective usage by organizations that handle big data.

Key Features and Capabilities:

1. **Managed Clusters:** EMR handles large amounts of operational and engineering work as it has fully managed clusters that can be provisioned and configured within minutes.
2. **Broad Ecosystem Support:** Much data processing is made possible with EMR which supports a plethora of big data applications such as Hadoop, Spark, Hive, among others.
3. **Dynamic Scaling:** EMR clusters have an efficient way of dynamically resizing to fit fluctuating workload requirements which allows resources to be used optimally.
4. **Integration:** EMR yields optimal benefits since it integrates well with other services such as S3, streaming data in real time with Kinesis and visualizing data with QuickSight.

7.3.1.1.2 Use Cases

Together with Pyspark, Amazon EMR is widely used with a lot of data analytics use cases that include:

a) **Data Transformation:** EMR is perfect for ETL processes that transform raw data which is useful to many organizations in need for data analysis.
b) **Log and event analysis:** EMR is used with application and system-generated logs and events for analysis for troubleshooting and monitoring purposes.
c) **Machine Learning:** As data scientists work with huge datasets, EMR gets applied for training ML models utilizing Apache Spark for distributed ML.
d) **Genomic Analysis:** EMR assists in the processing and analysis of genomics data in healthcare and life sciences for further research and diagnostics purposes.
e) **Recommendation Systems:** Through the analysis of user interaction data EMR may be used to develop recommendation systems.

g) **Amazon QuickSight**
Amazon QuickSight is a business intelligence (BI) cloud application which enables the pursuit of reports, dashboards and interactive data visualizations. Companies are able to extract data and perform sharing with audience in a simplified and attractive way.

Key Features and Capabilities:

- **Data Visualization:** QuickSight facilitates the generation of interactive data visuals like charts, data graphs and maps among others so that data can be more readable.

- **Data Exploration:** Users can perform data drilling, filtering and exploring to extract useful information.
- **Integration:** QuickSight permits integration with various data sources among them Amazon Redshift, RDS and Athena, providing all-round analysis.
- **Auto Insights:** This feature allows data practitioners to generate and offer insights and recommendations based on data analytics automatically.
- **Embedding and Sharing:** It allows automatic embedding of QuickSight dashboards and reports into applications and shares them securely with either inside or outside the organization.

7.3.1.1.3 Use Cases

Amazon QuickSight is utilized for a number of use cases such as the following:

- **Business Dashboards:** Organizations in construction build interactive dashboards using QuickSight embedding for Building business KPI and other metrics.
- **Data Exploration:** A data user goes through data trying to seek trends, patterns and anomalies to support decision-making process within the business which uses data.
- **Ad Hoc Reporting:** With QuickSight, it is easy to generate reports for adhoc analysis and reporting as they can be created on the spot.
- **Data Storytelling:** This feature aids in the narration of data stories through interactive narratives that render data insights in a more relatable and impactful manner
- **Cost Management:** It also aids in the monitoring and analysis of incursions and cost minimization, especially when used hand in hand with AWS billing and usage information.

h) AWS Glue

AWS glue is a serverless process that is ETL-based and automates the process of preparation of data for analysis. This is further complemented by a broad spectrum of tools designed to enhance data integration and transformation processes.

Key Features and Capabilities:

- **Data Catalog:** AWS Glue helps maintain a single repository of metadata that can assist in the complete cycle of data asset discovery, organization and comprehension both within and across data sources
- **Creating ETL Job:** By means of graphical or programmatic methods, users generate and manage ETL jobs that will be responsible for data manipulation, transformation and migration.
- **Automatic Schema Detection:** Semi-structured and structured data schema can be automatically detected by Glue which decreases the effort necessary for data integration.
- **Data Transformation:** It provides various data transformations capabilities including but not limited to data filtering and data aggregation, data enrichment.

- **Integration:** AWS Glue interacts seamlessly with other AWS services such as Amazon S3, Redshift and RDS and hence it is a key component of the AWS analytics stack.

7.3.1.1.4 Use Cases

AWS Glue is suitable for numerous data integration and ETL scenarios which include

- **Data Warehousing:** Glue is utilized in preparing and loading data into data warehouses such as Amazon Redshift and Snowflake.
- **Data Migration:** Organizations use Glue to replace information from a local site, other clouds, and so on AWS.
- **Data Lake ingestion:** It assists in data lake creation by simplifying the process of transforming unrefined data into an organized form ready for analysis.
- **Data Cleansing:** Glue helps to tidy up and harmonize data sources by eliminating duplicates, missing values and Applying Data Quality Policies.
- **Cross-Site Replication:** It provides means of replicating the data to facilitate disaster recovery, backup and constant change of the data.

In this section, we examined several cloud-based powerful ML and analytics tools including; Amazon SageMaker, Deep Learning AMIs, Deep Learning Containers, Rekognition, Redshift, QuickSight and AWS Glue services. These capabilities allow for the construction, training and deployment of ML models, the carrying out of complex data analysis as well as automating data-processing processes providing scale, flexibility and cost efficiencies. It is also possible for enterprises to enhance their AI and data-led approach by using these services, which improve performance and business results (Vora et al., 2016)

7.4 SERVERLESS DATA ANALYTICS PIPELINE REFERENCE ARCHITECTURE

Because it is inefficient and challenging to predefine constantly changing schemas and spend time negotiating capacity slots on shared infrastructure, business users, data scientists and analysts are now demanding straightforward, frictionless, self-service options to build end-to-end data pipelines for many use cases.

For the past decade, Serverless along with cloud technologies have become the preferred architecture for implementing a data workflow pipeline because of their cost-effective nature and effortless scalability. In a serverless environment, cloud providers automatically take care of the infrastructure provisioning, planning, scaling and maintenance. From the perspective of data engineers, this means that they can solely focus on building and implementing their data workflows. There is therefore no server provisioning or management, and operational complexity and cost is further lowered. Serverless data pipelines are highly automated and scale themselves to meet the needs of the workload at hand. These data pipelines can easily cope with increases in workload or incoming data without requiring any intervention. Additionally, serverless services function as a pay-as-you-go model. This allows businesses to scale up or down with ease. Serverless services are thus an economical solution for both small- and large-scale data operations.

In addition, serverless architectures ease the development work which allows for quicker deployment and iterations. It makes coordination with other cloud services simpler, which allows the automated combination of data storage and analytics tools with other services to create a singular workflow. With this level of abstraction, it becomes easier for teams to focus on using data effectively instead of maintaining the servers. Thus, serverless data workflow pipelines become an attractive alternative to businesses which want to be efficient, cost-effective, and scale their data operations.

Given the exploratory nature of ML and many analytics workloads, it is necessary to swiftly ingest fresh datasets and clean, normalize and feature engineer them without worrying about operational overhead when it comes to the infrastructure that supports data pipelines. A serverless data lake design may provide quick, self-service data onboarding and analytics for all data consumer roles in a company. Using AWS serverless technologies such as building blocks, data lakes and data-processing pipelines may be rapidly and interactively created to ingest, store, convert and analyse petabytes of structured and unstructured data from batch and streaming sources. As a result, no computational or storage resources need to be managed.

This section will discuss a serverless data platform that includes a data lake, pipelines for processing data, and a consumption layer that enables multiple analyses of the data in the data lake without transferring data, including exploratory interactive SQL, big data processing, predictive analytics, business intelligence (BI) dashboarding and ML. (*Let's Architect! Architecting For Big Data Workloads | Amazon Web Services*, 2022) (refer Figure 7.2).

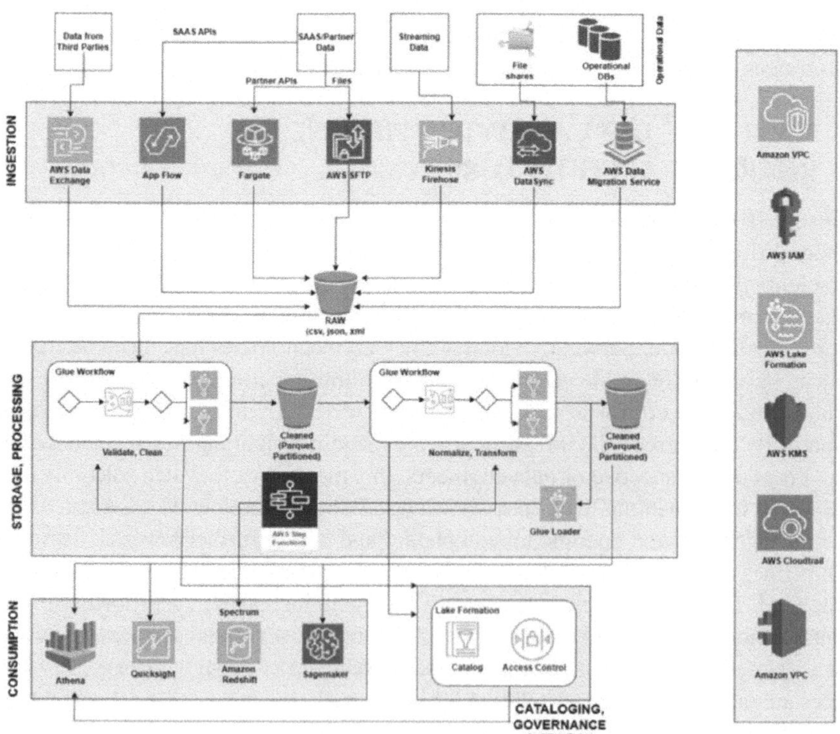

FIGURE 7.2 Data analytics reference architecture on AWS.

7.4.1 Ingestion Layer

Data entry into the data lake is handled by the ingestion layer. It offers a range of protocols for connecting both internal and external data sources. Both streaming and batch data may be ingested into the storage layer. The ingestion layer is also responsible for delivering ingested data to various locations in the data storage layer, including databases, warehouses and object storage. The distinct connection, data format, data structure and data velocity needs of operational database sources, streaming data sources and file sources are met by specific AWS services.

i) **Operational Databases:** Organizations often use a variety of relational and NoSQL databases to hold their operational data. Numerous functioning RDBMS and NoSQL databases may be connected to using *AWS Data Migration Service (AWS DMS)*, which can then ingest the data into Amazon Simple Storage Service (Amazon S3) buckets in the data lake landing zone. Firstly, the source data is imported into the data lake using AWS DMS and then changes happening in the source database can also be replicated into data lake. While storing S3 items in the data lake, AWS DMS encrypts them using *AWS Key Management Service (AWS KMS)* keys. AWS DMS is a robust, fully managed service that offers a large selection of instance sizes for database replication applications. To ingest data from AWS native or on-premises database sources into the landing zone in the data lake, *AWS Lake Formation* offers a scalable, serverless substitute known as blueprints. A Lake Formation blueprint is a pre-made template that, when given input parameters like the source database, target *Amazon S3* location, target dataset format, target dataset dividing columns, and timetable, creates an AWS Glue process for data intake. An efficient and parallelized data input pipeline is made up of crawlers, many parallel processes, and triggers that link them based on circumstances and is implemented via an *AWS Glue* workflow created from a blueprint.
ii) **Streaming data Sources:** To obtain streaming data from both internal and external sources, the ingestion layer makes advantage of *Amazon Kinesis Data Firehose*. A Kinesis Data Firehose API endpoint can be set up with a few clicks, allowing sources to deliver streaming data including clickstreams, application and infrastructure logs, and monitoring metrics, as well as IoT data like sensor readings and device telemetry. The following is what Kinesis Data Firehose does:

   - buffers incoming streams.
   - encrypts, alters, compresses and batches the streams.
   - keeps the streams in the data lake's landing zone as S3 objects.

   For real-time analytics use cases, Kinesis Data Firehose may send data to *Amazon S3, Amazon Redshift and Amazon OpenSearch Service*. It also interfaces directly with the security and storage layers. Kinesis Data Firehose doesn't need to be managed, is serverless, and has the ability to automatically scale to match the throughput of incoming data, making it ideal for real-time streaming data delivery to destinations like Amazon S3, Amazon Redshift, Amazon OpenSearch Service and third-party services such as Splunk.

iii) **File Sharing:** Data from file sources can be useful for organizational analysis as follows:
   - **Internal File Shares:** An *AWS DataSync* service, which transfers, schedules and queues automatic data syncs over networks, has been successfully utilized to move large volumes of information from NAS devices to Data Lakes while taking care of data integrity.
   - **Partner Data Files:** AWS offers transfers with SFTP and stores your data on Amazon S3, which allows for safe file sharing via AWS Transfer Family. It provides encryption backed up by AWS KMS and integrates both IAM and Active Directory for authentication purposes.

iv) **Data APIs:** Companies tap APIs from SaaS and partner applications in an effort to acquire 360 degrees business perspectives:
   - **SaaS APIs:** *AWS Appflow* enables serverless data collection and processing from SaaS applications such as Salesforce and Google Analytics without the need of servers. It allows event-based or predetermined flows of data and processes data validation, conditions and mapping; masking data before storing it. AppFlow also works with other Security, tokenization and wrapping services.
   - **Partner APIs:** Custom applications get partner API data and upload it into S3 via AWS SDKs. These applications are built in a docker container and hosted on AWS Fargate which is serverless compute with security and monitoring built in.

API based data ingestion tasks can be scheduled through *AWS Glue* Python shell jobs as servers are not needed, which facilitates API ingestion tasks on various workflows with libraries offered by the partner or native features.

7.4.2 Storage Layer

The storage layer is in charge of offering robust, scalable, safe and reasonably priced components for storing enormous amounts of data. It can store datasets of various types and structures as well as unstructured data. It allows source data to be stored in its original form without requiring it to be structured to fit a target schema or format. The storage layer can be easily and natively integrated with components from all other levels. The storage layer is divided into the following zones to store data according to its suitability for consumption by various personas within the organization:

Raw Zone: Components from the ingestion layer land data are stored in the raw zone. In this temporary space, data is consumed directly from sources. The data kept in this zone is usually accessed by data engineering personas.

Cleaned Zone: Data from the raw zone is transferred to the cleaned zone for long-term storage following the initial quality tests. Data is kept in its original format here. In the event of faults or data loss in downstream storage zones, it is possible to "replay" downstream data processing by permanently storing all data from all sources in the cleaned zone. Personas in data science and data engineering often work with the data kept in this area.

Curated zone: This area contains data that complies with data models and organizational norms and is in the best possible condition for consumption. The datasets in the curated zone are usually separated, grouped and stored in ways that allow the consuming layer to access them effectively and economically. After cleaning, normalizing, standardizing and enriching data from the raw zone, the processing layer generates datasets in the curated zone. The information kept in this area is used by all individuals in companies to inform business choices.

Amazon S3 constitutes the backbone of an extendible, economical serverless framework responsible for a dedicated data lake and S3 objects across landing, raw and curated zones. It guarantees 99.99% and 99.999999999% uptime and durability, respectively, and KMS keys encrypt the data while fine-grain access control is facilitated using IAM policies. Cost optimization is achieved automatically through lifecycle policies, intelligent tiering as well as colder storage tiers like *S3 Glacier an S3 Glacier Deep Archive*: S3 is appropriate for unstructured data in potentially any format and has no required schemas, allowing quick and easy ingestion of data in its raw format. Such an approach works well as schema-on-read and could be implemented by layer for both processes and consumption, for structured analysis. Partitioning makes the filtering more effective, allowing for easy cooperation with AWS services and third-party solutions.

7.4.3 Catalog and Search Layer

Business and technical metadata pertaining to datasets housed in the storage layer are stored by the cataloging and search layer. It offers the granular segmentation of dataset information in the lake as well as the capability to track schema. Additionally, it has means for tracking versions so that metadata changes may be monitored. By providing search capabilities, the layer improves data visibility in the storage space as the quantity of datasets grows.

The cataloging and search layer is important for metadata management in data lakes especially in the cases where partitions and schemas are subject to change. Lake Formation is the primary catalog that includes technical metadata – schemas, partitions, data locations – as well as business ones – ownership and sensitivity. It allows for schema-on-read in the processing and consumption layers as well as facilitates the self-service data discovery.

AWS Glue, EMR and Athena work on the same level with Lake Formation and thus promote automated metadata discovery and its registration. *AWS Glue* crawlers scan for schema changes and new partitions, so the catalog gets updated metadata during such activities. Lake Formation also provides a single-entry point for managing granular permissions like table- and column-level access and secure, role-based, data access across Athena, EMR and Redshift Spectrum servers.

7.4.4 Processing Layer

Through data validation, cleansing, normalization, transformation and enrichment, the processing layer is in charge of converting data into a consumable state. It is in charge of registering metadata for the raw and converted data into the cataloging layer and improving the datasets' consumption readiness along the landing, raw and curated zones. The processing layer consists of custom-built data-processing components that are tailored to the specific dataset features and processing job at hand. The processing layer supports a wide range of data formats, partitioned data, schema-on-read and large data volumes. Building and coordinating multi-step data-processing pipelines with specially designed components for each stage is another capability offered by the processing layer.

The processing layer encompasses the functionalities for creating stand-alone orchestrated pipelines and managing events for situations that warrant that such as ingestion of new data.

- ***AWS Glue*** provides functionalities for executing python jobs and spark cluster jobs (scala or python) as a managed server-less cluster ETL service on a pay-per-use basis. It simplifies data transformations by code generation workflows and is able to validate, clean, transform and enrich data in CSV, JSON formats. Glue also supports incremental updates to partitioned datasets and provides off-the-shelf classifiers for several formats. It creates a dataset containing crawlers that assist in dataset discovery, schema inference and dataset registration with the lake formation catalog. Glue pipelines are job-specific and can either run on schedule or be run on demand, which opens up possibilities for job degrees of parallelism through dependencies as well creating triggers and workflows.
- ***AWS Step Functions*** provides a server-less workflow orchestration solution for building intricate data workflows across other AWS services like *Glue, Lambda and ECS*. It depicts in graphical format workflows, oversees states, controlling checkpoints and restarts while ensuring that steps run in a set sequence. Built-in features such as try/catch make processes more dependable.

Both AWS services link storage, cataloging and security layers of AWS, and thereby enable strong and scalable data-processing workflows.

7.4.5 Consumption Layer

Scalable and effective techniques for extracting insights from the massive volume of data in the data lake are provided by the consumption layer. Through a number of specially designed analytics tools that enable analytical techniques, such as SQL, batch analytics, BI dashboards, reporting and ML, it democratizes analytics across all personas inside the business. The storage, cataloging and security layers of the data lake are all naturally integrated with the consumption layer. Components in the consumption layer allow schema-on-read, various data formats and topologies, and data splitting for cost and performance optimization.

The **consumption layer** leverages fully managed analytics services for SQL querying, business intelligence (BI), batch analytics and ML:

- **Interactive SQL:** In *Amazon Athena*, an appropriate schema is defined using Lake Formation, while *Amazon S3* data in CSV and Parquet formats is queried through ANSI SQL without the need for pre-loading. It is server-less and pay-per-use, and allows control over access using AWS security.

- **Data Warehouses:** With Redshift, *Amazon Redshift* allows petabyte-scale databases to petabyte-scale databases with quick latency queries. Redshift Spectrum expands queries to S3 data without having to import it and integrates cluster and external data collections.
- **Business Intelligence:** *Amazon QuickSight* allows intuitive dashboards and guess what, operated by ML and it connects to multiple data sources such as AWS services and SaaS. Its SPICE engine has a session-based pricing which involves allowing numerous users to experience quick performance for maximum benefits.
- **Machine Learning:** Organizations can build, train and deploy distinct ML models in *Amazon SageMaker* using cost-efficient EC2 Spot Instances. It has built-in algorithms and custom, automatic algorithm tuning, monitoring for model drift and accuracy.

7.4.6 Governance and Security Layer

The security and governance layer protects the data in the storage layer and the computing power in the other tiers. It offers tools for network security, tracking, auditing, encryption and access control. In addition, the security layer creates a thorough audit trail and keeps an eye on every component activity in other layers. The security and governance layer are natively integrated with components of every other tier.

This layer includes the security and governance that adds protection to data, identities and processing resources present across all the layers of architecture. The available security features are:

- **Authentication and Authorization:** IAM allows control of users and role access across various AWS services while also providing single sign-on and multi-factor authentication capabilities. With Lake Formation, database- and table-level access policies can be created in the data lake, enabling fine-grained access control and consistent policy enforcement across services like Athena, Redshift and QuickSight.
- **Encryption:** *KMS* has integrated with AWS to manage encryption at the data layer to protect data in the data lake. *IAM* allows controlling access to the keys as well as audit capabilities which are provided by *CloudTrail.*
- **Network Protection:** Possible IP addresses, subnets and gateways are manageable by users to build their private *VPC* allowing them to secure traffic between services and making it more compatible for deployment.
- **Monitoring and Logging:** *Cloudwatch* allows the transfer of logs and metrics for the purpose of creating analysis and alerts for abnormal activities. Event histories of user and service actions are captured by the Cloudtrail and this information helps in carrying out security analysis and tracking resources.

The serverless architecture offers big gains in data workflow pipelines, such as being easier to scale, cheaper and easier to manage. Because of the serverless approach, data teams can solely concentrate on building and optimizing workflows as there is no single detail related to infrastructure management that needs to be taken care of, which accelerates the data-processing cycle. As organizations continue to harness the power of cloud-based ML and serverless technologies, they will be better prepared to utilize technology to improve their decision-making skills, increase operational efficacy and remain on top in the seas of data. There is, however, unimaginable potential for the future of ML in the cloud if innovation and growth are to be anticipated across all these industries.

7.5 CONCLUSION

In the last few years, the amount of data available has indeed increased tremendously, and traditional data architecture struggle to meet the requirements in terms of scale and performance. Architectural data features enabled by ML together with the cloud services enable processing of enormous datasets in a far more efficient manner. This chapter considers the evolution of data architectures from traditional to cloud-based putting specific emphasis on data analytics. Some of the key services discussed include Amazon SageMaker, Deep Learning AMIs and AWS Lambda among others that integrate ML with data analytics. Other services discussed in this chapter include AWS Glue, Redshift, QuickSight and Rekognition which allow transforming, viewing and drawing insights from the data. Additionally, a serverless data analytics pipeline reference design is also discussed in detail. The development of data analytics will require deeper integration of AI and ML technologies with cloud-based systems. The increase in data will lead to a situation where companies will utilize sophisticated features such as automated data analytics and forecasting for decision-making. Cloud companies will further develop their products/services ensuring cheaper and more effective data analytical and processing solutions. Moreover, in the future, edge computing technologies (Feng et al., 2024) will enable the transfer of data processing to the nearest location and minimize the analysis time of real-time data. Also, the trend for the democratization of data analytics will persist, and more economical solutions for analytical framework management will efface the need for technical professionals to access and implement ML and AI.

REFERENCES

Berisha, B., Mëziu, E., & Shabani, I. (2022). Big Data Analytics in Cloud Computing: An Overview. *Journal of Cloud Computing Advances Systems and Applications, 11*(1). https://doi.org/10.1186/s13677-022-00301-w

Darwish, D. (2024). Big Data and Cloud Computing. In *Advances in Computer and Electrical Engineering Book Series* (pp. 219–252). https://doi.org/10.4018/979-8-3693-0900-1.ch012

Feng, P., Bi, Z., Wen, Y., Pan, X., Peng, B., Liu, M., Xu, J., Chen, K., Liu, J., Yin, C. H., Zhang, S., Wang, J., Niu, Q., Li, M., & Wang, T. (2024, October 2). Deep Learning and Machine Learning, Advancing Big Data Analytics and Management: Unveiling AI's Potential Through Tools, Techniques, and Applications. *arXiv.org*. https://arxiv.org/abs/2410.01268

Let's Architect! Architecting for Big Data Workloads | Amazon Web Services. (2022, August 10). Amazon Web Services. https://aws.amazon.com/blogs/architecture/lets-architect-architecting-for-big-data-workloads/

Machine Learning (ML) on AWS – ML Models and Tools – AWS. (n.d.). Amazon Web Services, Inc. https://aws.amazon.com/ai/machine-learning/

Manekar, A.K., & Pradeepini, G. (2015). Cloud Based Big Data Analytics a Review. In *2015 International Conference on Computational Intelligence and Communication Networks (CICN)*, Jabalpur, India, pp. 785–788. https://doi.org/10.1109/CICN.2015.160

Medvedev, V., & Kurasova, O. (2016). Cloud Technologies: A New Level for Big Data Mining. In *Computer Communications and Networks* (pp. 55–67). https://doi.org/10.1007/978-3-319-44881-7_3

Rajan, A.A., &. Vetriselvi, V. (2023). Systematic Survey: Secure and Privacy-Preserving Big Data Analytics in Cloud. *Journal of Computer Information Systems*, *64*(1), 136–156. https://doi.org/10.1080/08874417.2023.2176946

Vora, R., Garala, K., & Raval, P. (2016). An Era of Big Data on Cloud Computing Services as Utility: 360° of Review, Challenges and Unsolved Exploration Problems. In *Smart Innovation, Systems and Technologies* (pp. 575–583). https://doi.org/10.1007/978-3-319-30927-9_57

What Is a Modern Data Architecture? – Build Modern Data Streaming Architectures on AWS. (n.d.). https://docs.aws.amazon.com/whitepapers/latest/build-modern-data-streaming-analytics-architectures/what-is-a-modern-data-architecture.html

8 Data Analytics and Cloud Together

A Powerful Combination for E-Commerce and Supply Chain Logistics

Avita Katal

8.1 INTRODUCTION

Large and complicated datasets that are difficult to handle with conventional tools like spreadsheets are referred to as "big data". It consists of mixed datasets (like AI training), unstructured data (like social media postings) and structured data (like inventory databases). Large volumes of data can now be stored more cheaply due to technological developments, which help organizations make more accurate judgments. Finding value in big data, however, necessitates a process of discovery that includes asking the proper questions, seeing patterns, formulating well-informed assumptions and forecasting future behaviour. The term "big data analytics" describes the methodical processing and analysis of vast quantities of data, including complicated datasets, in order to derive insightful information. To assist analysts in making data-informed judgments, big data analytics makes it possible to find trends, patterns and correlations in vast volumes of raw data. Through sophisticated analytic approaches, this process enables enterprises to extract actionable knowledge from the rapidly expanding data created from a variety of sources, such as social media, financial transactions, Internet-of-Things (IoT) sensors and smart devices. Volume, velocity and variety – the "three Vs" – are the three properties that are commonly used to describe big data. Value and veracity, two more Vs, have surfaced in recent years, nevertheless. The increasing value of data as a resource is reflected in these additions (Ishwarappa & Anuradha, 2015).

- The term *"volume"* describes the vast amount of data, especially unstructured data from sensors and social media feeds.
- The quick pace at which data is collected and processed – often in real-time – is known as *velocity.*

 DOI: 10.1201/9781003396772-9

- *Variety* encompasses a range of data formats, including text, audio and video, both organized and unstructured.
- *Veracity* emphasizes quality and integrity while addressing the data's dependability and trustworthiness.
- In business, data is inherently valuable. However, until that *value* is found, it is useless.

Big data gathers both depth and breadth of insights; therefore, there are insights that can help the organizations somewhere in all of that data. This value can be external, like recommendations for customer profiles that can increase engagement, or internal, like operational procedures that could be enhanced.

Organizations were able to gather and manage vast volumes of unstructured data in the early 2000s because of the developments in technology and software. Big data frameworks were created by open-source groups to handle and store the vast amounts of usable data. Large data collections are processed and stored distributed over a network of computers using these frameworks. Big data frameworks can be utilized in conjunction with other tools and libraries for:

- Using statistical algorithms and artificial intelligence (AI) in predictive modelling.
- Statistical analysis to reveal hidden patterns and conduct in-depth data exploration.
- Using what-if analysis to model various situations and investigate possible results, handling a variety of datasets from many sources, such as structured, semi-structured and unstructured data.

There are four primary techniques for analysing data: *descriptive, diagnostic and predictive and prescriptive.* These are as follows:

- **Descriptive Analysis:** The goal of descriptive analytics is to summarize historical data to comprehend its fundamental features (the "what happened" stage).
- **Diagnostic analytics:** Analyses the data to determine the underlying reasons for patterns that have been seen (the "why it happened" stage).
- **Predictive analytics:** Predictive analytics forecast future patterns (the "what will happen" stage) by utilizing models and historical data.
- **Prescriptive analytics:** Makes suggestions for improving subsequent activities based on knowledge gained from earlier phases (the "what to do" stage).

One low-cost big data analytics model is cloud computing. NIST states that cloud computing is a methodology that makes it possible for on-demand, easy and widespread access to a common pool of configurable computer resources (such as servers, networks, storage and the cloud for Big Data analytics trends) that require little management work or communication with service providers and may be quickly provided and released (Mell et al., 2011).

These attributes can be described as:

- **Rapid Elasticity:** Easily and swiftly scale up or down to satisfy demand.
- **Pay as you go:** Pay according to usage for metered service.
- **On-demand self-service:** Customers have self-service access to all the IT resources they require.
- **Resource pooling:** It serves multiple clients, customers with provisional and scalable services.
- **Network Access:** All resources are available for access from a wide range of network devices, such as tablets, laptop, computers and mobiles.

Big data on the cloud is being adopted by an expanding variety of technologies. When big data and cloud technology come together, big data analytics in the cloud is a viable choice. To obtain superior analytical findings, businesses transfer the data to dedicated servers. Big data analytics – the process of breaking down massive amounts of structured or unstructured data to find patterns and improve business decisions – benefits greatly from the cloud's elastic properties. The reference design for an analytical environment is described by the Cloud Standard Customer Council, which emphasizes cloud architecture for Big Data and Analytics (Cloud Standards Customer Council, 2017).

In this chapter, how data analytics, machine learning (ML) and cloud synergize together for providing a suitable and ever-growing environment for e-commerce and logistics is discussed in detail. Cloud computing and analytics are revolutionizing the logistics and e-commerce sectors by giving companies the ability to make data-driven choices, improve customer experience and optimize operations. Real-time tracking, predictive analytics, inventory management and customized marketing are made possible by these technologies' capacity to handle enormous volumes of data. Big data analytics and cloud-based platforms work together to improve productivity, reduce procedures and keep businesses competitive in a market that is always changing.

8.2 UNDERSTANDING E-COMMERCE

To buy goods and services, consumers used to rely on physical stores, product catalogs and their reliable landlines. However, all of it was altered by the Internet. The way that companies and customers interact was revolutionized by early e-commerce platforms like eBay and Amazon. Since the turn of the century, e-commerce has rapidly increased in popularity due to the ease with which consumers can compare prices and place orders from the comfort of their homes.

By enabling Internet shopping for billions of individuals, mobile shopping revolutionized the market. Consumer attitudes shifted as a result, and a desire for convenience and customization emerged that brands were all too pleased to meet. As a result, there was a huge spike in popularity in the 2010s, and online shopping has continued to develop ever since. The difference between e-commerce and traditional sales is getting less.

Online trading is referred to as "electronic commerce" or "e-commerce". It includes every online transaction involving the purchase and sale of goods and services. Both business-to-business (B2B) and business-to-consumer (B2C) interactions are possible. E-commerce occurs when you visit your preferred Internet merchant to purchase a new pair of shoes. E-commerce also includes purchasing a ticket to a performance or booking a flight online. However, e-commerce isn't limited to desktop computers. Mobile devices account for most e-commerce traffic. Mobile commerce sales account for over 57% of e-commerce market share (*Mobile Commerce Growth (2017–2028) [Updated Aug 2024]*, n.d.) driven by the popularity of smartphones and the ease of online shopping.

How significant is Internet purchasing now for both consumers and businesses?

- By 2024, e-commerce is expected to account for 57% (*Highlights From the Second Edition: State of Commerce*, n.d.) of retail sales.
- The global population of digital shoppers is 2.6 billion (*How Many People Shop Online in 2024? [Updated Jan 2024]*, n.d.). It is like losing out on the opportunity to convert a large number of prospective customers if you are not selling online.
- Digital channels are preferred by more than half (57%) (*Mobile Commerce Growth (2017–2028) [Updated Aug 2024]*, n.d.) of all clients.

In the modern world, e-commerce has emerged as the best solution, not only to consumers who have been offered extreme convenience but also to businesses. With more of its promotion from technology such as AI and data analytics, it allows 24/7 operations and shop configurations, customization on clients, global reach. The COVID-19 pandemic has only brought forward its use and has altered the conventional retail brokerage and logistics operations. Companies like Amazon and Shopify make it possible to compete on the international level even for a small company. All in all, e-commerce has been integrated into the modern commerce world, which never looks back, along with its innovations.

8.2.1 Advantages of E-Commerce for Businesses and Customers

a) **Increased Market Accessibility and Reach:** Due to the extreme diversity of markets, physical retailers may find it difficult to connect with customers in various geographical areas. E-commerce, however, offers a distinct benefit in this respect. It's possible to effortlessly grow clientele and meet the wants of a wide range of consumers by utilizing the power of Internet platforms. Customers who reside in rural or isolated locations where traditional brick-and-mortar establishments might not be reachable can be reached through e-commerce. Additionally, it's possible to target clients with diverse cultural preferences, languages and geographic locations. The long-term viability of the business may depend on its ability to develop a more extensive and varied clientele.

b) **Cost-Effective:** Physical retail shops can be very expensive to run, mainly due to very high real estate and rental costs for prime locations. It is, however, possible to reduce these costs because of e-commerce systems and these resources can be utilized in other important areas of business operations. In the same spirit, e-commerce allows companies to have fewer employees because many processes can be performed automatically. This has the effect of minimizing the chances of human mistakes and help reduce costs (Al-Jaberi et al., 2015).

c) **Enhanced Interaction with Customers:** Due to the rise of social media and the Internet in the everyday functioning, customers are looking for more engagement from the companies now, and e-commerce makes it possible to meet these needs. Companies, through e-commerce platforms, have the ability to connect with consumers on a one-on-one basis and offer them personalized advertisements.
d) **Convenience for Customers:** Convenience ranks high among the factors influencing consumers, and e-learning marketing incorporates a variety of components that can enhance customers' buying experience. E-commerce websites are never closed as they can be accessed anytime throughout the day enabling consumers to purchase at their will and at different locations. In this scenario, customers who cannot go to physical shops due to time, distance, or other reasons will find such services useful.
e) **Individual Differentiation and Specialization:** e-commerce offers businesses yet another significant advantage, namely, the ability to customize and personalize. Companies can target specific segments for offering products and services, thereby purchasing their target audience's evaluation and meeting their needs.
f) **Reduced Complexity in Inventory Processes:** The high diversity of clients' needs in the very large and diverse market makes inventory control difficult. Other than countless opportunities, e-commerce platforms come with features which enhance inventory management and error minimization. One of these technologies is the automatic inventory management system that allows businesses to always monitor their inventory. When a company has limited quantities of a certain item, this feature will inform them so that they can order more before the item goes out of stock. This strategy allows firms to avoid stock-outs, which in turn helps in preventing lost sales opportunities and dissatisfied customers.
g) **Access to Data and Analytics:** e-commerce from various platforms is able to provide companies with information regarding the structure, lifestyle and other aspects of their target audience, which is an invaluable asset to the market and business practices. Analytics and access to data have many benefits, including the understanding of the company's clients in a more practical manner. Clients' behavioural patterns, purchase history, and their interaction with the goods make it possible for businesses to understand clientele sentiments. Such information can help improve marketing strategies. For instance, a company can create targeted campaigns and marketing strategies that match each customer's particular preferences, increasing the chances that they will become loyal customers.
h) **Higher Conversion Rates:** Conversion rates measure the ability of e-commerce stores in terms of the ratio of visitors of their e-commerce store to the amount of buys done. As with any e-commerce company, these owners

should seek to increase their conversion rates since such an increase will ultimately increase sales, hence making the company more successful and sustainable. One way in which this can be accomplished is through personalized advertisements (Alrumiah & Hadwan, 2021). Businesses analyse their clients to deliver precisely what they want to the appropriate audience. This strategy can result in more sales, better customer relationships and more active customers.

i) **Ability to Operate 24/7:** e-commerce has given us the opportunity whenever we want to reach out to any type of customer. Unlike the physical shop, where there are specific opening hours, the online shop does not have the same restriction. This means that even when the bricks and mortar stores are closed, sales can still be made. Additionally, as customers are able to make orders and inquiries at any time, the customer services will be improved, as communication is available as well. Providing such convenience to the customers will enhance sales for your business as well as giving you an edge over your competitors in the market.
j) **Connectivity with Other Business Systems:** Considering the intricacy of business procedures, it is unfortunate to note that e-commerce platforms do not coordinate with other business systems. By bridging the gap between e-commerce and the other business processes, such as accounting, inventory, or CRM, company's performance can be more precise and effective. This approach may save time and reduce expenditure by automating processes and improving the overall efficiency of the organization.
k) **Adaptability and Expandability:** Changes in the market are inevitable try as we may. Therefore, e-commerce operators must cope with those changes and face competition. The commerce platforms are quite flexible that the owners can add or remove products, change prices as well as the marketing strategies to suit the consumer needs. Changing pressures in the competitive environment in this way allow you to stay ahead of competitors and develop an enduring business. Also, the need to be able to adjust one's capabilities to the market as the company grows since it will create additional market needs. E-commerce platforms enable one to rapidly and conveniently expand a business without spending too much money.

8.2.2 Data Analytics Strategies to Enhance E-Commerce Experience

a) **Customer Demographics:** The analytics software can obtain information regarding the location, age and interests of the visitors via social media integration. In addition, they are also able to identify certain users or visitors who will most likely purchase any product or at least engage with the business in any manner. Through this, a marketer can develop content that is most relevant to his target audience in light of the information available on the site and the products or services they buy. It might also allow them to target consumers who are currently underrepresented, therefore improving their marketing strategies. For example, the user demographics of an Online shop may indicate that only a small percentage of the websites' traffic is older users but when these users visit the site the purchase opportunities are very high. In the e-business phenomenon, the user demographics have a crucial role in identifying marketing campaigns and even the purchasing environment. An online clothes retailer, for example might view its customers as separate segments including students, young and middle-aged working class, older people, while also considering the customers' geography, their income and gender. Then by looking into these demographics the company can easily offer customized promotions such as student promotions, bundled professional wear and premium wear collections. By engaging in strategic efforts, this strategy not only boosts sales but also develops brand equity and enhances customer satisfaction.

b) **Data on engagement and reach:** Reach and engagement are two essential components of social media marketing for e-commerce businesses. The number of individuals who view a social media post or receive emails from a business is known as the reach of a social media account. Members of email list, subscribers and people who view your content while online are all included in this figure. The frequency with which users connect with your postings by like or sharing them is known as social media engagement. An e-commerce website's revenue can rise by attracting more visitors through increased reach and engagement. To find patterns in reach and engagement, analytics software can examine a brand's email and social media marketing. While login into your account allows you to see how many people like or share a social media post, analytics software can provide you more detailed information by revealing how many people saw a post through surfing or on other people's accounts. An analytics program could inform you, for instance, that posts with videos receive 30% more views than posts with text. You may use this information to create a social media plan that increases the level of brand knowledge among your audience.

c) **Analysis of a basket or cart:** Online shoppers frequently purchase several related items on a single visit to an e-commerce website. A marketer can create new strategies to satisfy consumer demand by examining the products that customers frequently buy together. They might add incentives for customers who buy things together, which can drive more people to buy numerous items. Marketers might also advertise products jointly on social media postings and paid adverts. Lastly, they may incorporate a recommendation system into the online store, asking users whether they would want to add specific items depending on what they currently have in their shopping basket. The marketing team of the business can utilize data analytics to determine which items, such as shampoo and conditioner, clients most frequently purchase together. They can provide discounts to encourage more people to purchase these products simultaneously by discovering common items that customers group together.

d) **Information about referrals:** A marketer can improve their marketing spend by using data analytics to determine how customers find the online business. Reports from analytics solutions can display the links that users click to access the website, including links from email campaigns, social media posts, search engine links and hosted ads on other websites. By focusing on the locations that bring in the most customers at the lowest cost, a marketer can develop an effective advertising campaign. For instance, the marketing team of an online retailer may use a variety of strategies to drive traffic to the website, such as email campaigns, sponsored social media advertisements, pay-per-click advertising and non-paid social media interaction. The team may concentrate on expanding its database of email leads through free events and promotional offers if its data analytics platform indicates that email campaign ads have a greater click-through rate than pay-per-click advertising. Additionally, the marketing director may reallocate the advertising budget, allocating more funds to lead-generation initiatives and less to pay-per-click advertising.

e) **User Behaviour**: Once a customer reaches the company's website, data analytics can help a marketer understand how they behave. These platforms can gather information about how frequently users click on each link on the home page and how long visitors spend on each page of an online retailer's website on average. The analytics application can forecast the probability that a consumer will finish the transaction in a single visit when they add products to their online basket or shopping cart. The marketer can use this information to modify the company's website design or expedite the purchasing process. The website of an online retailer, for instance, may contain multiple steps between the home page and the online payment process. The percentage of visitors who finish the entire purchasing procedure and the point at which they may leave the website in search of a simpler option can be ascertained by an analytics program (Akter & Wamba, 2016). Using this information, a marketer may add buttons or banners to make the retail section of the website easier to access from the main page or combine purchasing stages. To entice users to stay longer, they may also include information on the home page or a campaign landing page.

f) **Efficiency in converting prospects into customers:** When a customer advances from one point of the sales funnel to another in a sequential manner, it is referred to as the conversion rate in e-commerce. Sales assistance or simplifying the checkout process are two methods that companies can apply to enhance their conversion rates. Marketers can improve comprehension of product offerings and make marketing and selling efforts more satisfactory to consumers when a firm's conversion coefficient is studied among different products. Suppose there is a financial service program's marketing site where people visit to learn more and of those people, half of them select a free software trial, which means the organization manages to have half of the website visitors convert, therefore, the conversion rate in this circumstance would be 50%. In such a case, the marketing team responsible for the promotion of the product may wish to increase this conversion rate further by including new advertisements that focus on the free trial, cut down the number of attainment steps required for registrants to fill in, or allow for the registration of visitors at different sights on the website.

8.3 UNDERSTANDING SUPPLY CHAIN LOGISTICS

From locating raw supplies to shipping completed goods to customers, supply chain logistics involves an intricate network of interrelated procedures. The necessity for effective and efficient supply chain management has never been higher due to the growth of globalization and e-commerce. Businesses may improve their supply chain operations, obtain insights and make wise decisions by utilizing the power of data. Let's enlist the critical role that data analytics plays in improving supply chain logistics in this section.

a) **Forecasting demand:** A crucial component of supply chain management and logistics is demand forecasting, which is made possible by the incorporation of artificial intelligence. AI gives businesses a competitive edge in inventory control and resource allocation by improving the accuracy of demand forecasts. AI examines past data, market trends, and outside variables using ML algorithms to find patterns and connections that conventional forecasting techniques might miss. This makes it possible to forecast demand in a dynamic and flexible manner, particularly in sectors where market conditions are changing quickly. Furthermore, AI systems can adjust to changing consumer habits and market conditions by continuously learning and improving their forecasts over time. This adaptability is crucial in the context of today's fast-paced business environment. This can avoid stockouts, cut holding costs and optimize inventory levels by utilizing AI's demand forecasting capabilities. By guaranteeing that products are constantly available when and when they are needed, this improves operational efficiency and raises consumer satisfaction.

b) **Optimization of Routes:** Another important area of strategic AI application in supply chain and logistics management is route optimization. Conventional route planning frequently uses static parameters and predetermined schedules, which results in inefficiencies and higher operating expenses. This method is revolutionized by AI, which dynamically analyses real-time data to determine the most efficient routes while taking delivery limits, weather and traffic conditions into account. AI regularly improves its route optimization models by using ML algorithms, which learn from past data and adjust to changing trends. This flexibility enables logistics firms to react quickly to developments, guaranteeing that routes are continuously improved for effectiveness. AI-driven route optimization optimizes vehicle fuel consumption and lowers emissions, which lowers transportation costs and lessens environmental impact. AI integration also improves fleet management overall by giving real-time insight into vehicle performance and maintenance requirements. By preventing malfunctions, this proactive strategy lowers downtime and improves supply chain operations' dependability.

c) **Inventory Management:** AI is essential to the transformation of supply chain and logistics operations' inventory management. Inventory management used to entail keeping stock levels in check to satisfy demand and prevent overstock. But by adding intelligence and predictive power to this process, artificial intelligence (AI) brings about a paradigm shift. AI examines enormous databases that include past sales, market trends and other pertinent information using complex ML techniques. By doing this, businesses may better predict demand, optimize inventory levels and steer clear of the costly traps of stockouts or surplus inventory. Additionally, real-time visibility into stock levels, warehouse conditions, and order fulfilment procedures is improved by AI-driven inventory management systems. More agile decision-making is made possible by this increased openness, which makes it easier to quickly modify inventory plans in response to shifting market conditions. By reducing holding costs and detecting slow-moving or obsolete material, AI's predictive analytics help free up funds for more strategic investments. Furthermore, the system helps with risk management by anticipating possible supply chain interruptions and enabling businesses to proactively lessen their effects on inventory availability (Cao et al., 2017).

d) **Automation in Warehouses:** Artificial intelligence-driven warehouse automation is revolutionizing the logistics and supply chain sector. Robotics, computer vision and ML are examples of AI technologies that are strategically used to improve and simplify warehouse operations. Intelligent robotics deployment is a major usage of AI in warehouse automation. These robots can select, package and sort while navigating warehouse areas with efficiency. These robots can learn from their experiences, adjust to changing circumstances, and continually improve their routes and procedures for optimal efficiency due to ML algorithms. Furthermore, by automating inventory movement tracking and providing real-time visibility into stock levels, artificial intelligence in supply chain management improves inventory management in warehouses. This guarantees correct order fulfilment, minimizes stock disparities and lowers mistakes. Demand-driven and dynamic storage methods are made easier by the incorporation of AI into warehouse operations, which optimizes the placement of items according to demand trends (Nair, 2013). Predictive maintenance powered by AI is also used to foresee and resolve any problems with warehouse machinery. By reducing downtime, this proactive strategy guarantees that automated systems operate at their best.

e) **Predictive Maintenance:** Artificial intelligence-powered predictive maintenance is a significant game-changer in the supply chain and logistics industry. Conventional maintenance procedures sometimes depend on set timetables or reactive approaches, which can result in downtime, unforeseen expenses and interruptions to operations. However, by utilizing ML algorithms and advanced data, AI-driven predictive maintenance revolutionizes this strategy. AI systems can forecast when assets or machines are likely to break down by tracking equipment continually and examining performance data from the past. By taking a proactive stance, businesses may plan maintenance exactly when required, reducing downtime and increasing operational effectiveness. By resolving problems before they become more serious, predictive maintenance also contributes to equipment longevity.

Large volumes of data are processed by AI, which allows it to spot minute trends and irregularities that conventional maintenance techniques can miss. This degree of understanding makes it possible to estimate maintenance needs more precisely and nuancedly, avoiding needless service and related expenses. Additionally, by lowering the need for urgent equipment repairs and lessening the effect of unplanned breakdowns, predictive maintenance helps save money. By keeping vital assets operational, this not only increases the overall reliability of the equipment but also strengthens the supply chain's resilience.

8.4 UNDERSTANDING IMPLEMENTATION OF E-COMMERCE AND SUPPLY CHAIN ON CLOUD PLATFORM

8.4.1 E-Commerce Architecture on Cloud-AWS

In this section, we will explore how cloud providers like AWS enable and support microservices-based architecture for e-commerce through their platform services (*Guidance for Building an Ecommerce Experience With Commerce tools on AWS*, n.d.). Figure 8.1 shows an example of one such kind of architecture for AWS through its services.

- **Amazon Route 53:** This highly accessible Domain Name System (DNS) service manages DNS queries to the e-commerce website.
- **CloudFront:** Amazon CloudFront is a content distribution network (CDN) having edge locations all around the world is. It can serve dynamic material from nearby sites with little latency and store both streaming and static content.
- **Frontend application:** AWS EC2 and auto scaling is used to install the e-commerce frontend application, which manages the specifics of load balancing, capacity provisioning, auto-scaling and application health monitoring automatically.
- **Amazon S3:** All static catalog material, including product photos, instructions and videos, as well as all microservices log files and clickstream data from Amazon CloudFront, are stored on Amazon S3.
- **AWS Fargate:** A group of polyglot microservices housed in Amazon Elastic Container Service (AWS Fargate) form the core of this architecture. These micro services represent domain components including users, orders, carts, items, and search and recommendation services.
- **Amazon DynamoDB:** Amazon DynamoDB is a NoSQL database service that is easy to set up, run and grow. It is completely managed and has excellent performance. Both the product database and a session store for persistent session data, such the shopping cart, are utilized. New product categories and characteristics can be added to the catalog with a great level of flexibility because DynamoDB doesn't have a schema.
- **Amazon ElastiCache:** This tool lowers I/O (and cost) on DynamoDB by serving as a caching layer for the product catalog and a session store for volatile data.
- **Amazon Elastic Search Index:** This Elastic Search service offers quick and incredibly scalable search capabilities, loads product catalog data.

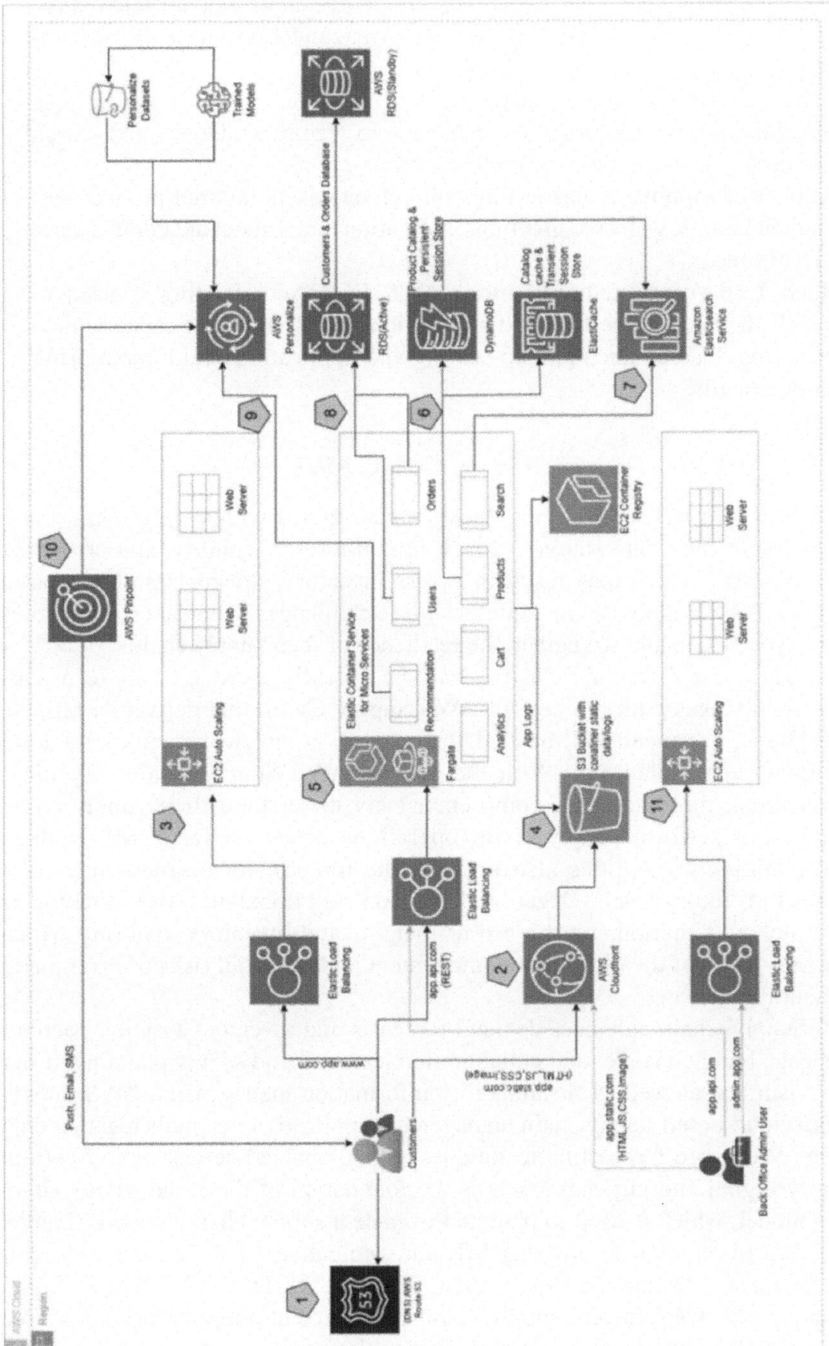

FIGURE 8.1 E-commerce architecture on AWS.

- **Amazon RDS:** To provide high availability, the user and orders databases are hosted redundantly on a multi-AZ (multi-Availability Zone) deployment of Amazon Relational Database Service (Amazon RDS) within private subnets that are isolated from the public Internet.
- **Amazon Personalize:** Amazon Personalize offers product suggestions based on user item interactions, related item recommendations and search re-ranking according to user preferences.
- **Amazon Pinpoint:** Amazon Pinpoint delivers users tailored product recommendations, welcome greetings and notifications about abandoned carts in real time.
- **Back End frontend application:** AWS EC2 Auto Scaling is used to install the back office frontend application, which manages capacity provisioning, load balancing, auto-scaling and application health monitoring automatically.

8.4.2 Supply Chain Architecture on Cloud-AWS

Organizations in a variety of sectors have long struggled with supply chain issues including fragmented data sources, a lack of end-to-end visibility, and erroneous demand forecasts, which may result in excess inventory, stockouts and decreased profitability. AWS Supply Chain addresses these challenges and enables companies to move beyond them and strengthen the resilience of their supply chains.

Organizations of different industries can successfully overcome long-term supply chain challenges with the help of AWS Supply Chain that delivers a reliable data backbone, advanced ML-backed forecasting, complete inventory tracking and optimal supply planning. With the help of AWS Supply Chain, organizations can break the data silos, comprehensively understand their supply chain processes, and perform supply chain operations based on facts. ML-enabled demand planning capabilities also improve the forecast for obsolescence costs and surplus inventory levels. Organizations can avoid imbalance, overstocking as well as stockout situations by the use of insights and inventory visibility which provide rare views of the distribution, movement and potential risks of inventories throughout the network.

AWS Supply Chain enhances demand forecasts and inventory visibility, actionable insights, bundled contextual collaboration, demand and supply planning, n-tier supplier visibility, as well as sustainability information management. AWS Supply Chain is a cloud-based supply chain management application that pulls together data and offers ML-based forecasting techniques. Cloud-enabled networking of certain third-party digital and physical assets is the foundation of the cloud supply chain business model, which is used to plan and oversee a supply chain network (Ivanov et al., 2022). In addition to utilizing ML and generative AI to convert and combine fragmented data into the supply chain data lake (SCDL), AWS Supply Chain can interact with your current supply chain management and enterprise resource planning (ERP) solutions. Without requiring replatforming, upfront license costs, or long-term commitments, AWS Supply Chain (*AWS Supply Chain Overview*, n.d.) may enhance supply chain risk management.

Key product features include:

- **Data lakes:** For supply chains to comprehend, retrieve and convert heterogeneous, incompatible data into a single data model, AWS Supply Chain creates a data lake utilizing ML models. Data from a variety of sources, including supply chain management and ERP systems like SAP S/4HANA, can be ingested by the data lake. Natural language processing (NLP) and ML are used by AWS Supply Chain to link data from source systems to the unified data model. Data from other systems may also be loaded into an Amazon Simple Storage Service (Amazon S3) bucket, where generative AI will automatically map it and then ingest it into the AWS Supply Chain Data Lake.
- **Insights:** Using the extensive supply chain data in the data lake, AWS Supply Chain automatically produces insights into possible supply chain hazards (such overstock or stock-outs) and displays them on an inventory visualization map. Additionally, AWS Supply Chain provides work order analytics to show maintenance-related materials from sourcing to delivery, as well as order status, delivery risk identification and delivery risk mitigation measures. In order to produce more precise vendor lead-time forecasts, AWS Supply Chain employs ML models that are based on technology that is comparable to that used by Amazon Supply planners can lower the risk of stock-outs or excess inventory by using these anticipated vendor lead times to adjust static assumptions included in planning models.
- **Demand Planning:** In order to help prevent waste and excessive inventory expenditures, AWS Supply Chain Demand Planning produces more accurate demand projections, adapts to market situations, and enables demand planners to work across teams. AWS Supply Chain employs ML to evaluate real-time data (such as open orders) and historical sales data, generate predictions and continuously modify models to increase accuracy in order to assist eliminate the human labour and guesswork associated with demand planning.
- **Supply Planning:** AWS Supply Chain Supply Planning anticipates and schedules the acquisition of components, raw materials and final products.
- **Suggested activities and cooperation:** When a risk is identified, AWS Supply Chain automatically assesses, ranks and distributes several rebalancing alternatives to give inventory managers and planners suggested courses of action. The sustainability impact, the distance between facilities, and the proportion of risk mitigated are used to rate the recommendation choices. Additionally, supply chain managers may delve deeper to examine how each choice would affect other distribution hubs around the network. Additionally, AWS Supply Chain continuously learns from your choices to generate better suggestions over time
- **N-Tier Visibility:** AWS Supply Chain N-Tier Visibility extends visibility beyond company to external trade partners by integrating with Work Order Insights or Supply Planning. By enabling this, they help to coordinate and confirm orders with suppliers, this visibility enhances the precision of planning and execution procedures.

- **Sustainability:** Sustainability experts may access the necessary documents and datasets from their supplier network more securely and effectively using AWS Supply Chain Sustainability, which employs the same underlying technology as N-Tier Visibility. Based on a single, auditable record of the data, these capabilities assist in providing environmental and social governance (ESG) information.
- **Supply Chain Analytics on AWS:** Amazon QuickSight powers AWS Supply Chain Analytics, a reporting and analytics tool that offers both premade supply chain dashboards and the ability to create custom reports and analytics. With this functionality, it's possible to utilize the AWS Supply Chain user interface to access data in the Data Lake.
- **Amazon Q:** By evaluating the data in AWS Supply Chain Data Lake, offering crucial operational and financial insights, and responding to pressing supply chain inquiries, Amazon Q in AWS Supply Chain is an interactive generative artificial intelligence assistant that helps to run your supply chain more effectively. Users spend less time looking for pertinent information, get solutions more quickly, and spend less time learning, deploying, configuring or troubleshooting AWS Supply Chain.

Figure 8.2 shows the architectural alternatives for creating an operational data hub for the supply chain with AWS services for supply chain management (*Guidance for Deploying a Supply Chain Data Hub on AWS*, n.d.) The hub incorporates information from hundreds of different sources, such as external sources for tracking shipments and internal sources for planning and execution. After then, the hub creates a

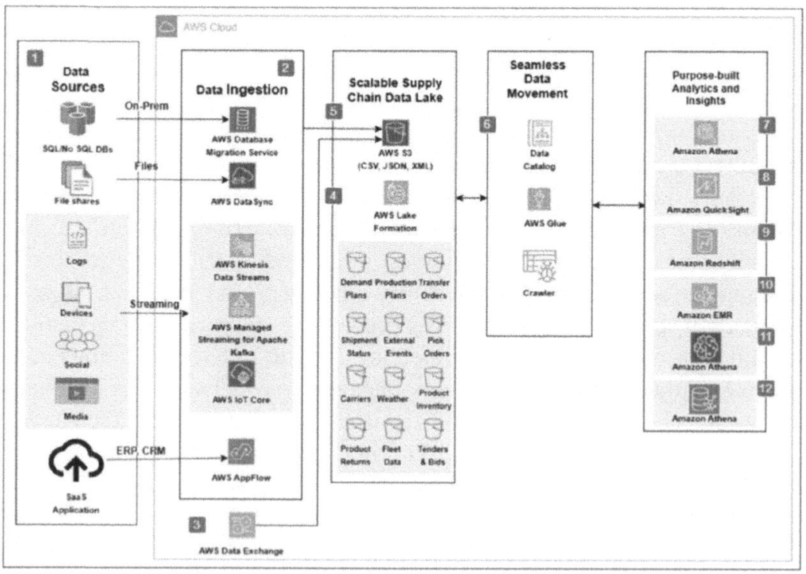

FIGURE 8.2 Operational data hub for the supply chain with AWS services for supply chain management.

unified view of the data. Real-time planning regarding demand projections, inventories and procurement may be facilitated by having visibility into data from many business and execution systems. The data centre assists supply chain companies in making data-driven choices that enhance customer happiness and delivery times.

Step 1: The company gathers supply chain data from a wide range of resources such as ERP and SaaS CRM applications, social media encompasses of tweets and Facebook posts, edges devices deployed on the manufacturing shop floor, logs and streaming media.

Step 2: The AWS-managed supply chain data lake receives data from sources such as Amazon Kinesis, Apache Kafka (Amazon MSK), AWS Database Migration Service (AWS DMS), AWS DataSync, AWS IoT Core and Amazon AppFlow depending on the source of data.

Step 3: The AWS Data Exchange uses other external data including weather data that can be applicable in predicting the ETA of shipments such data is directed to their supply chain data lake.

Step 4: The adaptable AWS Lake Formation is helpful in the creation of the supply chain data lake.

Step 5: The underlying solution for storage of the supply chain data lake is Amazon Simple Storage Service.

Step 6: Using AWS Glue, data from different data stores such as ERP, planning, and shipping visibility systems are extracted, transformed, classified and loaded.

Step 7: Amazon Athena is a serverless interactive query service examining data hosted in Amazon's object storage, S3 buckets, using standard SQL.

Step 8: While trying to help planners make each business decision in an informed way, Amazon QuickSight's dashboards are useful as they can analyse data related to supply chain planning, execution and real-time data on shipping.

Step 9: The Amazon Redshift cloud warehouse supports structured and semi-structured data.

Step 10: Big data can be processed by a variety of open-source tools through the EMR's huge cloud-based data platform provided by Amazon.

Step 11: Supply chain application intelligence is provided by the AWS AI services and ML model building, training and deployment is done by the Amazon SageMaker.

Step 12: The graph database from Amazon Neptune improves the accuracy and efficiency of network queries.

8.5 CHALLENGES

8.5.1 E-Commerce

a) **Risks to Security:** The rise in online purchases has also raised the risks of online fraud and security breaches. Hacking, phishing and malware attacks are just a few of the strategies that cybercriminals might employ to obtain private client data and company information. Customers may stop trusting you as a result, and your company's reputation may suffer. E-commerce companies must invest in strong security solutions like firewalls, SSL certificates and encryption to reduce these dangers. They also need to teach staff security best practices.

b) **Reliance on technology:** In a growing cross-border e-commerce industry, firms need to use various forms of technology, including online payments, website authoring applications, and even hosting services. As such, any breakdown in the system or technical glitch has the propensity to disrupt operations and incur costs. Moreover, because the nature of technology has been evolving at a rapid pace, it requires the firms to keep abreast of the latest changes which can also be quite resource and time exhausting. Such needs, the businesses or the entrepreneurs, should have alternate solutions to be able to overcome such technological failure's possibilities whereas adequate amount should be allocated towards maintenance and improvement in the current setting.

c) **Problems with Customer Service:** Among the key aspects of success for every e-commerce company is customer service which is quite challenging to get right. For online shoppers, for example it might be hard to find needed items, to find out how to navigate the website or how to make their payments. Customer feedback and bad reviews could also emanate from the delivery and shipping aspects of the items like when items are broken, or when they are late in delivery. To deal with these challenges, businesses must invest in easy-to-use websites, effective order management systems and efficient and timely customer contact.

d) **Increased Competition:** With the rise in e-commerce, businesses today face stiff competition not only from established players in the market but also from new entrants. Consequently, companies may find it hard to differentiate themselves and gain customers. If e-commerce players have any hope of gaining recognition in the Indian e-commerce marketplace, they will have to invest heavily in branding and advertising that communicates their unique value offer as well as providing perfect customer service.

e) **Lack of face-to-face engagements with the clients:** E-commerce firms have lesser occasions to physically meet their clients than the conventional brick and mortar business. This means that it would be difficult to establish long-lasting relationships and cultivate customer loyalty. However, companies are able to overcome this hurdle by engaging clients through emails and social media with personalized offers and incentives.

f) **Problems in Shipping and Handling:** Shipping and handling can be quite troublesome for Indian e-commerce enterprises. A timely and cost-effective delivery can be an issue due to the vast landmass, poor infrastructural development and regulatory problems. Businesses ought to develop efficient supply chain management systems to handle this. They must track inventory, optimize delivery routes and provide customers with updated information on the status of the orders. In addition, they must work with reliable logistics providers.

g) **Unfamiliarity and unwillingness to extend trust:** For success, trust is critical for e-commerce players with no prior experience in the industry.

A potential consumer, most likely to buy from an unknown company or website, appears to be far possible if he/she has no way to validate the standards or secure mechanisms in use. In this case, companies shall necessarily invest in establishing a strong reputation.

h) **Limited Perceptual Experience:** It is a limitation where e-commerce firms cannot provide clients with the experience of experiencing their products through touch, smell, etc. This lack of customers being able to experience the feelings of touching, smelling or even tasting products could be a disadvantage, especially in clothing, food and cosmetics. E-commerce firms are able to counter this disadvantage by providing detailed descriptions of items, good images and videos and customer opinions and ratings. Touch and feel experiences such as free trials or samples can also help build trust and loyalty to customers.

i) **Not Able to View the Items Physically:** Another disadvantage of e-commerce is the lack of facility to examine goods before purchasing them. Customers might therefore, be unwilling to purchase products online without physically viewing them, especially when it comes to costly products like jewellery and gadgets. Such a deficiency can be mitigated by e-commerce companies providing sufficient product information, images and videos, customer reviews and ratings and a clearly defined return and refund policy.

j) **Compliance with Law and Regulation:** E-commerce companies that are active in India need to follow several laws including taxation, consumer protection law and data privacy law. For small and medium-sized firms, for instance, failure to comply can cause heavy penalties, and lawsuits, etc., e-commerce companies should invest not only on the initial setup but also on the resources needed for research and compliance of the legal and regulatory framework applicable to their industry, region and country. Such complex legal and tax issues are best resolved in collaboration with financial and legal experts.

k) **Costs of the Initial Investment and Continued Maintenance:** A new e-commerce venture has costs associated with the undertaking that would include initial outlays for marketing, investments in technical infrastructure and design work for the website. While there are some such costs that would be classified as maintenance costs for example web hosting and site security, upgrades, etc. that are recurrent maintenance costs which can be quite considerable. To ensure their maintenance is not operating at a loss, e-commerce companies must clearly define their budget for the operation's costs and allocate funds appropriately. In this case, they should focus on an advertising campaign on the most effective ones and cut extra costs such as on utilizing cloud hosting together with open-source software.

As the world goes increasingly digital, business owners should carefully weigh these pros and cons with a proper perspective so that they can make informed decisions regarding their e-commerce strategies. E-commerce introduces technological limitations, increased competition and security risks, while also extending convenience and flexibility to customers, as well as enabling active participation by customers. This is also important to note that e-commerce has a bright future because the market is constantly progressing and developing. Businesses that will implement commerce practices are most likely going to witness increased sales and customer engagement as more people embrace online shopping. To remain competitive and provide the best experience to clients, it is very crucial to keep abreast of the latest trends and advancements.

8.5.2 Supply Chain

a) **Security issues:** Sensitive information such as financial data, supplier agreements and client data is embedded in cloud-based SCM solutions. Organizations will want to ensure that their cloud service provider has sufficient security infrastructure that will guard sensitive data against Internet risks or any unauthorized access.
b) **Integration problems:** It is imperative to integrate cloud-based SCM solutions with other company applications such as ERP, logistics, and warehouse management systems. The integration process might be made more difficult by different data structures, formats incompatibility and some hitches in compatibility.
c) **Dependency on Internet connectivity:** SCM using cloud technology makes it very convenient to access the systems. However, the SCM cloud application can only be accessed if the Internet availability and connection are guaranteed. Slow speed of the Internet connection or outages can disrupt supply chain processes, resulting in loss of time and efficiency and cost implication.
d) **Data ownership and control:** The companies should have structures in place to ensure that even supply chain data that is held on the cloud should be their property and they have control over the same. They also need to have specific agreements about data ownership, access and control through contracts and service-level agreements with their cloud provider.
e) **Vendor lock-in:** Businesses have to be careful in order not to be dependent on a certain cloud provider or proprietary technology. Vendor lock-in may have a detrimental effect on their long-term adaptability and competitiveness as well, because such restrictions will make system upgrades, provider changes or solution adaptations more cumbersome.
f) **Regulations and compliance:** There are some laws related to data security and privacy around the world, for example CCPA, GDPR, HIPAA which companies must adhere to (Karvela et al., 2021). They have to ensure that these standards are met by their cloud provider and that the processing and storage of their data is done in a manner that conforms to the standards established.
g) **Data backup and migration:** Organizations may experience problems shifting their data to the cloud and ensuring they have a regular backup of their data. There is a need for backup plans to be in place to ensure the recovery of data in the event of destruction or interruption of Operations. Since data relocation is likely to be difficult, tedious and riddled with the possibility of errors, backup procedures are essential.

h) **Skills gap:** Relating to the CC and SCM systems, businesses may have a shortage of labour. They must make sure that their workers are equipped with the appropriate tools and training needed in operating the cloud-based supply chain management systems.
i) **Worst common practice:** Cloud-based SCM solutions are challenged by existing consumer demand and supply in the market due to the worst common practice. Different providers have their own vocabulary, data and interface which lags the integration of the solutions across the supply chain.
j) **Change management:** Implementing cloud-based supply chain management solutions requires large-scale changes in the organization's structure, labour organization and business processes. Businesses need to have a well-detailed management strategy in order to cope with these changes as well as facilitate smooth transitioning to the cloud SCM systems.

8.6 CONCLUSION AND FUTURE SCOPE

The merging of Data Analysis, ML and Cloud Computing is set to enhance e-commerce and supply chain logistics, making the processes to be smarter, scalable and more efficient. These technologies are making it possible for companies to customize consumer engagement, enhance supply chains, control fraud and be proactive in the use of business intelligence. Despite the existence of data privacy issues, integration complexity and cost management, the potential is huge for the future. Trends such as advanced analytics through AI, edge computing and blockchain technology integration have the capacity to change the game for these industries. Autonomous Logistics systems, real-time hyper-personalized commerce in e-commerce and advancement of green computing strategies give more evidence of the changes that the industry will be able to achieve in the future. In the context of the fourth industrial revolution, the combination of data, AI and cloud is becoming increasingly important. It is only by combining these technologies that firms can respond to ever-increasing challenges. Such is the potential of advancements and continuous upcoming innovations that businesses can be able to thrive for many years to come.

REFERENCES

Akter, S., & Wamba, S. F. (2016). Big data analytics in e-commerce: A systematic review and agenda for future research. *Electronic Markets*, *26*(2), 173–194. https://doi.org/10.1007/s12525-016-0219-0

Al-Jaberi, M., Mohamed, N., & Al-Jaroodi, J. (2015). E-commerce cloud: Opportunities and challenges. In *2015 International Conference on Industrial Engineering and Operations Management (IEOM)*, Dubai, United Arab Emirates, pp. 1–6. https://doi.org/10.1109/IEOM.2015.7093867.

Alrumiah, S. S., & Hadwan, M. (2021). Implementing big data analytics in e-commerce: Vendor and customer view. *IEEE Access*, *9*, 37281–37286. https://doi.org/10.1109/ACCESS.2021.3063615

AWS Supply Chain Overview. (n.d.). [Video]. Amazon Web Services, Inc. https://aws.amazon.com/aws-supply-chain/

Cao, Q., Schniederjans, D. G., & Schniederjans, M. (2017). Establishing the use of cloud computing in supply chain management. *Operations Management Research, 10*(1–2), 47–63. https://doi.org/10.1007/s12063-017-0123-6

Cloud Standards Customer Council. (2017). *Cloud Customer Architecture for Big Data and Analytics V2.0.* www.omg.org/cloud/deliverables/CSCC-Cloud-Customer-Architecture-for-Big-Data-and-Analytics.pdf

Guidance for Building an Ecommerce Experience with Commercetools on AWS. (n.d.). Amazon Web Services, Inc. https://aws.amazon.com/solutions/guidance/building-an-ecommerce-experience-with-commercetools-on-aws/

Guidance for Deploying a Supply Chain Data Hub on AWS. (n.d.). Amazon Web Services, Inc. https://aws.amazon.com/solutions/guidance/deploying-a-supply-chain-data-hub-on-aws/

Highlights from the Second Edition: State of Commerce. (n.d.). Salesforce. www.salesforce.com/in/resources/research-reports/state-of-commerce/

How Many People Shop Online in 2024? [Updated Jan 2024]. (n.d.). Oberlo. www.oberlo.com/statistics/how-many-people-shop-online

Ishwarappa, N., & Anuradha, J. (2015). A brief introduction on big data 5Vs characteristics and Hadoop technology. *Procedia Computer Science, 48*, 319–324. https://doi.org/10.1016/j.procs.2015.04.188

Ivanov, D., Dolgui, A., & Sokolov, B. (2022). Cloud supply chain: Integrating Industry 4.0 and digital platforms in the "supply chain-as-a-service". *Transportation Research Part E Logistics and Transportation Review, 160*, 102676. https://doi.org/10.1016/j.tre.2022.102676

Karvela, P., Kopanaki, E., & Georgopoulos, N. (2021). Challenges and opportunities of cloud adoption in supply chain management: A SWOT analysis model. *Journal of System and Management Sciences.* https://doi.org/10.33168/jsms.2021.0311

Mell, P., Grance, T., & National Institute of Standards and Technology. (2011). *The NIST Definition of Cloud Computing. In NIST Special Publication 800–145 [Report].* National Institute of Standards and Technology. https://nvlpubs.nist.gov/nistpubs/Legacy/SP/nistspecialpublication800-145.pdf

Mobile Commerce Growth (2017–2028) [Updated Aug 2024]. (n.d.). Oberlo. www.oberlo.com/statistics/mobile-commerce-sales

Nair, P. R. (2013). Tackling supply chain through cloud computing: Management: Opportunities, challenges and successful deployments. In *Advances in Intelligent Systems and Computing* (pp. 761–767). https://doi.org/10.1007/978-3-319-03095-1_82

9 Data Analytics, Machine Learning and Cloud Together

A Powerful Combination for Healthcare and Education

Neelu Jyothi Ahuja

9.1 INTRODUCTION

The integration of data analytics, machine learning (ML), and cloud computing signifies a remarkable milestone within the contemporary technological framework. Individually, each of these components has played a crucial role in the progression of numerous sectors; however, their combined application presents substantial new prospects for revolutionizing our methods of engaging with and utilizing data-informed insights [1]. Two areas best placed to capitalize on this change of power are the fields of health and education, the two sectors most closely associated with the overall health and development of society. After that, we can then merge ML power built into these predictive analytics capabilities with immense space for data storage and accessibility in cloud computing for addressing historical issues in such areas even as it provides bespoke accessible solutions that contribute to improvement in quality, efficiency and personalized support. Harnessing the transformative potential of data analytics, ML and cloud computing data analytics forms the basis on which modern information support can transform the decision-making processes because it allows organizations to extract useful insights from large collections of data [2]. Improved with the inclusion of ML, since ML models can even discern patterns and even make predictions and auto-decisions based on complex datasets that would be difficult, if impossible, for humans to consider individually. Cloud computing could, in parallel, provide the very basic infrastructure necessary for such an approach of scalable, on-demand storage and processing capabilities. Cloud technology has improved to an extensive extent in the storage and analysis of vast amounts of data, rendering expensive on-premises solutions obsolete. It integrates insights gained from ML and cloud resources that enable absolutely fantastic possibilities for real-time data analysis; it makes room for timely interventions in fast-moving sectors like healthcare and education. These are expanding patient data

DOI: 10.1201/9781003396772-10

sources in the form of EHRs, wearable technologies and medical imaging [3]. Such sources come as aids through which a healthcare provider can continue monitoring and assessing patient health through intensive datasets stored in the cloud and ML algorithms providing meaningful insight into patterns in patients' health, early signs of diseases, and recommend preventative practices. It also allows complex analyses on vast datasets to be completed instantly, which is very critical in applications like remote patient monitoring and personalized medicine, using the inherent facility of speed in processing that is available with cloud computing. In this manner, data analytics, ML, and cloud computing can be integrated to achieve a new means of more proactive and individualized care for patients, making healthcare systems able to manage this increased cost and complexity surrounding the care of patients [4]. Like education, ML and data analytics offer similar transformative power to shape instruction for individual students in schools and other educational institutions. Such insights may emanate from data related to individual student performance during assessments, attendance and engagement. This shall enable insights into uniquely different learning styles and the challenges of students. Cloud computing facilities provide easy access to such analytics and models to empower the teacher in reaching out early to struggling students and implementing appropriate interventions. The instructor is empowered to focus on developing more inclusive and personalized learning environments that help tackle the needs of diverse student populations using a data-driven approach. Healthcare and education are perhaps two of the most basic aspects of a society where modern technological innovations echo much deeper than just mere operational efficiency in affecting individual experiences as well as broader social frameworks [5, 6]. They also embrace pressing needs for greater accessibility, effectiveness and customization in services through the use of data analytics, ML and cloud computing. High patient volumes; scarce resources; and increasing complexity of chronic diseases all challenge traditional models in healthcare. But the bright future lies in its predictive, risk-based identification of health problems and tailoring the treatment plan according to the patient's needs. Example: The data collected from wearable devices, for instance, smartwatches and fitness trackers, enables the ML algorithm to identify early signs of health deterioration, which thus enables early health interventions, reduces hospital admissions and decreases healthcare expenditure. Moreover, cloud-based ML applications allow healthcare professionals to analyse real-time data that emanates from different sources, hence, making informed and timely choices about managing care for the patient. With cloud-based solutions now becoming widely available, advanced health analytics and monitoring services would be rolled out to even the most remote or deprived locations.

The influence of ML and data analytics on education is deeply transformative. Due to being relatively rigid, traditional educational frameworks do little in adapting towards the diverse influences that learners usually show: speed, interests, and capability. The applications of ML can enable the analysis of a pattern in data from classroom interactions, assessment and student engagement to yield trends and personalized feedback that fosters an adaptive learning environment. The cloud is used in enhancing this adaptability, where most online learning platforms are accessible anywhere, making education more inclusive and more scalable [7]. Aggregated data can also be utilized to estimate the outcomes of education for schools and policymakers, thus better allowing informed decisions regarding the development of curriculum and the management of resources. With integration into data analytics, ML and cloud computing, therefore, strong solutions to specific challenges will be offered for the healthcare and education sectors, thus facilitating kinds of developments that result in both operational improvement and significant social transformation [8]. These tools will shift to tomorrow on the premise of preventive healthcare, leapfrogging over-reactive methodologies and student-centred education from one-size-fits-all approaches.

9.2 THE ROLE OF ML IN DATA-DRIVEN HEALTHCARE

Guided by Data ML has become a new basis for healthcare development, together with improved access to large datasets, the growth of computing power and the perception of the need for more personalized and cost-effective care. Using pattern discovery and prediction-making algorithms on large amounts of data, the use of ML can enable various healthcare providers to make better decisions and refine care processes. This chapter discusses transformative applications of ML in data-driven healthcare, namely predictive analytics, personalized treatments, medical imaging and operational efficiency that will accelerate the sector.

9.2.1 Predictive Analytics: Early Detection and Pre-Emptive Management

A particularly transformative application is predictive analytics, which enables healthcare providers to forecast and mitigate potential future health problems. Analysations of EHRs, wearables and genetic information are used to detect trends and patterns that would otherwise go unnoticed by a human – for example predictive models may identify the predisposed patients suffering from diseases such as diabetes or heart disease, so early treatment and lifestyle changes may be intervened in advance to prevent such disease [9, 10]. Similarly, ML-based predictive tools are applied in predicting readmissions and hence placement planning for care and reduction of readmission rates and outcomes may be enhanced. An example of this is using RNNs in time-series data, like tracking the patient's blood pressure or glucose or heart rate. Hence, anomalies can be brought to the patient's notice and appropriate action to be done in real time with ease. In the final analysis, proactive treatment reduces reactive treatment and improves health outcomes significantly while significantly decreasing its costs.

9.2.2 Personalized Medicine and Personalized Treatment Solutions

It changes the paradigm of personalized medicine by providing the basis for sophisticated treatment strategies tailored according to an individual's genetic composition, medical history and lifestyle factors. In contrast to conventional healthcare mechanisms, general treatment protocols cannot serve the needs of every individual whereas advanced ML algorithms can scan vast amounts of data generated through clinical trials, patient profiles and pharmacological research to prescribe specific treatments. For instance, ML-based platforms would analyse genomic data to predict the response a particular patient might have to certain medications. This aids doctors in selecting the right drugs as well as their dosages and, at the same time, reduces side effects and leads to less trial-and-error prescribing [11]. Biomarkers for cancer ML models have thus proved to be extremely useful for oncology. With the help of such models, other applications in IBM Watson Health use NLP and ML to automate extraction of insights from medical literature and patient records and provide clinicians with customized evidence-based recommendations about each specific case [12].

9.2.3 New Technologies in Medical Imaging and Diagnosis Industry

One of the most significant domains in which ML has shown substantial effectiveness is in medical imaging. Conventional diagnostic methods primarily rely upon the skills and expertise of radiologists and pathologists to detect abnormalities present in the imaging data, such as X-rays, MRIs or CT scans. Recently, it has been noticed that algorithms based on ML, and deep learning architecture typically CNNs, have been very accurately diagnostic of medical conditions, such as tumours, fractures and neurological disorders [13]. For example Google's DeepMind designed models that could diagnose eye diseases with a high degree of precision based on retinal scans like a human doctor. The ML tool is applied in the analysis of mammograms for the detection of early cases of breast cancer [14]. During diagnosis, false positives are reduced and the detection accuracy maximized. Besides detection, ML models are also found to be used in image segmentation, which enables quantification of areas of interest in the images – for instance, how big is a tumour or what percentage of tissue damage lies within an image. This is useful not only for diagnosis but also in the course of treatment planning and monitoring the disease progression.

9.2.4 Operational Efficiency and Expense Reduction

ML increases efficiency in productivity within healthcare systems and automates most tasks, optimizing workflow processes while foreseeing trends in resource utilization; this leads to reduced operating expenditures and improves the quality of care [15]. For example ML models can predict which patients are likely to be admitted to hospitals and help the hospitals really plan and ensure adequate staffing, beds and resources. ML-based chatbots are being used to automate routine administrative activities such as scheduling appointments and answering questions from inquiring patients, thus unburdening the healthcare staff. Predictive analytics is also helpful in the supply chain handling of healthcare. With predictive analytics, resources such as medicines, equipment and vaccines would be available at the right place and time to support service delivery. Proper resource distribution would indeed make the difference between life and death in such emergencies as a pandemic.

9.2.5 Redressing Inequality in Access and Equity

ML also leads to a reduction in the disparities regarding the accessibility and equity of healthcare, especially among underserved populations. Cloud-based ML solutions provide remote patient monitoring and telemedicine services for bringing quality care to remote and rural regions [16]. For instance, an ML algorithm within a wearable device can measure the patient's vital signs and send that data to healthcare providers for timely interventions without needing a long-distance journey by the patient. However, models trained on a diverse dataset can enable the identification of disparities in healthcare delivery and outcomes, thereby making a difference in addressing systemic inequities between policymakers and healthcare providers. For example predictive models can identify a susceptible population for a certain disease so targeted public health interventions can be invoked.

9.2.6 Challenges and Ethical Dilemmas

While ML promises tremendous changes, it poses subsequent challenges related to the healthcare sector itself: accountability/breaches of patient data, quality of training datasets and risks of algorithmic bias. Compliance with regulations, such as the Health Insurance Portability and Accountability Act, is foundational to protecting private patient information [17]. Healthcare providers also have to be heedful of ethical considerations of ML so that algorithms are explainable, transparent and equitable.

9.3 ML AND DATA ANALYTICS IN SCHOOL MANAGEMENT

The fields of ML and data analytics are fundamentally transforming the educational landscape by facilitating increased personalization, streamlining administrative functions and elevating overall educational outcomes. Educators and educational institutions that leverage substantial datasets are able to extract valuable insights that improve pedagogical strategies, identify students at risk of underperformance, and anticipate future trends in educational requirements [12]. The subsequent section deals with the disruptive impacts of ML in education: personalized learning, predictive analytics for student success and operational efficiencies of academic institutions.

9.3.1 Custom-Focused Education and Adaptive Frameworks

ML facilitates personalized education by customizing learning experiences according to individual requirements, preferences and progress. Adaptive learning platforms employ ML algorithms to assess a student's performance and recommend customized content or activities [18]. These systems adjust levels of difficulty and pacing in real-time, making them helpful in sustaining engaged student learning at the appropriate level of challenge. For example Coursera and Khan Academy both use ML algorithms to suggest courses, quizzes and other learning resources based on individual users' usage of these resources. ML-based tools can also analyse patterns of students' problem-solving approaches, providing targeted feedback and recommendations for improvement.

Key applications include:

a. **Intelligent Tutoring Systems (ITS):** ITSs are designed to simulate individualized tutoring situations by providing personified support and feedback.
b. **Recommendation engines:** Learners get learnable resources based on the student's progression and preference through recommendation engines.
c. **Gamified Learning:** Adaptive algorithms will develop game-oriented educational frameworks that modify challenges to maintain participant engagement.

9.3.2 Student Performance Predictive Analytics

These institutions are increasingly using ML to predict and achieve better output from students. Predictive analytics involves analysing historical data in order to identify trends and specific forecasts regarding the success of the student. Predictions inform educators about proactive measures to address issues such as dropouts and declining performance.

Examples include:

a. **Early warning:** ML models use attendance, grades and engagement data to determine which students are at risk so that early interventions are implemented through mentoring or tutoring.
b. **Career Pathway Predictions:** ML algorithms analyse student skillsets and interests to recommend career paths or courses, helping students make informed decisions.
c. **Examination of Learning Behaviour:** Online observations reveal trends in study practices, which provide teachers with insights to adapt their instructional methods.

9.3.3 Improving Educator Efficiency and Decision-Making Mechanisms

Educators derive advantages from ML and data analytics by utilizing tools that streamline routine tasks and generate actionable insights, thus facilitating informed decision-making processes [19]. This technological advancement alleviates administrative burdens, permitting instructors to dedicate more time to teaching and mentoring activities.

Primary Usage:

a. **Automated Grading Systems:** Utilize NLP and ML algorithms in scoring the essays and assignments while giving accurate feedback to the students.
b. Dashboards for classroom analytics provide timely insights related to student engagement and progress, aiding educators in identifying aspects that necessitate improvement.

c. **Professional Development Recommendations:** Teacher's performance should be evaluated and proper training programs suggested.

9.3.4 Effectiveness in the Effective Operation of Educational Organizations

Training institutions use ML to operate their resources efficiently and plan strategically [20]. This often benefits schools and colleges dealing with vast datasets, as it increases operational efficiency, saves costs and improves the delivery of services.

Applications include:

a. **Enrolment Management:** Future enrolment projections will aid the proper use of resources.
b. **Facility Optimizations:** Utilizing the data on classroom usage, facilities ensure optimal space utilization.
c. **Financial Aid Distribution:** The algorithm separates scholars who are eligible for funding and scholarships.

9.3.5 Accessibility and Equity in Educational Contexts

Some inequality in education can be defeated by the use of ML to construct an accessible and inclusive learning environment. Equally, assistive technologies empowered by ML assist all students with disabilities while data analytics reveal areas of inequity in educational opportunities [5].

Examples are

a. **Speech-to-text tools:** Accommodate students who are deaf.
b. **Language translation systems:** Supporting systems for non-native language learners.
c. **Equity Analysis:** Precisely determine the equity groups that require additional focused interventions.

9.3.6 Ethical Issues and Challenges

Integrating ML with the education sector has attached itself to data privacy issues, bias in algorithm and ethical usage. In that regard, most institutions must ensure that they adhere to the data protection regulations and use transparent and fair models for ML [20].

Major issues:

a. **Data Privacy:** Student and teacher data must be safe from unauthorized access.
b. **Algorithmic Bias:** Ensuring that ML models do not just exacerbate existing inequalities.

c. Expenditure towards Implementing It: Balancing the benefits of ML against the resources required to implement it.

9.4 THE CLOUD AS AN ENABLER

Data analytics and ML merge with cloud computing that is finally revolutionizing health and education through intelligent systems' capabilities to process huge datasets and deliver actionable insights to present personalized solutions. These technologies make great contributions in healthcare, especially towards the advancement of personalized medicine where ML models learn to predict therapy outcomes based on suggestions about treatment plans given through recommendations from the cloud-stored patient data [19, 21]. They also include real-time analytics that enables an early disease diagnosis and prediction of the outbreak. Telemedicine and remote monitoring utilize cloud-based platforms for the storage and processing of data streams from wearable devices to offer personalized care uninterruptedly. Predictive analytics of health operations further optimize resource allocation and hospital management with resultant reduction in costs and improvements in efficiency. Similarly, in education, these technologies drive the need for personalized learning by analysing student performance data to tailor content and pacing to individual needs. ML models automate assessments, offering immediate feedback that lets educators concentrate on teaching strategies. Cloud-based data analytics evaluates course effectiveness and supports curriculum optimization. Some of its other advantages for distance learning with cloud-based platforms include hosting virtual classrooms and providing access to resources from anywhere in the world, thus broadening accessibility. Despite these benefits, data privacy issues, incompatibility with other healthcare systems present today, and differences in educational access thwart the rapid mainstream adoption of this service.

Both domains shall utilize these technologies to make real-time decisions and to do predictive analytics. For instance, healthcare can predict patient deterioration while education identifies at-risk students for timely intervention. The knowledge-based and innovative system of cloud platforms encourages hospitals, schools and research institutions to innovate together. Novel developments in federated learning train ML models on the local device while aggregating the insights into the cloud, thus addressing privacy concerns over sensitive domains [4, 22]. Edge computing in conjunction with cloud services accelerates processing for applications where every minute counts critical applications like patient monitoring or immediate feedback in virtual classrooms.

A concept map shown in Figure 9.1 to represent the benefits of Cloud computing and ML in education, healthcare and efficiency. Major benefits include personalization of learning experience, learning pathways, assessment automation, analytics, patient information security, real-time health monitoring, predictive diagnosis and storage scalability. Nodes with arrows point out some of the factors, such as accessibility, administrative benefits, efficient data handling and improvement in research and development.

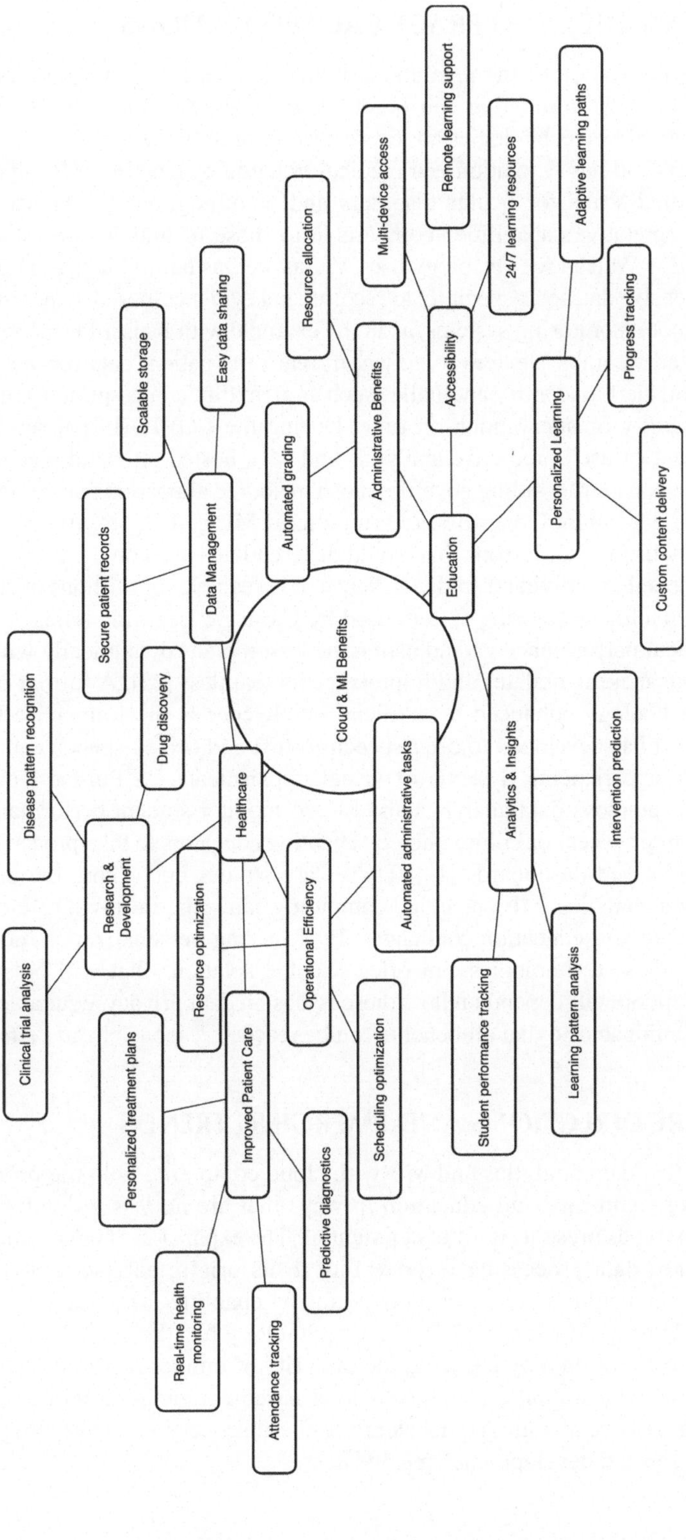

FIGURE 9.1 Advantages of cloud computing and machine learning: A conceptual diagram illustrating uses in educational settings, healthcare and operational effectiveness.

9.5 CASE STUDIES AND PRACTICAL APPLICATIONS

An additional illustration of the revolutionary applications emerging from data analytics, ML, and cloud computing can be observed in the sectors of healthcare and education, where these technologies address critical issues. In the realm of healthcare, Google's DeepMind has revolutionized medical imaging by enabling ML algorithms to analyse retinal scans for ocular disorders and mammograms for breast cancer, achieving interpretative capabilities comparable to those of human specialists [23]. Meanwhile, IBM Watson for Oncology uses ML as well as natural language processing across extensive datasets especially to recommend evidence-based, cancer-specific therapies. Remote monitoring systems, as in the example with Kaiser Permanente, use cloud-connected wearable devices to collect in real-time patient data for analysis by ML models and alert to identify anomalies such as arrhythmia or respiratory problems with the possibility of intervention on time. During the COVID-19 pandemic, platforms like BlueDot used predictive analytics and ML, hosted on cloud platforms, to forecast outbreak patterns, aiding governments in resource allocation and containment efforts [24]. In education, DreamBox Learning used ML and cloud infrastructure to provide personalized math lessons that would differentiate based on the type of learning style and speed of individual students; hence, it is scalable for millions of students. Similarly, the intelligent tutoring system used by Carnegie Learning relies on ML in analysing student performance and adjusting the lesson plans dynamically with cloud computing, thus making updates and improvements seamless [25]. A further instance of assistive technology enhanced by artificial intelligence is the Immersive Reader, which Microsoft has developed to offer speech-to-text and text-to-speech capabilities for individuals experiencing dyslexia or visual impairments. At Purdue University, Course Signals employs data analytics and ML to monitor student performance and forecast academic success or failure, thereby enabling educators to take proactive measures via cloud-based dashboards [14]. These case studies underscore the profound impact that data analytics, ML and cloud computing can bring in solving a cross-section of healthcare and education challenges. By fostering personalization, efficiency and inclusion, these technologies can offer scalable solutions that will bolster outcomes, but adoption will depend on how these issues on data privacy, equitable access and ethics are mitigated so that all benefits can be reached responsibly and effectively.

9.6 FUTURE DIRECTIONS AND EMERGING TRENDS

And it's here that data analytics and ML with cloud computing hold the promise of revolutionizing healthcare and education in ways that are no less groundbreaking. Cross-domain trends present significant potential. The expansion of edge computing, which facilitates data processing in proximity to its origin, enhances cloud computing within the health and education domains by enabling faster data processing with reduced latency. Moreover, blockchain technology has the capacity to provide enhanced security for data by ensuring the integrity of tamper-resistant patient history records and educational credentials. Cloud-based computation will unlock the speed of drug discovery with AI, accelerating the discovery of viable drug candidates so as to shorten development time and cost.

In education, ML-based adaptive learning systems will be used to evolve hyper-personalized content delivery, taking into account both the students' cognitive and emotional states. Cloud-based architectures will integrate gamification and immersive technologies – the use of AR and VR – to create a state of engagement in learning. It will advance collaborative learning tools using real-time data analytics for peer-to-peer engagement and to promote group problem-solving activities. Moreover, as global access to Internet infrastructure expands, cloud-powered educational platforms will bring high-quality education to underserved regions, narrowing the digital divide. Cross-domain trends also hold great promise. The proliferation of edge computing, which will process data closer to where it is created, supports cloud computing in the health and education sectors with quicker data processing at lower latency. Blockchain technology can offer greater security over data through tamper-proof patient history records and academic credentials. With each passing day, sustainability will fuel "green cloud computing" initiatives that further reduce the already lowered environmental impact of data storage and processing.

Ethical considerations will thus be the bedrock of the future, whereby such frameworks will be put in place to ensure fair use and unbiased use of these technologies. Innovation needs always to be balanced by privacy, fairness and transparency so that stakeholder trust can be built. With these challenges addressed, the combination of the potential of data analytics, ML and cloud computing continues to redefine healthcare and educational landscapes while producing smarter, more inclusive systems for generations yet to come.

9.7 CONCLUSION

The synergistic integration of data analytics, ML and cloud computing is reshaping the frameworks of healthcare and education by creating opportunities for enhanced efficiency, individualized approaches and greater accessibility. It is evident that a number of the most innovative technologies, when amalgamated, will demonstrate significant progress in predictive analytics aimed at early disease identification, customized treatment strategies, operational effectiveness in healthcare systems and adaptable learning environments within educational contexts. They will possess the capability to provide precise and economically viable solutions that address urgent demands for equitable access and quality, by fully utilizing extensive data resources alongside the computational capabilities offered by cloud platforms. Although these developments have been made, data privacy issues, algorithm bias and ethical problems remain critical for handling. Among the promising directions related to the abatement of these problems are federated learning, explainable AI, and edge computing, including data security, transparency and faster decision-making. Immersive technologies, blockchain and green computing drive these innovations towards wider societal benefits beyond the domains where they can be applied immediately. Deep synergies exist between data analytics, ML and cloud computing; therefore, future healthcare and education will be shaped in a profoundly new way. Trust can therefore be earned by responsible use in ennobling more inclusive, intelligent and impactful systems that shape the best possible future where innovation serves more human-centric goals.

REFERENCES

[1] Gupta, Urvashi, and Rohit Sharma. 2023. "A Study of Cloud Based Solution for Data Analytics in Healthcare." https://doi.org/10.1109/ISCON57294.2023.10112083.

[2] Atikom, Srivallop. 2024. "A Comparative Analysis of Cloud-Based Healthcare Platforms through Effective Machine Learning Approaches." *Journal of Information Technology and Digital World*. https://doi.org/10.36548/jitdw.2024.3.002.

[3] Adams, J., Rafal Cymerys, Karol Szuster, Daniel Hekman, Zoryana Salo, Rutvik Solanki, Muhammad Mamdani, Alistair E. W. Johnson, Katarzyna Ryniak, Tom Pollard, David Rotenberg, and Benjamin Haibe-Kains. 2024. "Health Data Nexus: An Open Data Platform for AI Research and Education in Medicine." https://doi.org/10.1101/2024.08.23.24312060.

[4] Huang, Rui, and Shucheng Fang. 2024. "Machine Learning and Big Data Analytics in the Cloud Environment." *International Journal of Cloud Computing and Database Management*. https://doi.org/10.33545/27075907.2024.v5.i1a.53.

[5] Jawaharbabu, Jeyaraman, and Muthukrishnan Muthusubramanian. 2022. "The Synergy of Data Engineering and Cloud Computing in the Era of Machine Learning and AI." *Online*. https://doi.org/10.60087/jklst.vol1.n1.p75.

[6] Dhiyanesh, B., Makwana Rameshkumar, K. Karthick, and R. Radha. 2023. "Cloud Computing and Machine Learning for Analysis of Health Care Data Based on Neuro Fuzzy Logistic Regression." *Journal of Intelligent and Fuzzy Systems*. https://doi.org/10.3233/jifs-223280.

[7] Ang, David, Kiranmai Naineni, and Johnny C. Ho. 2023. "Healthcare Data Handling with Machine Learning Systems: A Framework." https://doi.org/10.1109/csce60160.2023.00223.

[8] Janani, S.R., R. Subramanian, S. Karthik, and C. Vimalarani. 2023. "Healthcare Monitoring Using Machine Learning Based Data Analytics." *International Journal of Computers Communications & Control*. https://doi.org/10.15837/ijccc.2023.1.4973.

[9] Sanat, Popli. 2024. "Cloud Computing, Artificial Intelligence, and Machine Learning in Healthcare: The Future of Patient Care." *International Journal for Multidisciplinary Research*. https://doi.org/10.36948/ijfmr.2024.v06i03.23841.

[10] Joy, Zihad Hasan, Arfan Uzzaman, Md Abdul Ahad, and Mahfuzur Rahman. 2024. "Integrating Machine Learning and Big Data Analytics for Real-Time Disease Detection in Smart Healthcare Systems." *Deleted Journal*. https://doi.org/10.62304/ijhm.v1i3.162.

[11] Juli, Kumari, and Ela Kumar. 2023. "A Structured Analysis to Study the Role of Machine Learning and Deep Learning in the Healthcare Sector with Big Data Analytics." *Archives of Computational Methods in Engineering*. https://doi.org/10.1007/s11831-023-09915-y.

[12] Milan, Vukicevic, Sandro Radovanovic, Miloš Milovanović, and Miroslav Minović. 2014. "Cloud Based Metalearning System for Predictive Modeling of Biomedical Data." *The Scientific World Journal*. https://doi.org/10.1155/2014/859279.

[13] Ajegbile, Mojeed Dayo, Janet Aderonke Olaboye, Chikwudi Cosmos Maha, Geneva Tamunobarafiri Igwama, and Samira Abdul. 2024. "Integrating Business Analytics in Healthcare: Enhancing Patient Outcomes Through Data-Driven Decision Making." *World Journal of Biology Pharmacy and Health Sciences*. https://doi.org/10.30574/wjbphs.2024.19.1.0436.

[14] Kaledio, Egon, and Karl Letho. 2023. "Machine Learning in Healthcare Education: Preparing the Future Workforce." https://doi.org/10.31219/osf.io/yxg42.

[15] Chukwudi, Cosmos, Maha Taiwo, Olabode Kolawole, and Samira Abdul. 2024. "Harnessing Data Analytics: A New Frontier in Predicting and Preventing

Non-Communicable Diseases in the US and Africa." *Computer Science & IT Research Journal*. https://doi.org/10.51594/csitrj.v5i6.1196.

[16] Popli, Sanat. 2024. "Cloud Computing, Artificial Intelligence, and Machine Learning in Healthcare: The Future of Patient Care." *International Journal for Multidisciplinary Research*. https://doi.org/10.36948/ijfmr.2024.v06i03.23841.

[17] Palayanoor, Seethapathy Ramapraba, Moorthy Radhika, Sokkanarayanan Sumathi, Jayavarapu Karthik, and Nachiappan Senthamilarasi. 2024. "An Efficient Healthcare System by Cloud Computing and Clustering-Based Hybrid Machine Learning Algorithm." *Indonesian Journal of Electrical Engineering and Computer Science*. https://doi.org/10.11591/ijeecs.v34.i3.pp1698-1707.

[18] Chelladurai, Fancy, Krishnaraj Nagappan, K. Ishwarya, G. Raja, and Shyamala Chandrasekaran. 2024. "Modelling of Healthcare Data Analytics Using Optimal Machine Learning Model in Big Data Environment." *Expert Systems*. https://doi.org/10.1111/exsy.13612.

[19] Deora, Mahipal Singh. 2024. "Analytics of Machine Learning in Healthcare Industries." https://doi.org/10.1007/978-981-97-1329-5_1.

[20] Joy, Zihad Hasan, Arfan Uzzaman, Md Abdul Ahad, and Mahfuzur Rahman. 2024. "Integrating Machine Learning and Big Data Analytics for Real-Time Disease Detection in Smart Healthcare Systems." *Deleted Journal*. https://doi.org/10.62304/ijhm.v1i3.162.

[21] Manivasagam, Anshu Kumar, and Mohd Murshleen. 2023. "Application of Machine Learning and Cloud Computing for Observing Health Status of Patients Remotely in Healthcare System." https://doi.org/10.1109/icaiccit60255.2023.10466171.

[22] Pragathi, Penikalapati, and Nagaraja Rao. 2020. "Healthcare Analytics by Engaging Machine Learning." https://doi.org/10.31763/SITECH.V1I1.32.

[23] Ria, Maheshwari, Kartik Moudgil, Harshal Bharatkumar Parekh, and Rupali Sawant. 2018. "A Machine Learning Based Medical Data Analytics and Visualization Research Platform." https://doi.org/10.1109/ICCTCT.2018.8550953.

[24] Nakayiza, Hellen, and Marvin Ggaliwango. 2023. "Learning Analytics for Cloud-Based Education Planning." https://doi.org/10.1109/ICOEI56765.2023.10125698.

[25] Rui, Huang, and Shucheng Fang. 2024. "Machine Learning and Big Data Analytics in the Cloud Environment." *International Journal of Cloud Computing and Database Management*. https://doi.org/10.33545/27075907.2024.v5.i1a.53.

10 Security and Privacy Issues for Data Analytics Using Machine Learning in Cloud Computing

Avita Katal

10.1 INTRODUCTION

Cloud computing has brought a significant change in the way organizations store and handle data and processes. The availability of limitless resources on demand along with the web provides organizations with the capacity to have and store a lot of information, complex calculations to be done and scale operations. Such strategic reorientation has made cloud become one of the key technology strategies for both advanced data analytics and active technological and organizational change. Users equipped with cloud-based data analytics tools can analyse very large amounts of data in real time which allows us to make decisions based on emerging trends.

Machine learning (ML) or any application for that matter seems to be built on artificial intelligence logic extends its horizons as it has the potential of transforming the data analytics landscape. ML models allow systems to acquire knowledge from data inputs, construct models, and give outputs with no high level of coding instructions. The concept of ML with cloud computing takes the possibilities of data analytics a notch higher by providing reliable frameworks, expandable architecture and already developed models which ameliorate the building and execution of advanced applications. Other emerging cloud technologies such as auto scaling, storage or serverless computing make it easier and cheaper to utilize ML-based analytics.

Nonetheless, there are inherent issues in terms of security and privacy with the mass adoption of cloud-based data analysis and ML. In cloud environments, data is usually stored and processed in multiple locations, increasing the attack surface. Important problems are multi-tenancy feature in which many users are sharing the same infrastructure which could result into the potential threats of cyber-attacks; losing control since the owners of data depend on external service providers regarding the possible provision of the infrastructure; and trust deficit as the organizations have to make sure that the providers are compliant with the policies regarding information security as well as the data privacy laws (Butt et al., 2022)

 DOI: 10.1201/9781003396772-11

It is common for individuals to use the terms privacy and security interchangeably, but that should not be the case, especially in a setting that entails cloud computing as well as data protection.

- Security is concerned with protecting information as well as systems from unauthorized access, attacks, destruction or theft, malicious or otherwise. Security is too often characterized as the ability to shield information technology systems infrastructure from failure through attacks or system weaknesses and it tends to be centred around protecting data from illegitimate use.
- Privacy, by contrast, is the prerogative that individuals or organizations have in the respect that they seek to limit how their sensitive or personal information is treated, more specifically how it is gathered, applied, and distributed. It is also important to understand that privacy encompasses the right to restrict how and where data collected is used, while data protection emphasizes the legal compliance of the processes performed on the individual's or organization's data.

Security is about protecting data from unauthorized access and attacks. Privacy is about ensuring that data is used and shared according to the data subject's consent and legal rights.

This chapter considers the fundamental confidentiality and security concerns with data analytics in a cloud computing environment. It assesses the threats that this new paradigm presents including, among other things, unauthorized access, theft of data, noncompliance with laws and regulations and unauthorized internal data breaches. The chapter also outlines the means of averting these risks such as encryption, multilevel authorizations safeguards, accountable privacy-protecting ML methods, and shared responsibility between cloud providers and customers (*Shared Responsibility Model – Amazon Web Services (AWS)*, n.d.). Tackling these issues will allow the organizations to use cloud-based data analytics and ML techniques without fear as they will retain effective security and privacy measures. This chapter, through an in-depth study, helps readers understand the challenges of securing cloud-based AI/ML data analytics and outlines the necessary steps to overcome them.

10.2 SECURITY ISSUES IN CLOUD-BASED DATA ANALYTICS

For cloud computing to be secure and reliable while maintaining sensitive data protection, the CIA Triad (Confidentiality, Integrity and Availability) is vital as it remains one of the most widely applied models in the field of information security.

- Confidentiality refers to the restriction of access to sensitive data to the people or systems that are supposed to protect such data. This becomes quite imperative in the cloud environment. It means that data can be accessed only by people, systems or processes which are permitted to do so. This is crucial in situations in which data is stored in a cloud infrastructure and several users or companies utilize it to stop information leaks or even breaches.

- Integrity primarily deals with the safeguarding of data and the degree of accuracy of data. In the context of cloud computing, reliability refers to the storage, processing, or transmission of information, which is neither interfered with nor modified, whether accidentally or intentionally.
- Availability emphasizes that authorized users should be able to reach cloud services and data at times when they need them. Even in difficult situations, such as hardware breakdowns, network assaults, or abrupt demand increases, it guarantees the highest possible uptime and the permanent operation of cloud assets.

The security aspects can be categorized as follows.

10.2.1 Infrastructure Security

Infrastructure security is core to infrastructure, which includes physical servers, virtual machines, containers, storage, networking elements, etc., in which the data analytics are being performed. The infrastructure includes physical servers or storage and virtual machines, networks and cloud components. Infrastructure security can be divided into network level, host level and application level.

10.2.1.1 Network Level

If you use public cloud services, changing security requirements will require changes to your network topology. You must address how your existing network topology interacts with your cloud provider's network topology. There are four significant risk factors in this use case:

- Ensuring the confidentiality and integrity of your organization's data-in-transit to and from your public cloud provider.
- Ensuring proper access control (authentication, authorization and auditing) to whatever resources you are using at your public cloud provider: An enterprise that uses a public cloud risks a considerable increase in the risk to its data since part or all the resources are accessible to the Internet. Even after the event, it's likely impossible to audit how your cloud provider's network is operating, much alone perform any real-time monitoring, as on your own network. Access to pertinent network-level logs and data will be reduced, and the capacity to carry out in-depth investigations and collect forensic material will be constrained. Reused (reassigned) IP addresses are one illustration of the issues related to this second risk element.
- Ensuring the availability of the Internet-facing resources in a public cloud that are being used by your organization or have been assigned to your organization by your public cloud providers: Because more data or more employees of a company increasingly rely on externally hosted devices to guarantee the availability of cloud-provided services, there is a greater need for network security. An excellent illustration of this third risk aspect is provided by Border Gateway Protocol (BGP), prefix hijacking (also known as the fabrication of Network Layer Reachability Information) and Domain Name System (DNS) assaults.

- Replacing the established model of network zones and tiers with domains: The previous architectural framework, where various network zones and tiers were practiced ensured deep isolation separating development from production systems, or, web presentation from the database, have been radically transformed particularly on public IaaS and PaaS clouds. The traditional model used segregation of cross-tier communication between databases and network systems to barge tier access and in effect increased security. However, in public clouds, that has been replaced with groups, security domains or virtual centres which are safe but inefficient. As an example, AWS creates security groups whereby virtual firewalls are used to filter out traffic from certain IP addresses according to packet types and designated ports. In the same vein, names of domains are utilized in other cloud platforms like Google App Engine for such purposes, but they do not ensure complete separation of systems. In the past, the same technologies were implemented in production systems with unquestionable logical separation on both the network and the host systems, where development and production were completely different, but with cloud computing, this physical separation is achieved mostly on the hosts with hypervisors, allowing more than one domain on a single physical server. This has a negative impact on security since separation is purely logical, which is weaker than zone separation.

10.2.1.2 Host Level

As nearly all of today's IaaS service offerings are implemented through host-based virtualization, host protection in IaaS can be classified as follows:

- Security of the hypervisor or the virtualization software
- Protection of the guest OS or individual virtualized servers

Protection of the guest OS or individual virtualized servers refers to the virtual instance of an operating system, such as different versions of Linux, Microsoft and Solaris, that is supplied on top of the virtualization layer/hypervisor to the customer for doing their tasks.

The software layer that allows users to build and remove virtual instances is placed on top of bare metal. This software is called Hypervisor or Virtual Machine Monitor (VMM). Virtualization at the host level can be achieved using any of the virtualization models, such as hardware-based virtualization (Xen, VMware, Microsoft Hyper-V), paravirtualization or OS-level virtualization (Solaris containers, BSD jails, Linux-VServer). Protecting this software layer between the virtual servers and the hardware is crucial.

10.2.1.3 Application Level

Although many firms have not completely addressed it, application security is an essential part of an enterprise's overall security policy. Current security procedures must be changed for apps intended for cloud platform deployment. Applications range from straightforward single-user programs to intricate multi-user systems, such as e-commerce platforms. Organizations frequently use web applications like wikis, content management systems and bespoke solutions (written using frameworks like PHP, .NET, J2EE, Ruby on Rails and Python). In the past, criminals focused on different attack routes, but as online vulnerabilities like cross-site scripting (XSS) have become more prevalent, attackers are increasingly making use of web programming errors to make money. Since browsers (like Firefox, Internet Explorer and Safari) are now used to access web applications, security programs

10.2.2 Operating System Security

Among all factors involved in overall system security in cloud setups, perhaps the most critical factor is how secure the operating system (OS) images used on virtual servers are. Each virtual machine (VM) images services or applications to be used in a virtualized environment using OS images as the starting point. To mitigate the risks that these images may pose to virtual servers that they power, such images need to be adequately secured.

OS security is clearly about OS images also because their regular and periodic update and patching to eliminate known vulnerabilities is important. Attackers may get into the system using unpatched or outdated OS images. The OS image should also be hardened as a part of the security process by employing measures such as disabling unnecessary services, adhering to the least privilege principle, and ensuring that irrelevant applications are not installed.

Physical security of OS images, number one in this list, is also concerned with their transport and storage. This means that while conducting installation or relocating OS images to other servers or into cloud environments, the OS images must be encrypted and secure transmission must be used for transferring the images to storage.

OS image security assists in maintaining the health of virtual machines as well as making sure the whole cloud framework is protected against threats such as viruses, unwarranted intrusions, or even incorrect settings. By ensuring the safety of the OS images, organizations can mitigate risks and maintain a secure and trustworthy cloud environment.

10.2.3 Data Security

Data security in the cloud serves to keep the data safe from unauthorized access, deletion or alteration – although it is resting, being transferred, or being worked on. But given that cloud data and its resources are distributed across several sites, a more thorough approach which covers issues like encryption, access management, integrity of the data and compliance controls is necessary to enhance data security.

10.2.3.1 Data at Rest

Data at rest are data that is not in current use and that is sitting idle in databases, data warehouses or file systems such as Amazon S3, Amazon RDS, or Amazon glacier. The following techniques can be used to protect this data:

- **Encryption of Data:** It is necessary for data to be encrypted while in the storage to ensure that unauthorized parties do not gain access. There are various storage services available on cloud platforms which include SSE-S3

(Server-Side Encryption For S3) and SSE-KMS (Key Management Service) on AWS which ensure that data is encrypted when at the store.

- **Access Control:** There are services such as IAM (Identity and Access Management) with strict access control mechanisms in place, so only authorized users or systems can access the data that is stored.
- **Redundancy:** Data that is at rest state should be stored in backup and enclave at least two different availability zones for potential high availability and Fault Tolerance.

10.2.3.2 Data in Transit

Any data being transferred between systems, such as between services and end users or inside your workload, is referred to as data in transit. For the security and integrity of the data in your workflow to be maintained, data protection in transit is essential.

Methods to Encrypt Data

i **SSL/TLS:** When a client and a server send information, the secure sockets layer (SSL) as well as its successor, the transportation layer security (TLS) encrypts the data to prevent any form of eavesdropping.

ii **VPNs:** Virtual private networks establish an encrypted channel between an on-premises infrastructure and the cloud, thereby protecting proprietary information.

iii **End-to-End Encryption:** Through this method, data can only be accessed at its intended endpoint and not elsewhere, as it is encrypted at the source and can only be decrypted at the end point.

Secure Communication Channels

i **HTTPS:** Hypertext Transfer Protocol Secure allows cloud applications to access Internet with encrypted connections.

ii **SSH:** The use of Secure Shell allows secure data transfer and remote connections to the cloud systems.

iii **IPSec Tunnels:** Internet Protocol Security secures the communication on a direct link mode for data transfer.

Network Isolation

i **Virtual Private Clouds:** VPCs grant distinct network domains that enhance security in the exchange of information across the cloud resources inside the VPC.

ii **Segmentation:** Network policies and Routing policies at the subnet level assist in restricting the traffic to approved routes thereby ensuring that information travels only over secured links.

Access Control Mechanisms

i **Identity and Access Management (IAM) Policies:** Management of Identity and Access, in a secure way, restricts system access to only the permitted users and applications.

ii **Role-Based Access Control (RBAC):** Access to databases and other sensitive tasks is done on the basis of that user's role and responsibilities in the organization, further minimizing the chances of unauthorized data exposure.
iii **Multi-Factor Authentication (MFA):** Single and most important factor providing security for user credentials is increased.

Monitoring and Logging

i **Traffic Monitoring:** AWS VPC Flow Logs and Azure Monitor logs network traffic for guidance analysis and threat identification.
ii **Intrusion Detection Systems (IDS):** Monitor for malicious activities during data transmission.
iii **Event Logging:** Tools such as AWS CloudTrail permit the documentation of who accessed or modified information or data, thus creating accountability.

Verification of Integrity

i **Checksums and Hashing:** During data transmission, algorithms such as SHA-256 help to ensure that gateways do not alter data which could result in loss of integrity.
ii **Digital Signatures:** Applied to secure communication by identifying the sender and verifying the physical message sent.

Policies about Secure DNS

i **DNSSEC:** Domain Name System Security Extensions aims to eliminate the risks associated with DNS spoofing and ensure safe transmission of domain names.
ii **Private DNS Zones:** Restrict the resolution of domains to a secure cloud space, thus safeguarding them from external threats to some degree.

Secure API Communications

i **API and Application security, Access control and Authentication:** OAuth and OpenID Connect protocols play critical roles in securing API access.
ii **Signed Requests:** Requests to the API are signed for their proof of origin with the help of certain cryptographic means.
iii **Dedicated Connectivity Options:** Secure, private access to large enterprise systems and cloud services is made possible through AWS Direct Connect, Azure ExpressRoute, or Google Cloud Interconnect, without having to pass through the public Internet.

10.2.3.3 Processing Data, Multi-Tenancy

Cloud providers specialize in offering their infrastructure as a service in the form of cloud platforms. Such platforms can be set up as multi-tenant environments in which multiple users will share resources. This fast-changing and decentralized infrastructure makes large-scale-load management not only effective but also quick to scale in response to demand. But the problem of multi-tenancy is ensuring that specific data and resources such as "compliance with GDPR and HIPAA" would not be shared. Security Mechanisms such as secure memory – isolation, access controls and confidential computing protect data while it's being processed. Auditing combined with anonymization and in-use encryption techniques not only improves security but also increases accountability. Data and resources allocated on a logical basis to each specific tenant allow proper data processing without compromising applicable privacy requirements or reducing the efficiency of processing.

Some of the techniques used include:

- **Virtualization:** As the name suggests, the process of virtualization consists of creating multiple virtual machines on a physical server thereby allocating each VM to a different tenant. The process looks after creating separate environments for data processing which in turn means that a tenant's environment cannot be disturbed by the neighbouring tenant.
- **Containerization:** Containerization consists of combining applications and their associated components into lightweight units called containers, in which application processes perform isolated functions but share a single OS kernel. This technique strengthens security by partitioning each tenant's processes.
- **Resource Quotas and Limits:** By incorporating monitoring techniques, resources such as CPU, memory or storage can be monitored by the administrators and their quotas and limits adjusted, accordingly allowing each organization using the cloud service to fairly allocate these resources without interference from other organizations
- **Network Isolation:** During data transfer, one of the most vital issues of inter-tenant communication must be indiscernible which means ensuring high data and traffic security, this can be achieved by a well-devised plan that includes implementing techniques of network segmentation and isolation.
- **Role-Based Access Control (RBAC):** RBAC segregates any access privileges to specific resources or services of the system according to a specific user within the organization thereby reducing the level of exposure of the sensitive resource.
- **Data Encryption:** Encryption prevents the data from being read by unauthorized individuals or mechanisms due to the lack of relevant key, irrespective of whether the data is being used or in a dormant state.

These methods enable secure, efficient and equitable access and use of data in multi-tenant cloud environments, keeping the tenants' space and any sensitive information secure.

10.2.3.4 Data Lineage

Data lineage is the process of tracking and documenting the movement of data through several processing stages in a cloud-based system or service. Data lineage tries to show the whole data flow from start to finish and displays the data life cycle.

Data lineage is the process of understanding, recording and visualizing data as it flows from data sources to data consumers. This includes the approach, the changes performed and the justifications for each change the data underwent during the process. To understand how raw data is imported, altered and finally used to generate reports on a cloud-based data analytics platform, for example data lineage may be crucial. By providing insights into the procedures and changes made to the data, this documentation aids in data assurance, auditing and troubleshooting.

Businesses may use data lineage to:

- Track errors in data processing.
- Adjust processes to be less risky.
- Execute system migrations with confidence.
- Integrate data discovery with a deep comprehension of metadata to create a data mapping framework.

Various techniques to achieve data lineage in cloud security entails being able to track the flow of data throughout its lifecycle. In addition, data processing, data origins and transformations can all be geo-located through centralized metadata management and data cataloguing thereby achieving substantial transparency. On the other hand, data events are recorded by logging and auditing while historic records of dataset and workflow changes are upheld through version control. Apart from the aforementioned techniques, data lineage and workflow management techniques allow for the design of computational pipelines and graphs for data transformation, respectively. Data movement between components is documented by API and integration logs, and ensures data quality. Tracking these data-processing processes and visually handling lineage is made easier through data profiling checks at different stages. Together, all these strategies are boosting traceability, governance and enforcing data security in cloud systems.

By leveraging data lineage, users can be confident that their data has been effectively translated, loaded to the correct location, and is coming from a trustworthy source. Data lineage becomes essential when strategic decisions require precise information. Data verification is almost impossible, or at the very least exceedingly costly and time-consuming, when data processes are not accurately tracked. Data lineage concentrates on verifying the accuracy and consistency of data by allowing users to search both upstream and downstream, from source to destination. This enables users to identify and correct anomalies.

10.2.3.5 Data Provenance

In a cloud-based system, data provenance aims to document and maintain information about the origin and history of data. Data provenance, for instance, might track the sources of experimental data, the methods used for analysis, and any modifications made during the study in a cloud-based scientific research endeavour. This information is useful for ensuring repeatability, meeting regulatory criteria and validating results.

Despite their varied applications, data provenance and data lineage are closely related ideas. Data lineage tracks how an individual or collections of data move through various systems, processes and applications. It focuses on data flows and changes. Data provenance is the record of metadata from the original source of the data that provides historical context and legitimacy. While data lineage helps with data pipeline efficiency and debugging, data provenance helps with data validation and auditing. Data provenance employs a number of techniques to improve data dependability. It comprises tracking data from its creation via several transformations to the present, meticulously documenting the lifecycle of every data asset. Data dependencies offer a comprehensive view of the provenance of the data and illustrate how changes to one component of the data pipeline may impact other components. Additionally, they highlight the connections among datasets, transformations and procedures. Dependencies help pinpoint the exact technique, writer, or data collection that led to a discrepancy in the data.

- Algorithms are extensively used in this process to automatically capture and document data flow across many systems, reducing errors and eliminating human work. They vouch for accuracy and consistency by standardizing data processing and enabling real-time tracking of data transformations.
- The use of APIs enables seamless communication and integration across different tools, systems and data sources. By making it easier to automatically collect, share and update provenance data across several platforms, they enhance the accuracy and completeness of provenance records.

10.2.3.6 Data Remanence

This is the depiction of data that may still exist even after attempts to delete or destroy it have been made. This is particularly crucial in shared or virtualized scenarios. "Data remanence" refers to the ability of a computer's memory to hold data for longer than intended. This typically occurs when you attempt to remove a file since the operating system only removes the reference to the data, not the data itself. Even though it makes some forensic procedures simpler, this poses a problem for companies that save sensitive data. This usually makes the information available to dishonest people who wish to use it improperly. Considering that devices with insufficient security endanger both you and your business. Unintentionally sharing user data can have detrimental effects, including a decline in trust and liability issues. Fortunately, businesses may use a range of secure data disposal solutions to get around data remanence. Consider a virtual machine (VM) in a cloud environment as an example. Even after the virtual machine (VM) has been stopped or the data has been deleted, it may still be present in the underlying infrastructure. Cloud providers use secure data erasure processes to lessen the risk of data remanence, ensuring that private information is safely erased when it is no longer needed. These techniques consist of:

- **Overwriting:** This technique sanitizes data by substituting random ones and zeroes for stored data, making any information that remains useless. Because overwriting is non-intrusive, devices can be reused or sold. If verified in a certified wiping and quality control method, overwriting is a less secure option since, if done improperly, there is still a chance that some data may be missed.

- **Using encryption:** Unauthorized users find it more difficult to access a physical storage device when a digital encoding method known as encryption is used. One of the best qualities of encryption is that it is reasonably priced and allows companies to reuse equipment with no security risk. However, the primary disadvantage of encryption is that it does not completely remove data from the device. If a cybercriminal were to figure out the security key for the encryption, they would have full access to the data. Furthermore, encryption removes the possibility of reuse because it blocks access, even to trustworthy vendors who might skilfully remove any remaining data and reset the device for new users.
- **Shredding:** For those who wish to be certain that their data is erased forever, industrial shredding is an alternative. When you shred your hard drive, you may rest easy knowing that all of the data on the storage device is gone forever, making all attempts at recovery pointless. While it may be tempting to shred your own data, it is recommended to choose a professional agency that can oversee the entire process and guarantee that all of your data is destroyed.

10.2.4 Application Security

The phrase "application security" describes security measures that are put in place at the application level with the intention of preventing the theft or hijacking of data or code inside the app. In addition to systems and methods to safeguard apps once they are deployed, it encompasses security considerations that arise during the design and development of applications. Routers that prevent people from viewing a computer's IP address from the Internet, software that detects or reduces security flaws, and protocols are examples of hardware application security. Another popular source of application security measures is software; protocols and other application security routines are examples of processes.

Application security is the process of developing, incorporating and testing security features into applications to protect against security vulnerabilities and threats, such as unauthorized access and modification. Cloud app security, or cloud application security, is a collection of policies, practices and controls that enable enterprises to protect data and applications in shared cloud environments.

Applications nowadays are more vulnerable to security lapses and assaults since they are often distributed over several networks and linked to the cloud. Application security is therefore essential. Ensuring application security in addition to network security is becoming more and more important. This can be explained, in part, by the fact that hacker attacks now target programs more frequently than they used to. By locating application-level vulnerabilities, application security testing can assist in thwarting these assaults. Examples of several types of application security features include authorization, encryption, logging, authentication and application security testing. Developers may build applications to reduce security vulnerabilities.

The process by which programmers add guidelines to an application to ensure that only authorized users may access it is known as authentication.

- **Authentication:** Authentication processes ensure that a user is who they say they are. Making an application login process that requires the user to provide their username and password is one approach to do this. Multi-factor authentication requires many forms of authentication, which might include things you possess (a mobile device), know (a password), and are (a fingerprint or facial recognition).
- **Authorization:** After successfully completing the authentication process, a user may be given authorization to access and use the program. The system can check if a user is allowed to access the software by comparing the user's identity with a list of authorized users. Authentication must take place before permission for the program to match the approved user list with just confirmed user credentials.
- **Encryption:** After a user has been granted permission to use the software, further security measures can stop sensitive data from being accessed or even used by a cybercriminal. Cloud-based apps can encrypt traffic to secure sensitive data while it is being sent between the cloud and the end user.
- **Logging:** Logging can help identify who accessed the data and how in the case of an application security breach. A time-stamped record of the features that users have utilized and when they were accessible is provided by application log files.
- **Testing for application security:** Ensuring that all these security mechanisms are functioning as intended requires testing for application security.

The application security is divided mainly into these three categories:

- **Web Application Security:** Ensuring the safety of web applications, websites or web apps as well as APIs from cyberattacks is the focal point of web application security. It seeks to ensure that there is no data breach, no espionage and no unethical competition. Since the web is universal, web applications and APIs have many attack vectors. The most prominent vulnerabilities encompass broken access control, cryptographic issue, injection vulnerabilities, insecure design, security misconfiguration, legacy components, broken authentication, broken integrity, poor logging supervision and server-side request forgery. Typically, these vulnerabilities are contained in the OWASP Top Ten which makes recommendations on how to prevent common security shortcomings in web applications.
- **Application Programming Interface (API) Security:** The practice of API security aims at protecting Application Programming Interfaces which are central to the backend architecture of web and mobile applications. APIs transport confidential information and are therefore susceptible to broken object-level authorization, broken authentication and excessive resource availability. It is important to integrate several measures when implementing API security such as proper authentication levels, limitation of input data, rate limiting of requests and encryption of data during transmission and while stored. Furthermore, it is important to maintain a constant watch

of the activities of the APIs and map any suspicious activities which pose the risk of data leakage or other illicit actions. Also, with the accelerated adoption of APIs into modern business processes, dedicated tools appear to scan and rectify the flaws present in the APIs.

- **Cloud Native Application Security:** The term 'cloud-native security' refers to set of security measures and tools that are particularly targeted at applications that are designed and used in cloud, in other words it is an approach to security that requires a comprehensive thinking on the application security by moving away from traditional security paradigm that requires the use of network-based techniques. Rather a focus is on workload security, identity Access Management (IAM), container security, continuous monitoring and endless response.

Using a combination of serverless framework, virtual machines and containers to design microservices applications is what we call cloud-native apps. Due to the nature of microservices architecture, cloud-native apps are composed of multiple interconnecting components which are sometimes replaced by new ones. Hence the security of such applications is a complex problem. As a result, it is difficult to track every part of a Cloud Native system, let alone the entire system itself.

A declarative configuration used for configuring environments in cloud native apps is known as an Infrastructure as code (IaC) this enables the creation of an application and its environment from a single repository. The application and the environment are configured by the application developers and so security measures must be implemented at both levels. Dedicated cloud native security tools are needed, able to instrument containers, container clusters and serverless features, alert developers to security flaws, and give them quick feedback loops.

Security should be carefully incorporated into the design principles of cloud-native applications. These considerations encompass securing containers (securing container images and runtimes), securing the network (segmentation and encryption), securing identity and access (service identities and Role-Based Access Controls [RBAC]; Attribute-Based Access Controls [ABAC], etc.), compliance and governance (Tabrizchi & Rafsanjani, 2020), securing and monitoring, and responding to incidents.

Recently, several cloud-native security approaches have surfaced, each with varying levels of efficiency. Among them are

- **Shared Responsibility:** In this approach, clients assume the responsibility of safeguarding the data, applications and access to the cloud while cloud providers take care of the hardware. This concept underlies every other modern cloud-native security approach. This approach will be discussed in detail in the coming sections.
- **Multi-cloud and serverless security:** A typical cloud service comprises seven layers; the premises, network, hardware, OS, Middleware, application and the user. Close loop security is deployed on all levels for detection and prevention of leakages of security gaps. This approach encompasses numerous software add-ons including but not limited to cloud-aware firewalls and

end-to-end encryption methods. However, managing these numerous tools could be a challenge.

- **Cloud-agnostic security systems:** These are apparently the universal best approach for dealing with security requirements of cloud native systems. They can optimize alerting and tools of the beleaguered security practitioners, mitigate cloud vendor lock-in and allow cross ecosystem views.

10.3 PRIVACY ISSUES IN CLOUD-BASED DATA ANALYTICS

In contemporary society, it has become vital to have cloud data storage systems. The concept of cloud-based data analytics refers to the processing and analysis of such large datasets residing in the cloud. This solution, however, comes with privacy issues including the nature of cloud environments and the types of data being processed. These concerns are related to data privacy, data control, data abuse and legal compliance. Below are key privacy issues in cloud-based data analytics:

- **Data Confidentiality:** The kind of data that is stored and processed in remote servers is sensitive in nature which means that it is accessible by unauthorized individuals. If encryption and access control features are not implemented, then it is highly probable that intruders will take advantage of existing loopholes and weaknesses leading to a leak of data. Cloud providers must strive to secure sensitive data, be it email addresses or any company's IP, throughout their lifespan (Choudhary et al., 2023). As an example, breaches of healthcare data could expose sensitive patient information, violating privacy regulations like HIPAA.
- **Data Location and Legal Framework:** Information can be held in several jurisdictions, since cloud providers are able to store data in several different countries or regions. Within different regions, data protection and privacy laws differ, such as the General Data Protection Regulation (GDPR) for the EU, and the California Consumer Privacy Act (CCPA) for the state of California. For instance, a US-based cloud provider may use a data centre located in the EU to host European customer data which, however, does present privacy challenges of meeting US and EU legal requirements.
- **Data Ownership and Control:** Cloud environments have shifted some aspects of data sovereignty norms, with individual users losing some control over their data. The cloud service provider is responsible for the infrastructure and data hosting which may be in different places around the globe. Even so, issues of data possession, access and procedures to reclaim or purge users' information bubble to the surface (Ali et al., 2024). For instance, a user might upload data onto a cloud provider's platform only to forget that it is impossible to offload the data from the server which the provider leased.
- **Data Anonymization and De-identification:** To maintain one's privacy, anonymization or de-identification of data is a common practice. Nevertheless, as the use of advanced methods of analysis has grown, there is a threat that the anonymized data could be subject to re-identification, for example

where there is a set of combined anonymized customer information with outside data or information, such individuals could be pinpointed against privacy protection.

- **Security of Cloud Service Providers:** Security of data offered by cloud providers is a security mechanism which is significant for upholding the secrecy of the data. Similarly, lack of security on the part of the provider may result in data exposure. For example in cases where the level of a cloud provider's database is protectively low, the database can be breached thereby exposing important details concerning customers, for example their credit card numbers.
- **Compliance and Regulatory Requirements:** For cloud-based data analytics confidentiality principles including, but not limited to, the GDPR and HIPAA must be adhered to. Non-compliance with these regulations incurs penalties and reputational damage. For instance, a cloud analytics provider in the healthcare industry must abide by HIPAA requirements when utilizing cloud analytics on patient data to avoid incurring costly penalties.
- **Employee Access and Insider Threats:** Beginning at the top, one of the most crucial components to be understood and managed is what is referred to as "Insider Threats" to privacy, which includes employees from both the cloud provider and the client organization. Despite Take Elephants' efforts to protect user data according to their privacy policy, there is always a chance of abuse of this trust by the employees of a service provider that has access to data and assets. For instance, an employee with the right clearance might abscond with data they ought not to have access to or leak that backend development information, hence jeopardizing the protection of all users' data.
- **Data Lifecycle Management:** Failure to have cloud backup and organize data in such a way that, once captured, it is easy to transfer throughout the content supply chain is another cloud challenge relating to management, data needs to be managed from the time it is collected all the way through its storing, processing and even its disposal. This appears to be a common issue as companies might leave unintentional exposure, especially when data has outlived its purpose, where, for instance, they say, a business fails to wipe off obsolete pieces of information, only for such events to prompt accidental sharing or leaking of said data.
- **Transparency and User Consent:** As already mentioned with regard to privacy issue, lack of transparency with respect to data practices can do just the opposite. There should be optimal disclosure to the users about the amount and the extent of data collected, how it is going to be used and who will be privy of that. For instance, a cloud provider collects personal information in the belief that it would be sufficient for disclosing the data sharing policy. Otherwise, there is a good chance of breaching users' trust and privacy legislation.

An approach that has not been put into practice yet is to notify users how their data is to be used. However, there is a potential problem with sharing user data; it could violate trust and privacy regulations if users are not properly informed regarding data collection procedures and terms. To counter these apparent privacy concerns, institutions may undertake the following strategies:

- **Encryption:** Ensure strong encryption methods for information data during transmission and storage.
- **Regulatory Compliance:** Deployment of compliance frameworks and audit mechanisms for adherence to privacy standards such as GDPR, CCPA, HIPAA, etc.
- **Anonymization Techniques:** Incorporate the methodologies of anonymization and de-identification of the personal identifiers while retaining its analytical value.
- **File Ownership Policies:** Develop comprehensive file ownership and access policies that will allow control over the files to the users.
- **Privacy-Enhancing Technologies:** Employ technologies that allow a data object to be encrypted even when it's being used. An example of this is homomorphic encryption.
- **Regular Auditing:** Check and evaluate data access regularly to avoid breach by- insiders and outsiders.

10.4 BEST PRACTICES FOR SECURING DATA ANALYTICS PIPELINES – AWS

Customers and AWS share responsibility for security. This is referred to as cloud security under the shared responsibility model:

- **Security of the cloud:** AWS oversees safeguarding the AWS Cloud's infrastructure, which powers AWS services. Additionally, AWS offers services that customers may utilize safely. As part of the AWS Compliance Programs, third-party auditors evaluate and confirm their security on a regular basis.
- **Security in the cloud:** The AWS service being used by the customer determines their obligation. Other considerations that fall under the customer's purview include the confidentiality of their data, the needs of their business and any legal and regulatory obligations.

This separation of duties may lead to misunderstandings and security flaws. Misunderstanding these duties might lead to negligence, incorrect setup, or disregard for crucial security precautions. Furthermore, Employing the shared responsibility paradigm requires that enterprises communicate, be clear, and have a common commitment to robust security procedures (Ahmadi, 2024). Figure 10.1 shows the shared responsibility model for different cloud service models like IaaS, PaaS, SaaS and FaaS. In an on-premises setup, the customer is fully responsible for all aspects, including data security, applications, networking, host infrastructure and physical security. With IaaS (Infrastructure as a Service), the cloud provider takes over physical security and host infrastructure, while the customer manages everything else. In

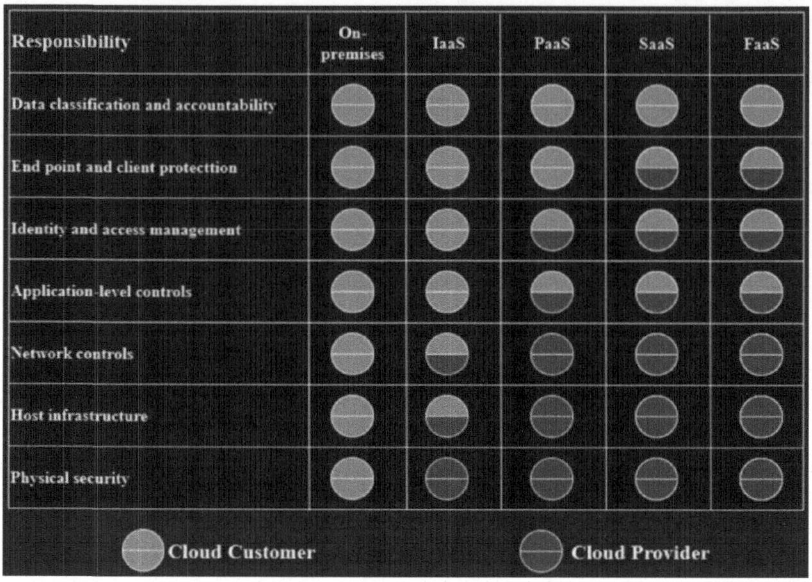

FIGURE 10.1 Shared responsibility model for different cloud service models Infrastructure as a Service (IaaS), Platform as a Service (PaaS), Software as a Service (SaaS) and Function as a Service (FaaS).

PaaS (Platform as a Service), the provider also handles network controls and application infrastructure, leaving data and application security to the customer. For SaaS (Software as a Service), the provider assumes most responsibilities, except for data classification and identity/access management, which are managed by the customer. Finally, in FaaS (Function as a Service), the provider takes on nearly all responsibilities, requiring minimal involvement from the customer. This progression demonstrates how the burden of management shifts from the customer to the provider as we move from on-premises to FaaS models, enabling customers to focus more on their core applications and less on infrastructure.

10.4.1 Data Protection

AWS suggests that customers should avoid sharing the AWS account root access credentials. Instead, they should follow the principle of least privileged and should create separate accounts as Identity and Access Management (IAM) (*Access Management- AWS Identity and Access Management (IAM) – AWS*, n.d.) users with policies attached through AWS services like AWS IAM Identity Centre or AWS IAM. AWS recommends the following restrictions on your data or application:

- Split AWS account into several parts and enable multi-factor authentication (MFA) for every user.
- Use SSL/TLS to communicate with AWS resources
- Log the API calls or user events using AWS Cloudtrail.

- Remain compliant with applicable sections in relation to the use of AWS services, always alongside the entire set of information security controls offered as a matter of course with all AWS services.
- Leverage enhanced managed security services such as Amazon Macie, where it will assist to identify and protect sensitive info that is kept in Amazon S3.
- If you are using AWS via the command line interface or programmatic interface and need to connect using an FIPS 140–2 validated cryptographic module, seek out an FIPS endpoint.
- Supported AWS Data Pipeline includes IMDSv2 Enabled for Amazon EMR and Amazon EC2 resources.

10.4.2 Identity and Access Management

People within an organization can jointly create and manage the available pipelines by granting the organization access to the pipelines. However, for instance, this might be required:

- Identify what users can use the certain specific pipelines.
- Avoid having a modification on the production pipeline engage inadvertently.
- Share a pipeline with an auditor only on read mode and not editing.

AWS Data Pipeline works in tandem with AWS Identity and Access Management (IAM) and has numerous advantages:

- Create users and groups in your AWS account.
- Share resources available in your AWS account with ease to the users within it.
- Each user is given his/her own security credentials.
- Define a user's access to services and resources
- Consolidate billing for all users in your AWS Account

10.4.3 Logging and Monitoring

AWS CloudTrail, a service that keeps track of the activities made by a user, role, or AWS service within AWS Data Pipeline, relates to AWS Data Pipeline. All AWS Data Pipeline API calls are recorded by CloudTrail as events. Code calls to the AWS Data Pipeline API operations and calls from the AWS Data Pipeline UI are among the calls that were recorded. Customers may enable continuous delivery of CloudTrail events, including those for AWS Data Pipeline, to an Amazon S3 bucket by creating a trail.

10.4.4 Configuration and Vulnerability Analysis

In AWS, clients share responsibility for configuration and IT controls.

10.4.5 Incident Response

AWS oversees handling incident responses for AWS Data Pipeline. Incident response is governed by a formal, published policy and procedure at AWS. The AWS Service

Health Dashboard displays AWS operational concerns that have a wide-ranging effect. Through the Personal Health Dashboard, operational difficulties are also posted to individual accounts.

10.4.6 Data Pipeline's Resilience

AWS regions and availability zones serve as the foundation for the AWS global infrastructure. Multiple geographically distinct and isolated availability zones are offered by AWS Regions, which are linked by highly redundant, high-throughput and low-latency networking. With availability zones, it's possible to design and operate applications and databases that automatically fail over between zones without interruption. Availability Zones are more highly available, fault tolerant and scalable than traditional single or multiple data centre infrastructures.

10.4.7 Security of the Data Pipeline Infrastructure

AWS Data Pipeline may be accessed via the network using AWS's published API calls. Transport Layer Security (TLS) 1.0 or later must be supported by clients. TLS 1.2 or later is what they recommend. Additionally, clients need to support cipher suites with perfect forward secrecy (PFS), including Elliptic Curve Ephemeral Diffie-Hellman (ECDHE) and Ephemeral Diffie-Hellman (DHE). These modes are supported by most contemporary platforms, including Java 7 and beyond. Requests also need to be signed using a secret access key linked to an IAM principal and an access key ID. Alternatively, you can create temporary security credentials to sign requests using the AWS Security Token Service (AWS STS).

Many useful measures are recommended to ensure maximum security in data analytics pipelines in organizations. This includes employing strong encryption techniques that protect the data both in storage and during transmission, that is, when it is 'in motion'. In order to prevent the risk of exposing sensitive data, IT security with least access rights, MFA and role-based access are mandatory. PII should not be exposed during such analysis, thus techniques like data masking and anonymization may be utilized to protect individual privacy. In order to avoid data leakage, pipelines should have operational features that secure the data in an encrypted storage and secure zones. As part of regular checks, tests designed to uncover weaknesses such as vulnerability assessments, audit logs and active monitoring are essential. To safeguard information from outside entities, automated validation and tests that seek out and rectify inconsistencies must be employed. In addition, since many attacks focus on APIs and microservices, it is necessary to protect them with proper authentication and authorization mechanisms. Emphasizing container security also implies using means of securing containerized platforms and strategizing around its deployment safely. If there is a failure, then backup and disaster recovery must be alleviated to improve the survival of the company. To mitigate potential legal risks, compliance with global standards including the CCPA, GDPR as well as HIPAA is mandatory. Using behavioural analytics and advanced threat detection systems (IDS/IPS) also helps in the detection of abnormal behaviours such as insider threats or illegitimate accesses. Using cloud-specific security configurations such as VPCs, private subnets and security groups for cloud-based pipelines improve the infrastructure's security. Together, these safeguards guarantee that data analytics pipelines continue to be safe, legal and robust against internal and external threats.

10.5 SECURITY OF AI/ML PIPELINES

Most businesses say that they are early adopters of ML, while some of enterprises are assessing the usage of ML. But this quick uptake has revealed a hidden danger: security flaws in ML pipelines. For security teams, these intricate, multi-step procedures that absorb, develop and train ML models frequently turn into blind spots. This gives cybercriminals a new avenue of attack, allowing them to take advantage of pipeline flaws to obtain private information without authorization, alter outputs, or stop whole processes. Wide-ranging repercussions may result, including monetary losses, harm to one's image and even safety risks.

Data and IT infrastructure were the main targets of security measures in the past. For many years, this method worked successfully for enterprises, guaranteeing the availability, confidentiality and integrity of vital information systems. However, ML pipelines have emerged as a new attack surface as a result of the increasing use of ML. These intricate, multi-step procedures frequently include flaws that hackers might take advantage of.

i) **Complexity of Pipelines:** Because ML pipelines are multi-step processes that include a variety of tools, scripts and settings, they introduce security flaws that are challenging to detect and fix.
ii) **Sensitive Data Access:** Pipelines frequently manage enormous volumes of sensitive data, including financial records, medical records and consumer information. This private information might be made public by a pipeline data breach.
iii) **Changing Methods of Attack:** To take advantage of ML flaws, cybercriminals are creating new techniques. These consist of:
   - **Data Poisoning Attacks:** These attacks include the introduction of modified data into the training dataset by malevolent actors. As a result, the model could pick up the wrong patterns and generate biased or erroneous results. A data poisoning assault on a loan approval algorithm, for example may result in the refusal of loans to worthy candidates.
   - **Model Hijacking:** In this technique, an attacker takes over a trained model and modifies its behaviour to suit their objectives. This can entail providing the model with hostile inputs that are intended to produce unexpected results.

Let's presume that there is a face recognition security system that has been compromised to allow unauthorized user access. Such a case is catholic to a healthcare facility which is using an ML batch that assist in the interpreting of medical images to help a doctor diagnose various diseases. The pipeline includes steps like Data Ingestion, Pre-processing, model training and model deployment. The attacker targets the system during the data ingestion phase by placing edited medical images into the training set.

These synthetic images may depict healthy tissue artificially altered to appear cancerous. Consequently, the ML model is trained in a way in which it acquires biases due the data it has been trained on. The result of the damage brought on by this approach is that the deployed models flag healthy patients as patients who are ill and subsequently need medical treatment to be provided to them. This leads to unnecessary medical protocols and undue stress for the patients. To prevent such events, it is imperative to safeguard the information while on the pipeline against alteration and unwarranted access. Moreover, thorough training data validation is critical to address inconsistencies or bias that need to be corrected. Apart from data poisoning and model hijacking, adversaries may exploit other weaknesses in the ML pipeline, such as:

- **Focusing on the Pipeline:** The security gaps in the pipeline may stem from the cloud storage or compute assets that support it, which can be utilized to break into the system or cripple its functions.
- **Vulnerabilities due to Improper Design:** Designing codes without sufficient care within the pipeline framework can provide loopholes for attackers. Recognition of these distinct vectors of attack is key when developing a robust strategy in regard to the security of your ML pipelines.

The risks posed to ML pipelines can be reduced to a degree, provided that certain measures are taken. Key ML pipeline security best practices include:

- **Set up access control lists:** Apply the principle of least privilege when granting access to the pipeline and its components. This ensures that only those with permission may access sensitive information.
- **Data Security all along the Pipeline:** Use strong data security measures during the entire lifecycle of the pipeline, including the data phase, model phase and even the deployment phase. This includes but is not limited to encryption, anonymization and data lineage tracking.
- **Active surveillance:** Keep track of the system for unusual or suspicious behaviour and possible areas of exploitation. Try and implement unused tools for anomaly detection and threat intelligence.
- **Model validation and testing:** Ensure that you run adequate tests on your ML models before use. This includes measuring the performance of the model on test data as well as other more unorthodox methods.
- **Get security training:** Security policies should be in place for personnel involved in development and deployment of the ML pipeline. This enhances security practices within the organization.
- **Exploit the security expert's understanding:** These cyber service providers can also assist in efficient vulnerability assessments and penetration testing VAPT for your ML pipeline. Also, realm SOC continues monitoring and active threats detection.

The most typical list of AI vulnerabilities and assaults that attackers might employ against the GenAI Model and conceptual AI pipeline (*Google's AI Security Framework – Google Safety Centre*, n.d.)

- **G1: Timely Injection:** To force your model to do something you don't want it to, an attacker will attempt to insert malicious data or information into the prompt, such attempting to access the underlying operating system or produce humiliating results that may be published on social media.
- **G02: Exposure to Sensitive Data:** This occurs when an attacker gains access to the underlying tech stack either due to inadequate curation of training data or by exploiting vulnerabilities in the underlying technology stack.
- **G03: Failure of Data Integrity:** Once an attacker has access to the underlying tech stack, they can use this to insert hostile data into the model or embedding database.
- **G04: Inadequate Access Management:** In this case, the attacker can download the model because the underlying tech stack lacks enough access control, or the APIs were not created with access control in mind.
- **G05: Inadequate Hallucination and Prompt Filtering:** In this situation, either common data hallucinations or prompt filters have not been sufficiently tested or red-teamed with abuse cases.
- **G06: Agent Excessive Access:** This is the case when a public-facing agent has access to financial systems, private/restricted internal APIs, or private/restricted models.
- **G07: Attacks on the Supply Chain:** AI tech stacks, like software development tech stacks, depend on several third-party libraries, especially
- **G07: Attacks on the Supply Chain:** AI tech stacks, like software development tech stacks, depend on several third-party libraries, especially Python libraries. If open-source libraries were used, malevolent third parties might have compromised them. Furthermore, it's possible that third-party AI model repositories were compromised. It is important to keep in mind that if the model is constructed with Python, it may come with a default configuration of data and code, which could potentially execute malicious code when installed.
- **G08: Denial of Service Attacks:** Here, either load balancing is insufficient or there is no throttle or rate limitation in place.
- **G09: Inadequate Record-Keeping:** Like typical tech stacks, there are multiple locations where valuable logging information may be collected and transmitted to a centralized SIEM, which could help defenders see an assault in progress. For AI pipelines, logging is frequently an afterthought.
- **G10: Unsecure Deployment That Faces the Public:** Instances of insecure public-facing deployment include models that are made directly downloadable or put on an unprotected inference server. Additionally, an Inference Web Service or API may be outdated, unpatched and vulnerable, and service accounts on inference servers may have too many permissions.

Google released the Secure AI Framework or SAIF (*Google's AI Security Framework – Google Safety Centre*, n.d.), which is a conceptual approach to AI safety. As any other framework, it also has its underlying principles that define its purpose – best practice standards and AI-centric forecasting. The six principles that form SAIF are as follows:

- Strengthening the existing security pillars to the AI ecosystem
- Broaden the scope of detection and response to include AI within an organization's threat landscape
- Automate defenses to emerging and current threats
- Standardization platform controls to achieve consistent security across the organization
- Customize security measures to better mitigate risks and have faster feedback loops for AI deployment.
- AI system risk – business processes mapping

Figure 10.2 shows the AI/ML pipeline attack surface. When it comes to the AI/ML pipeline, threat hunting revolves around systematic and proactive approaches to managing cyber risks that are targeted explicit cases. This shift from a passive mode of "waiting for alerts" to a more active mode of "looking for evidence of compromise" indicates a major evolution in an organization's security posture. This move is critical in finding new, undetected threats in AI/ML systems as well as proves invaluable in the alert-less world.

- **Assess:** The aim is to gather data supporting or disproving a hypothesis to assist in recognizing a weak point in the AI environment. Threat hunters formulate hypotheses about potential attacks and choose the target timeframe of their hunts.
- **Acquire:** Hunters collect pertinent information to support their theories. To identify abnormalities and automate warnings for prompt detection, it is essential to comprehend which tools in the AI pipeline offer visibility and how to use the data effectively.
- **Analyse:** Signs of compromise in the data are searched, and evidence is collected along the attack paths like the ones in GAIA top 10. Any suspicious evidence is appropriately investigated and validated ensuring proactiveness to threats.
- **Action:** In case of a confirmed attack, all necessary steps are taken to limit collateral damage. A response plan such as an attack communication strategy with relevant stakeholders is key to reducing the damage.

Threat hunting is useful when it comes to ensuring the safety of the AI pipelines by detecting issues that are often left unnoticed by security tools offering a proactive approach to threat detection. Seeking out threats means the attacker's "dwell" time is minimized and reduces the opportunity attackers have to exploit the situation. Regular threat hunting increases the AI system's strength by patching the threats before they can be used which ultimately increases the security of the pipeline.

Identifying and prioritizing the protection of critical assets within the AI pipeline is the first step in threat hunting. This step is required because without securing important components, we cannot enhance threat hunting capabilities. Organizations

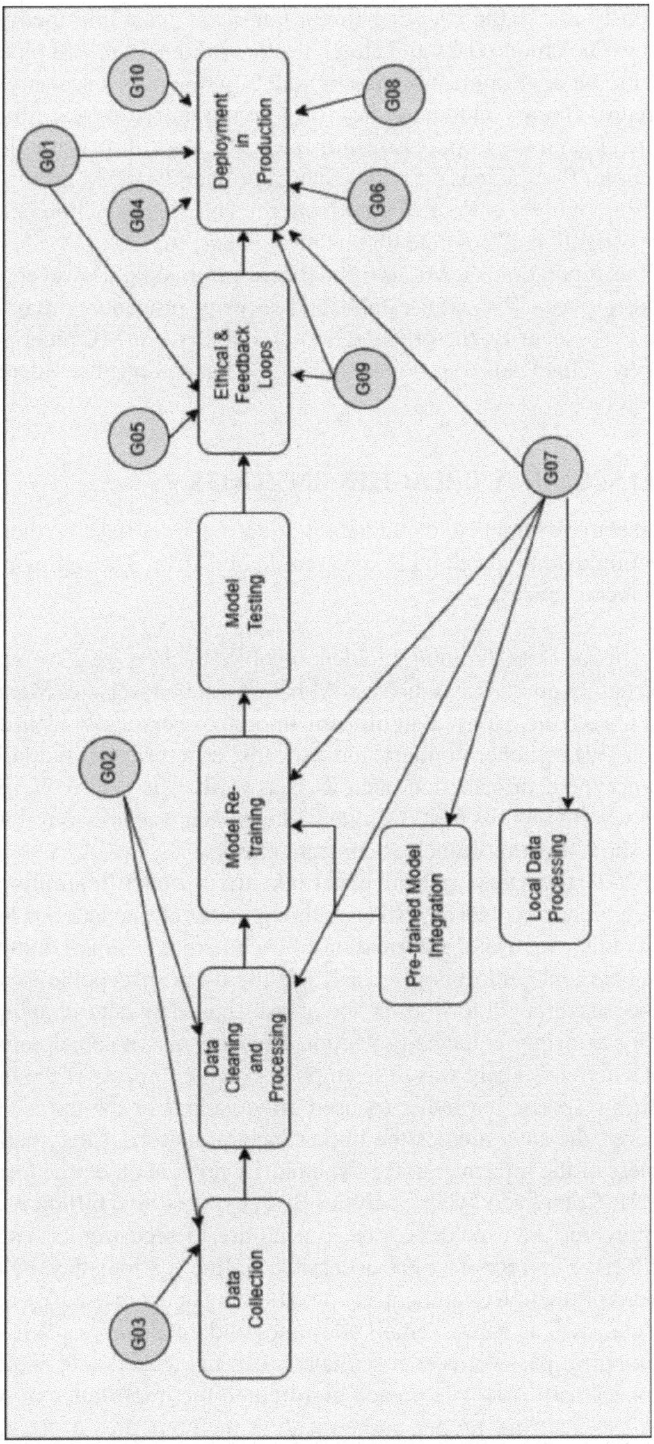

FIGURE 10.2 AI/ML pipeline attack surface.

need to continuously assess the evolving threat landscape, enabling them to adapt security measures. The unique risks and attack vectors present in the AI pipeline can be understood with the development of attack models, while robust security controls can mitigate threats. Threats and anomalies must be monitored in real time so that the response is quick, and the impact is minimized. ML algorithms, combined with rule-based detection of suspicious activities, can significantly speed up the identification process. Employing a variety of data from the entire AI pipeline enables the detection and investigation of possible threats more efficiently.

Admittedly, the reputation of ML is immensely promising. However, security practices must keep pace. With well-established security procedures married with the right skill in cybersecurity, the organization can implement ML pipelines without undue exposure. This leads to productive invention and controlled advancement of ML across sectors.

10.6 CLOUD SECURITY BREACHES: INSIGHTS

The recent cybersecurity threats to cloud data mining pipelines have further emphasized why protecting data in the cloud is an essential objective. The following events are some notable occurrences:

- The 2019 Alibaba Data Scraping Incident involved hackers stealing over 1.1 billion usernames and passwords from Alibaba's Taobao website (Marzouk, 2021). The breach did expose a significant amount of Personally Identifiable Information (PII), phone numbers and user ids, however, substantially no sensitive encrypted information such as passwords was said to be in the mix. After several months post the attack, the breach was uncovered which goes on to show the importance of constant checks.
- In the year 2021, there was an incident at LinkedIn in which 700 million user profiles were breached (Morris, 2021). Although most of the data was leaked out to the public eye, useful information of such nature as email addresses, phone numbers and geolocation records left the users susceptible to social attacks. The case brought forth the scale of risks posed by data scraping and the necessity to firmly enhance protection mechanisms on social networks against such activity. There was little emphasis on the impacts of the breach in LinkedIn's response but rather focused on violations of the terms of service. However, the case stresses the importance of platform safety and user consciousness of the information they voluntarily provide on online forums.
- In June 2021, Cognyte, a cyber analytics firm, exposed five billion records detailing previous data incidents due to a failure in securing its database (Rashid, 2021). The records were accessible online for four days without any password protection or authentication, allowing hackers to easily access sensitive data, such as names, email addresses and data sources. While the precise number of passwords exposed is unclear, the leaked data presented a long-term security risk. The breach highlighted the importance of securing databases, ensuring proper authentication methods are in place, and safeguarding sensitive information to prevent long-term exploitation.

- A breach occurred on Facebook sometime around August 2019, but the company chose to wait until April 2021 to alert the more than 530 million users that their personal information had been taken and then uploaded to a public database (Bowman, 2021). Phone numbers, complete names, addresses, a few email addresses and other information from user accounts were among the data. Facebook's reputation was damaged, even though the firm eventually published an account regarding the hack on its blog. Facebook claims to have identified and resolved the problem right away, but creator Mark Zuckerberg was also impacted. To resolve a privacy lawsuit with the Federal Trade Commission, which involved business paying a $5 billion penalty, he had to answer federal officials. The incident highlights the importance of timely user notifications, robust data security and compliance with privacy regulations to safeguard trust and mitigate reputational risks.

10.7 CONCLUSION AND FUTURE DIRECTIONS

This chapter addresses the essential security components required to protect cloud-based data analytics pipelines. It focuses on the critical steps that are essential to secure sensitive information, starting with the understanding of the shared responsibility model and implementing strong security measures across the different cloud architectural layers. By placing emphasis on protecting data in transmission and at rest, designing and addressing multi-tenancy issues and compliance with privacy regulations, organizations can enhance the security and privacy of their analytical pipelines. Ultimately, this chapter impresses upon the readers the relevant knowledge and techniques for building secure, effective and privacy – respecting cloud data analytics infrastructures. The future of data pipeline security is likely to focus on automating security compliance validation, enhancing encryption techniques to protect data that is becoming more and more dispersed, and embedding advanced ML models for anomaly detection as the cloud and data analytics technologies mature. Also, further developments on privacy-preserving analysis such as federated learning and homomorphic encryption (Mahato & Chakraborty, 2021) will be significant as the global privacy environment becomes stricter. Due to the growing complexity of multi-cloud and hybrid cloud environments, enhanced cross-platform security management strategies and tools are also required. Therefore, to ensure deep security over the cloud-based data analytics pipelines, any such future initiatives must concede to these new challenges.

REFERENCES

Access Management- AWS Identity and Access Management (IAM) – AWS. (n.d.). Amazon Web Services, Inc. https://aws.amazon.com/iam/

Ahmadi, S. (2024). Systematic Literature Review on Cloud Computing Security: Threats and Mitigation Strategies. *Journal of Information Security*, *15*(2), 148–167. https://doi.org/10.4236/jis.2024.152010

Ali, R. F., Shehzadi, A., Jahankhani, H., & Hassan, B. (2024). Emerging Trends in Cloud Computing Paradigm: An Extensive Literature Review on Cloud Security, Service

Models, and Practical Suggestions. In *Advanced Sciences and Technologies for Security Applications* (pp. 117–142). https://doi.org/10.1007/978-3-031-52272-7_5

Bowman, E. (2021, April 10). After Data Breach Exposes 530 Million, Facebook Says It Will Not Notify Users. *NPR*. www.npr.org/2021/04/09/986005820/after-data-breach-exposes-530-million-facebook-says-it-will-not-notify-users

Butt, U. A., Amin, R., Mehmood, M., Aldabbas, H., Alharbi, M. T., & Albaqami, N. (2022). Cloud Security Threats and Solutions: A Survey. *Wireless Personal Communications*, *128*(1), 387–413. https://doi.org/10.1007/s11277-022-09960-z

Choudhary, C., Vyas, N., & Kumar Lilhore, U. (2023). Cloud Security: Challenges and Strategies for Ensuring Data Protection. In *2023 3rd International Conference on Technological Advancements in Computational Sciences (ICTACS)*, Tashkent, Uzbekistan, pp. 669–673. https://doi.org/10.1109/ICTACS59847.2023.10390302.

Google's AI Security Framework – Google Safety Centre. (n.d.). https://safety.google/cybersecurity-advancements/saif/

Mahato, G. K., & Chakraborty, S. K. (2021). A Comparative Review on Homomorphic Encryption for Cloud Security. *IETE Journal of Research*, *69*(8), 5124–5133. https://doi.org/10.1080/03772063.2021.1965918

Marzouk, Z. (2021, June 16). Alibaba Data Breach Exposes 1.1 Billion Pieces of Data. *ITPro*. www.itpro.com/security/data-breaches/359897/alibaba-data-breach-exposes-11-billion-pieces-of-data

Morris, C. (2021, June 30). LinkedIn Data Theft Exposes Personal Information of 700 Million People. *Fortune*. https://fortune.com/2021/06/30/linkedin-data-theft-700-million-users-personal-information-cybersecurity

Rashid, H. (2021, June 20). Cybersecurity Firm Exposes 5 Billion Data Breach Records. *Hackread – Latest Cybersecurity, Tech, Crypto & Hacking News*. https://hackread.com/cybersecurity-firm-expose-data-breach-records/

Shared Responsibility Model – Amazon Web Services (AWS). (n.d.). Amazon Web Services, Inc. https://aws.amazon.com/compliance/shared-responsibility-model/

Tabrizchi, H., & Rafsanjani, M. K. (2020). A Survey on Security Challenges in Cloud Computing: Issues, Threats, and Solutions. *The Journal of Supercomputing*, *76*(12), 9493–9532. https://doi.org/10.1007/s11227-020-03213-1

11 Future Trends for ML-Based Data Analytics in the Cloud

Seema Rawat and Praveen Kumar

11.1 INTRODUCTION

At once, the coalescence of machine learning (ML) and cloud computing has reshaped the very framework on which data analytics rests. Cloud computing, with its scalability and flexibility, has therefore become a natural partner for ML, which by its nature, is adept at finding patterns and making predictions. This powerful pairing empowers organizations to address complex business problems and innovate like never in industries from health to retail.

With businesses increasingly adopting data-driven frameworks for decision making, cloud-based ML solutions have laid the foundation for digital transformation. This empowers organizations to use their data to gain insights by giving them access to sophisticated analytics tools. The chapter covers cloud ML infrastructure evolution, domain adaptive ML in the cloud, ML as a service, the cloud and edge convergence in the future cloud, benefits and ROI of cloud ML, cloud ML trends and challenges for enterprises and vendors, providing a deeper understanding to achieve sustained success.

11.2 EVOLUTION OF ML IN THE CLOUD

11.2.1 Pre-Cloud Era and Its Challenges

Before cloud computing came to be, ML was well suited to enterprises with large on-premise infrastructures. The need for expensive hardware and specialized knowledge create very high barriers for all but the largest companies. Moreover, on-premise setups had limitations in handling burst workloads, leading to scalability issues in ML projects [1].

Example: A pharmaceutical company attempting to analyse clinical trial data faced delays and high costs due to the limitations of its in-house computing resources.

11.2.2 Emergence of Cloud-Native ML

Cloud computing changed the ML ecosystem, enabling any business to leverage advanced analytics. Applications of these frameworks are then running on cloud platforms like the AWS, Azure, Google cloud: they offer a range of services that can

DOI: 10.1201/9781003396772-12

be easily integrated into ML workflows, allowing for businesses to train, deploy and scale models quickly [2].

Case Study: Airbnb uses Google Cloud's ML services to deliver personalized recommendations to millions of users globally, optimizing customer experience.

11.2.3 Key Milestones in Cloud ML

- **2006:** Launch of AWS S3 and EC2, enabling scalable storage and computing.
- **2010s:** The rise of open-source ML frameworks like TensorFlow and PyTorch democratized AI development.
- **2020:** The proliferation of edge computing combined IoT and ML capabilities, enabling real-time analytics at the data source [3].

11.3 CORE ADVANTAGES OF CLOUD-BASED ML

11.3.1 Scalability and Elasticity

One of the significant advantages of cloud platforms is their scalability; organizations can scale resources up or down based on workload needs. This elasticity is key to supporting large-scale deep learning workloads [4].

Example: Tesla leverages AWS for training its Autopilot models, utilizing massive datasets collected from its fleet of vehicles.

11.3.2 Cost-Efficiency

Pay-as-you-go pricing models reduce the initial investments required to get started with ML, and enable smaller companies as startups and small and medium enterprises (SMEs) to adopt this technology, with advanced options like spot instances and reserved instances to further optimize costs.

11.3.3 Enhanced Collaboration

Cloud-based platforms support better collaboration between data scientists, engineers and business analysts. Shared development environments such as JupyterHub on Kubernetes or Google Colab make developers share and contribute to a codebase, making them more productive [5].

11.3.4 Global Reach with Local Optimization

Azure Availability Zones and other features provide low-latency access to ML services, allowing organizations to deploy models at a global scale while also complying with regional data compliance policies.

11.4 FUTURE TRENDS IN ML-BASED CLOUD ANALYTICS

11.4.1 Hyperautomation and AI-Orchestrated Workflows

Hyperautomation refers to ML infusion in robotic process automation (RPA) to automate the end-to-end process of business operations with minimum human involvement and maximum efficiency [6].

Example: An e-commerce platform uses AI-driven RPA to manage inventory, optimize supply chains and process returns automatically.

11.4.2 Edge AI and Federated Learning

With edge AI, data is processed locally on devices, which lowers the latency and alleviates data privacy issues. Federated learning trains a shared model across multiple decentralized devices or servers holding local data samples, without exchanging them [7].

Case Study: Google's Android devices use federated learning for improving Gboard's typing suggestions while preserving user privacy.

11.4.3 The Proliferation of Industry-Specific AI Models

Cloud platforms are working up tailored pre-trained models, which can reduce the time-to-market for AI applications [8].

Example: AWS Comprehend Medical extracts insights from medical records, assisting healthcare providers in diagnostics and patient management.

11.4.4 Explainable AI

With the expansion in ML adoption, the need for transparency is also on the rise. Explainable AI (XAI) tools such as SHAP and LIME make sure that ML models are interpretable, bringing trust and compliance with regulations [9].

Example: In banking, XAI explains credit scoring decisions, helping institutions adhere to regulatory standards.

11.5 APPLICATIONS ACROSS INDUSTRIES

11.5.1 Healthcare and Biotechnology

ML in the cloud is revolutionizing healthcare with predictive analytics, precision medicine and medical imaging [8].

Example: IBM Watson Health analyses patient data to recommend personalized treatment plans, leveraging cloud-based ML for scalability.

11.5.2 Retail and E-Commerce

Cloud ML is used by retailers to optimize pricing, to predict demand, and to improve customer experiences [2].

Case Study: Amazon's recommendation engine, powered by ML, accounts for 35% of its revenue by delivering personalized suggestions to users.

11.5.3 Smart Cities and Urban Planning

Other industries are leveraging Cloud ML solutions as well; for instance, smart cities developing IoT devices can analyse data using Cloud ML solutions, for energy optimization, public safety analytics, traffic management, etc. [10].

Example: Singapore uses AI-powered analytics for real-time traffic monitoring, improving urban mobility.

11.5.4 Financial Services

Cloud-hosted ML models enable better fraud detection, automate risk assessments and produce personalized banking services for improved customer experience [6].

Example: JP Morgan Chase employs ML for fraud detection and customer retention strategies, leveraging Azure's ML capabilities.

11.6 CHALLENGES AND SOLUTIONS

11.6.1 Data Privacy and Security

Challenge: Cloud environments are susceptible to unauthorized access or breaches and data leaks, particularly when sensitive data like healthcare records or financial transactions are involved [11].

Example: The 2021 LinkedIn data breach exposed personal information of over 700 million users, highlighting the need for robust cloud security measures.

Solution:

1. **Federated Learning:** Data is kept on edge devices and only model updates are sent to the cloud so sensitive data is never travelling outside its source.
2. **Advanced Encryption:** Advanced encryption techniques such as homomorphic encryption enable computations to be carried out on encrypted data while preserving privacy throughout the entire ML workflow.
3. **Zero-Trust Architecture:** Establish a policy that validates every user and device, wherever they are located, before granting access.
4. **AI-Driven Threat Detection:** Use AI to identify and respond to potential threats in real time, improving comprehensive cloud security.

11.6.2 Talent and Skills Gap

Challenge: Data Scientists and ML Engineers are in short supply, leading to ML adoption being hampered in the Cloud. This framework is especially pressing for SMEs that struggle to attract talent due to a tighter budget.

Solution:

1. **AutoML Platforms:** Tools such as Google AutoML and Azure ML allow less experienced users to build powerful solutions by simplifying the process of model creation.
2. **Training and Certification:** Cloud vendors like AWS and Google provide certifications, bootcamps and hands-on lab targets to train employees.
3. **Collaborative Ecosystems:** Pre-configured environments and shared notebooks from cloud platforms enable the development of shared expertise rather than relying on an individual.

11.6.3 Environmental Sustainability

Challenge: So at least the cost of running these large ML models, like azure GPT-4, and BERT, it has a high impactful carbon emissions contribution. One example is the training of GPT-3, it took 1,287 MWh and gave [12] off 552 metric tons of CO_2 emissions.

Solution:

1. **Green Data Centres:** Facilities powered by renewable energy sources (Google Cloud's carbon-neutral data centres are an example).
2. **Optimized Model Training:** Pruning, quantization or transfer learning to lessen calculation load.
3. **Dynamic Workload Allocation:** Contract workloads to regions with renewable energy availability, resulting in a carbon-negative footprint.
4. **Research in Efficient Algorithms:** Foster development of light algorithms (TinyML, etc.), as needed in resource-limited environments [13].

11.6.4 Integration Complexities

Challenge: Integrating cloud-based ML with legacy systems, disparate data sources and cross-platform applications often involves complex and error-prone processes.

Solution:

1. **Standardized APIs and Frameworks:** Use standardized APIs and frameworks, such as REST or GraphQL, to promote integration.
2. **Data Wrangling Tools:** Infrastructure such as AWS Glue and Google Dataflow that automates data preparation and pipeline management.
3. **Hybrid Architectures:** Utilize hybrid cloud to your advantage to create seamless integration with existing systems hosted on-premises.

11.6.5 Vendor Lock-In

Challenge: Click here to set up and download the new prototype. This dual-provisioning, though, is a single-point-of-failure.

Solution:

1. **Multi-Cloud Strategies:** Use orchestration tools such as Kubernetes to spread workload over various cloud providers.
2. **Open Standards:** Use frameworks such as TensorFlow or ONNX to facilitate model portability.
3. **Exit Strategies:** Prepare robust strategies to facilitate migration of data, apps and workflows should a transition to competing platforms be necessary.

11.6.6 Cost Management

Challenge: Without limits, these cloud resources incur cost, which can scale quickly for compute-heavy ML workloads [14].

Solution:

1. **Monitoring and Optimization:** Tools such as AWS Cost Explorer and Azure Advisor aid to monitor and optimize resource consumption.
2. **Serverless Architectures:** Embrace serverless computing models that allow organizations to pay solely for the resources consumed during model inference or training.
3. **Budget Controls:** Put caps on costs and alerts in place to avoid cost overruns.

11.7 EMERGING TECHNOLOGIES DRIVING FUTURE GROWTH

11.7.1 Quantum Computing

Quantum computing can optimize complicated problems and speed up ML workloads [15].

Example: Azure Quantum offers researchers a platform to test quantum-accelerated ML algorithms.

11.7.2 Blockchain and ML Integration

It also improves the security and traceability of ML workflows, which is critical in terms of data integrity in such cases [11].

Example: Financial Institutions build decentralized data lakes where they can do analytics with high trust and transparency.

11.7.3 Multi-Cloud and Hybrid Strategies

Multi-cloud strategies are helping organizations avoid vendor lock-in and increase redundancy. Serverless Architecture on Kubernetes

11.8 ETHICAL CONSIDERATIONS IN CLOUD ML

11.8.1 Bias in ML Models

Challenge: ML algorithms can build on top of the biased data and repeat or even amplify social inequality across many types of action and decisions [16].
Example: Facial recognition systems have reported greater error rates for people whose skins are either dark or lighter than average, thus flagging both fairness and accountability as areas of concern.

Solutions:

1. **Bias Auditing:** Use tools such as IBM's AI Fairness 360 to regularly assess datasets and model outputs for fairness.
2. **Diverse Data Sources:** Include datasets that cover a broad spectrum of demographics, cultures and geographies.
3. **Adversarial Debiasing:** Use adversarial methods during training that reduce bias in model predictions.

11.8.2 Lack of Transparency

Challenge: Decisions taken by Black-box ML models are challenging to interpret, leading to lower trust and accountability.

Solutions:

1. **Explainable AI (XAI):** Tools such as SHAP and LIME help understand the decision-making process of models, promoting transparency.
2. **Model Documentation:** To document the intended use, limitations and evaluation metrics of ML models, employ frameworks such as Google's Model Cards.
3. **Interactive Dashboards:** Use visual tools to allow stakeholders to query and understand model predictions

11.8.3 Regulatory Compliance

Challenge: Cloud-based ML systems must comply with worldwide data protection legislation like GDPR, HIPAA and CCPA, which can statute for stringent validation of data storage, processing and transfer [17].

Solutions:

1. **Geolocation of Data:** Place data within specific regions to adhere to local laws, leveraging features such as Azure Availability Zones.

2. **Privacy-Preserving ML:** There are techniques like differential privacy which allow for training ML models with sensitive data but without exposing the sensitive data itself.
3. **Comprehensive Compliance Audits:** Utilize cloud-native compliance tools such as AWS Artifact to create audit reports and maintain voltage with standards.

11.8.4 Accountability in ML Workflows

Challenge: ML-driven decisions can fail or produce an unexpected outcome, determining who is responsible can be incredibly complex – particularly when working in a multi-cloud or hybrid environment.

Solutions:

1. **Version Control:** Use it to track changes in datasets, models and code.
2. **Traceability Frameworks:** Use logging and auditing mechanisms to track all actions taken during the life cycle of ML.
3. **Ethical Review Boards:** Create cross-functional committees to assess the social implications of the implementation of ML models before preparing the deployment.

11.8.5 Dual-Use Risks

Challenge: ML systems might be exploited for nefarious reasons, like generating deepfakes or conducting cyberattacks automatically.

Solutions:

1. **Restricted Access:** Restrict sensitive ML tools usage to verified users with role-based access control (RBAC).
2. **Anomaly Detection:** Identify and flag suspicious behaviour or unauthorized access using ML.
3. **Global Standards:** Support initiatives that advance the ethical use of AI, such as the OECD AI Principles.

11.9 RECOMMENDATIONS FOR BUSINESSES

Adopting ML and cloud computing has the potential to boost your business operations in terms of growth, efficiency and innovation. Yet to fully capitalize on the promise of these technologies, organizations must design strategies to maximize adoption, utilization and sustainability over the long term. Here are a few tips for businesses to successfully exploit cloud-based ML.

11.9.1 Adopt MLOps Practices

MLOps (Machine Learning Operations) is the essential practice that helps organizations scale and automate the ML workflow, from development to deployment and monitoring. MLOps empowers the continuous iterations and development of ML models in AI and builds more reliable AI systems faster leading to reduced time-to-market for ML applications and improved model accuracy.

- **Automation of Workflow:** Digest incoming data with algorithms which may include training, testing and deployment steps. Examples of integrated MLOps tools for the complete ML lifecycle can be found in the cloud platforms such as AWS SageMaker, Azure ML and Google AI.
- **Continuous Integration and Continuous Deployment (CI/CD):** Establish CI/CD processes for ongoing integration, testing and deployment of the model, allowing enhancements to be swiftly reached by users.
- **Model Monitoring and Retraining:** Consistently monitor models in production for drift or underperformance and retrain them using updated data, ensuring the quality of predictions and outputs over time.

11.9.2 Leverage Pre-Trained Models for Faster Deployment

Cloud-based ML has a significant advantage, that is pre-trained models can be deployed without significantly altering the framework flow, which enables a dramatically shorter development time and potentially a better system performance. Fine-tuning these models allows businesses to build industry-specific applications or leverage general-purpose, pre-trained models to bring AI solutions into production without reinventing the wheel.

- **Tailored Solutions:** In many cloud systems, pre-trained (or even low-shot trained) models are available that are tuned to specific industry verticals (such as healthcare, retail, finance and automotive). AWS website, for example mentions Amazon Comprehend Medical to analyse medical texts and Google Cloud Vision that provides out-of-the-box image analysis.
- **Fine-Tuning:** Utilize transfer learning to adapt these pre-trained models with company-specific data to yield better results for the unique use case in question without the heavy lifting of building a model from scratch.
- **Quick Proof of Concept:** The pre-trained model allows the organization to create prototypes or proofs of concept, in a much shorter time, and validate the product idea before large-scale deployment.

11.9.3 Prioritize Data Security and Compliance

As data privacy and regulatory compliance concern rises, so should businesses do significant measures to ensure data is secured while operating a cloud-based ML solutions. By implementing strong security measures, you can protect sensitive data and preserve customer trust.

- **Data Encryption:** Encrypt sensitive data in transit and at rest. Most cloud platforms and public infrastructure as a service (IaaS) provider has built-in encryption services including AWS Key Management Service (KMS) or Azure Key Vault.

- **Access Control:** Enforce strict access controls and role-based access to minimize exposure and only allow designated personnel to access sensitive data or models.
- **Compliance with Regulations:** Keep an eye on data privacy regulations across the globe (GDPR, HIPAA, CCPA, etc.) and build your cloud ML options with these compliance in mind. Use any compliance tools offered by your cloud vendors (such as AWS Artifact or Google Cloud's Compliance Resource Center).

11.9.4 Invest in Employee Training and Upskilling

Management should bring their organizations up to speed on the types of AI technologies working well in the field, while IT centres of excellence should work to ensure ML is successfully integrated in the cloud. Continuous training would make sure that your team will be well-equipped to handle and streamline these systems.

- **Certifications and Training Programs:** Regional employees can take part in cloud-specific certification programs like AWS Certified ML – Specialty or Microsoft Azure AI Engineer Associate.
- **Collaborative Learning:** Foster a culture of collaboration by employing collaborative infrastructure tools like Google Colab or Azure Notebooks, enabling team members to discover, learn and fine-tune their models together.
- **External Partnerships:** Collaboration with universities, colleges, research institutions, or training providers to provide internal workshops, boot camps and other resources on available cloud-based ML tools and techniques.

11.9.5 Implement Ethical AI Practices

With this increasing use of AI in enterprise applications, there needs to be an emphasis on ethical AI. These include but are not limited to fairness, transparency and accountability of the ML systems being built and deployed.

- **Bias Mitigation:** Regularly monitor your datasets and models for biases that may result in discriminatory outcomes. Use tools such as IBM AI Fairness 360 or Google's What-If Tool to discover and mitigate the biases in your models.
- **Explainability:** Implement explainable AI (XAI) techniques to give insights into how models make decisions. It will also promote transparency and confidence especially in regulated sectors like finance and healthcare.
- **Ethical Frameworks:** Clearly define an ethical approach to ML implemented and including how data will be collected, used and shared. Improve customer awareness around AI usage and provide mechanisms to address any and all feedback received.

11.9.6 Foster a Data-Driven Culture

For ML and AI cloud-based tools to perform efficiently, companies must adopt a data-driven culture. Decisions must rely on data-based intelligence and inferences, not feelings or assumptions [18].

- **Leadership Buy-In:** Ensure support for the adoption of data-driven decision-making and ML among executive leadership which creates a tenor for the whole organization.
- **Data Democratization:** Make data available to all employees in all departments by centralizing data and leveraging self-service analytics tools.
- **Data Quality:** Focus on ensuring that the data is of high quality, accurate and up to date so that the ML models are getting the right inputs to perform. Regularly clean and refresh datasets to avoid the "garbage in, garbage out" problem.

11.9.7 Adopt Hybrid or Multi-Cloud Strategies

To mitigate vendor lock-in, redundancy and take advantage of the best features of multiple cloud providers, hybrid and multi-cloud strategies are becoming widespread across organizations. This helps organizations optimize their ML workloads while keeping the flexibility [15].

- **Cloud Flexibility:** This means that once a business uses multiple cloud providers (e.g. AWS, Microsoft Azure, Google Cloud), businesses must choose the most appropriate services and features for specific use cases, which help ensure that their MLSolution is designed to be scalable, reliable, and cost-efficient.
- **Seamless Integration:** Tools like Kubernetes, Apache Kafka, or Terraform can help integrate cloud seamlessly for cross-cloud orchestration and scaling.
- **Risk Mitigation:** Multi-cloud approaches reduce dependence on a single provider, providing more reliability and less downtime during outages.

11.9.8 Stay Agile and Continuously Improve

ML and Cloud landscapes are changing at a lightning speed, and one has to stay agile to compete. Review your approaches, models and technologies periodically to stay updated with the changes in the industry and advancements in technology.

- **Iterative Development:** ML models should be improved regularly utilizing newfound datasets, feedback loops and performance indices. Use agile approaches that allow you to develop items iteratively and adapt faster to market needs.
- **Feedback Loops:** Act like a customer, anticipate their questions, and think of prospective people using your solution.

- **Explore New Technologies:** Keep your ear to the ground on buzzword technologies like quantum computing, 5G and edge AI, which hold the potential to massively optimize your cloud-based ML in the future.

11.10 CONCLUSION

The interplay of ML and cloud computing is a tectonic shift in how organizations use and exploit data. With the increasing dependence of organizations on data-driven decision-making, it is imperative to process and analyse large volumes of information more efficiently. Combined with powerful ML algorithms, the cloud offers the infrastructure required for dynamically scalable resources that can analyse and act on this data, driving predictive analytics, automation and overall more intelligent decisions.

These technologies are colliding to generate new opportunities for innovation. Incorporating cutting-edge technologies such as edge AI, the practice of processing data at the source rather than the cloud, and quantum computing, delivers a paradigm shift in processing power and capability of analysis for businesses to maintain an edge and avoid social engineering and phishing attacks. This leads to new use cases that, until now, simply weren't possible or practical. But organizations that are harnessing the transformative power of ML and cloud computing need to navigate a myriad of challenges as well. As companies amassing more sensitive data, data privacy concern is still a major issue. As the amount of this data collected increases, to be able to keep up the customers' trust and comply with the regulations like GDPR, HIPAA, etc. Also, the expansive environmental effects on training large ML models must be considered and moved towards sustainable education; examples include energy-efficient data centres and the use of renewable energy sources.

In addition, companies need to promote a culture of lifelong education and flexibility since the field of cloud-based ML is increasingly dynamic. Organizations that effectively adopt emerging technologies, invest in strong security practices, and proactively monitor regulatory changes will be best positioned to drive innovation and maintain a competitive advantage in an increasingly data-driven landscape.

The role of ML and cloud computing in business strategy is a critical and not optional part of remaining competitive. If organizations confront the challenges directly and realize the full potential that these technologies can offer, they can be positioned to achieve new efficiencies, deliver personalized customer experiences, and drive operational effectiveness. In conclusion, the thoughtfully orchestrated combination of ML and cloud computing will enable organizations to not just survive but flourish in the digital age, paving the way for sustainable growth and industry leadership in their respective industries [19].

REFERENCES

[1] Tesla AI. (2023). *Tesla Autopilot and AI Innovations*. Retrieved from www.tesla.com/AI

[2] Xu, W., & Zhao, L. (2022). Explainable AI in finance: A survey of methods and applications. *Financial Innovation*, 8(1), 34. https://doi.org/10.1186/s40854-022-00316-y

[3] Amazon Web Services (AWS). (2023). *AWS Cost Management*. Retrieved from https://aws.amazon.com/cost-management

[4] Mell, P., & Grance, T. (2011). *The NIST Definition of Cloud Computing*. NIST Special Publication 800–145. Retrieved from https://doi.org/10.6028/NIST.SP.800-145
[5] Ivanov, D., Dolgui, A., & Sokolov, B. (2022). Cloud supply chain: Integrating Industry 4.0 and digital platforms in the "Supply Chain-as-a-Service." *Transportation Research Part E Logistics and Transportation Review*, 160, 102676. https://doi.org/10.1016/j.tre.2022.102676
[6] Williams, H., & Howard, D. (2022). Green AI: Balancing innovation and sustainability in machine learning. *Journal of Environmental Informatics*, 38(2), 123–138. https://doi.org/10.1016/j.jenvinf.2021.102611
[7] Zhang, X., & Li, Y. (2021). Blockchain for cloud computing: A systematic review. *Journal of Cloud Computing: Advances, Systems, and Applications*, 10(1), 12. https://doi.org/10.1186/s13677-021-00246-z
[8] Watson Health. (2023). *IBM Watson Health and Cloud AI Applications*. Retrieved from www.ibm.com/watson-health
[9] Cao, Q., Schniederjans, D. G., & Schniederjans, M. (2017). Establishing the use of cloud computing in supply chain management. *Operations Management Research*, 10(1–2), 47–63. https://doi.org/10.1007/s12063-017-0123-6
[10] Azure AI. (2023). *Azure Machine Learning Documentation*. Retrieved from https://learn.microsoft.com/en-us/azure/machine-learning
[11] PayPal. (2023). *AI and ML for Fraud Detection*. Retrieved from https://paypal.com/business
[12] IBM. (2022). *AI Fairness 360: An Open-Source Toolkit*. Retrieved from https://aif360.mybluemix.net
[13] Google Cloud. (2023). *Federated Learning Documentation*. Retrieved from https://cloud.google.com/solutions/federated-learning
[14] Google AI. (2023). *Explainable AI (XAI) Tools*. Retrieved from https://ai.google/explanations
[15] Microsoft Quantum. (2023). *Azure Quantum Documentation*. Retrieved from https://azure.microsoft.com/en-us/products/quantum
[16] TensorFlow. (2023). *TensorFlow Model Optimization Toolkit*. Retrieved from www.tensorflow.org/model_optimization
[17] Zhou, T., & Liu, Z. (2023). Ethical challenges in AI adoption for smart cities. *AI Ethics*, 4(3), 245–259. https://doi.org/10.1007/s43681-022-00112-9
[18] OpenAI. (2023). *GPT-4 Technical Documentation*. Retrieved from https://openai.com/research
[19] Netflix Technology Blog. (2023). *How Netflix Personalizes Your Experience with Machine Learning*. Retrieved from https://netflixtechblog.com

Index

Note: Page numbers in *italics* indicate a figure, and page numbers in **bold** indicate a table on the corresponding page.

D

E

Q

R

S

T

U

V

W

Y